The
Clay Pigeons
of St. Lô

Glover S. Johns, Jr.

with a new foreword by
Joseph Balkoski

STACKPOLE
BOOKS

Published by
STACKPOLE BOOKS
5067 Ritter Road
Mechanicsburg, PA 17055
www.stackpolebooks.com

Printed in the United States of America

Distributed by NATIONAL BOOK NETWORK

ISBN 978-0-8117-1782-3

Library of Congress has cataloged the previous edition as follows:

Johns, Glover S., 1912-
    The clay pigeons of St. Lo / Glover S. Johns, Jr.
        p. cm.
    Originally published: Harrisburg, PA : Military Service Publ. Co., 1958.
    Includes bibliographical references and index.
    ISBN 0-8117-2604-5
    1. Saint-Lo (France)—History—Siege, 1944. 2. United States. Army. Infantry Regiment, 115th—History. 3. World War, 1939–1945—Regimental histories—United States. 4. Johns, Glover S., 1912-5. World War, 1939–1945—Personal narratives, American. I. Title.

    D756.5.S2 J6 2002
    940.54'1273—dc21

                                                    2001055043

DEDICATION

To

THE BIG RED TEAM
(1st Battalion, 115th Infantry,
29th Division)

Foreword 2002

THE SOIL OF NORMANDY holds many secrets.

In 1944 young Americans came thousands of miles across the sea to this, the unchanging land of *bocage*, the legendary hedgerows and labyrinthine sunken lanes, the ancient Romanesque churches and turreted chateaus, the tiny jigsaw piece pastures tilled for centuries by weather-beaten French farmers. In the grand scope of world history, what these young men achieved here was magnificent. But the passing of more than half a century dims memories and lessens passions: do Americans of the new millennium remember? In the sometimes cynical world of the twenty-first century, military service is routinely disparaged and the warriors' art ridiculed as nothing more than a terrible reflection of a flawed human psyche. Even cynics, however, cannot deny that what happened in Normandy in 1944 represents nothing less than the salvation of Western civilization at a moment when it stood on the brink of a barbaric new Dark Age.

Glover Johns and the 800 men of the 1st Battalion, 115th Infantry, 29th Division, U.S. Army, were among the leading waves of young Americans to fight their way ashore in Normandy as part of what Gen. Dwight D. Eisenhower labeled "The Great Crusade." A shockingly large number of them lie there still, never having had a chance to grow old, to feel the warmth of a new family, to sit by the fireside with buddies to talk of the old days, or to enjoy the fruits of American democracy taken for granted by later generations. Abraham Lincoln's enduring Gettysburg Address applies as appropriately to them as to the Union soldiers killed at Gettysburg: They "gave their lives that that nation might live."

Glover Johns was both a witness and an important contributor to the military events in Normandy in the summer of 1944, and in his classic book *The Clay Pigeons of St. Lô*, he saw to it that the devotion of his beloved warriors would never be forgotten. Yes, there are many secrets in the soil of Normandy, but *The Clay Pigeons of St. Lô* divulges many of them.

I have spent much time in Normandy over the past decade researching the World War II activities of the 29th Infantry Division, much of it in the St. Lô area, walking the pastures, woods, and lanes so vividly portrayed by Johns in *Clay Pigeons*. What Johns's soldiers endured and accomplished in 1944 was powerfully demonstrated to me during my many sojourns over 29th Division battlefields fifty or more years later. *The Clay Pigeons of St. Lô* is devoted in its entirety to a month-long battle in an area no bigger than six square miles. To accomplish its mission, Johns's battalion fought yard-by-yard with little or no respite against some of the most skilled fighters on earth, suffering almost unthinkable casualties, but successfully pressing on to the objective of St. Lô. The extraordinary difficulty of this mission is exemplified by the fact that a present-day traveler can walk from the Bois de Bretel, the place where Johns's narrative begins, to the city of St. Lô, where his story closes, in little more than an hour. In 1944 the 29th Division endured more than 30 days of hard fighting to traverse that distance and in his classic book, Johns explains to mesmerized readers exactly why it took so long.

I rarely read books twice; however, over the years, I have lost track of the number of times I have read *The Clay Pigeons of St. Lô* from cover to cover, but I can declare with certainty that there is no book in my library that I have read more. A friend first introduced me to Johns's work in 1977. In those days I commuted to and from work on long New York City subway rides, and I vividly recall my initial reading of *Clay Pigeons* in dilapidated and stuffy cars underneath the streets of Manhattan. Most of the time the trains were too crowded for me to find a seat, but as the first few pages of *Clay Pigeons* had convinced me that it was one of those extraordinary books that simply could not be put down, I read much of the book standing, with one arm wrapped around a pole for balance as the subway roared and shuddered down the tracks.

From a writer's perspective I can imagine no greater satisfaction than having one's words inspire others to write. I do not have the slightest doubt that Glover Johns and his memorable book had that effect on me: In 1988 I took a year off from work to write a history of a U.S. Army division and its wartime experience in the Normandy campaign, and it is no accident that the unit I chose to write about, the 14,000-strong 29th "Blue and Gray" Infantry Division, included Glover Johns's battalion within its ranks. The book, entitled *Beyond the Beachhead: The 29th Infantry Division in Normandy,* was published in 1989 by Stackpole Books, whose Military Service Publishing Company imprint published the original edition of *Clay Pigeons* in 1958. Those who are familiar with *Beyond the Beachhead* already know the name of Glover Johns, as he figures prominently in that book.

For me, a face-to-face interview with "the Major" (as Johns refers to himself in *Clay Pigeons*) would have been of immense significance, but sadly such a meeting never took place as Johns was no longer living by the time I started writing *Beyond the Beachhead.* Johns's influence on my work, however, was profound. First, and probably most important, *Clay Pigeons* is highly accurate. I have been dedicated to Normandy research now for more than a quarter of a century, and I can most assuredly declare that virtually all of what Glover Johns writes in *The Clay Pigeons of St. Lô* truly happened as he describes it. I know this because I have examined almost every pertinent historical document in the National Archives, visited the actual Norman battlefields depicted by him, and talked to as many men as possible who served with him. Even now I am stirred by memories of standing at the exact spot occupied by Johns on June 17, 1944 when, in the very first page of his book, he describes observing his battalion "carrying their rifles at the high port, [moving] out of the trees, across the narrow lane . . ." Similarly, I have walked down the steep stone steps of the Famille Blanchet mausoleum in the St. Lô cemetery, deeply moved by Johns's vivid description of this ad hoc battalion command post at the end of *Clay Pigeons.*

I believe Johns's work has successfully stood the test of time because it is undeniably a captivating read. Cynics may presume that warriors are not adept with the written word. A reading of *The Clay Pigeons of St. Lô,* however, will change that assumption, for even those who know little of World War II history cannot help but be impressed with Johns's expertise with the pen. If a writer's goal is to achieve the widest possible audience with enthralling prose, I submit that Glover Johns fulfilled that goal admirably. I consider this a notable achievement, as Johns was for most of his adult life a professional soldier, not a writer—and in fact was actively soldiering when he penned *Clay Pigeons* in 1958. I would consider myself privileged if one of my books were still in print nearly half a century after its initial release. With this reprint of *The Clay Pigeons of St. Lô*, Glover Johns has achieved that lofty status.

The Clay Pigeons of St. Lô also fascinates because of its unique perspective of war. In *Beyond the Beachhead*, I describe a pre–D-Day meeting in Tavistock, England called by the commander of the 29th Infantry Division, Maj. Gen. Charles H. Gerhardt. Addressing his assembled senior officers, Gerhardt growled, "This war is won at battalion level . . . A year from today, one out of every three of you will be dead, and the toll will be higher if senior commanders don't know their stuff!" It is notable that Glover Johns was a battalion commander and served under "Uncle Charlie" Gerhardt for almost the entire length of the war in northwest Europe from June 1944 to May 1945. As a consequence, *The Clay Pigeons of St. Lô* is a valuable historical document because it so realistically portrays the level of fighting rightly defined by Gerhardt as the key to military victory in World War II. Battalion commanders like Johns were connectors between the front line fighting soldiers and the top brass behind the lines. This was a very delicate task: Johns had to interpret orders from rear area command posts into practical objectives that could be easily comprehended by his infantrymen at the front. As Johns makes clear in *Clay Pigeons*, sometimes orders from the rear made little sense, but they had to be executed in any case. Furthermore, General Gerhardt, like most division commanders in World War II, was not an easy man to please, and when battalions in the 29th Division did not achieve objectives, it was always the battalion commander, not the fighting soldier, who bore the brunt of the general's wrath.

To do their job effectively, Johns and his fellow battalion commanders in the 29th Division had to remain very close to, if not directly in, the front lines. There they were subject to enemy machine gun fire, artillery barrages, and all the physical discomforts associated with living outdoors in the middle of a terribly violent conflict. Amid all this chaos, they had to ponder their decisions carefully, as every order could mean life or death to hundreds of men. Herein lay the heart and soul of battalion command, which Johns so successfully depicts in *The Clay Pigeons of St. Lô*: to create an effective fighting unit, a commander had to establish a genuine bond between himself and his men; but to become an effective commander, he had to harden himself to the unfortunate fact that it was his job to send the men he so deeply respected into mortal danger day after day.

Glover Johns's quietly respectful portrayal of the men of the 1st Battalion, 115th Infantry, 29th Division in *The Clay Pigeons of St. Lô* was published at a time when the soldiers he describes were still young men. Those lucky enough to have survived the war went on with their lives and thought little, if at all, of their impact on history. Only four decades later would observers coin the phrase "The Greatest Generation" to define these selfless warriors. Had Johns lived to witness the profound change in America's perception of its wartime generation, he doubtlessly would have muttered "Amen," and "It's about time." In truth Glover Johns was one of the first writers to advise the American public that its World War II soldiers were highly deserving of such tribute.

Shortly after the United States entered World War II in December 1941, Prime Minister Winston Churchill of Great Britain addressed a joint session of the U.S. Congress in Washington, D.C. For the Allies, war news was bleak: Churchill's 1940 avowal to his people that he had "nothing to offer but blood, toil, tears, and sweat" had come true and now these ominous words applied to America as well. A long, hard road to ultimate victory lay ahead. Referring to the German, Italian, and Japanese enemy, Churchill posed a question to his American listeners: "What kind of people do they think we are?"

Glover Johns knew exactly what kind of people we are, and in *The Clay Pigeons of St. Lô*, he ensured that all of us would know too.

Joseph Balkoski
Baltimore, Maryland
November 2001

Foreword

THE CLAY PIGEONS OF ST. LO is a true story of an American infantry battalion in combat in Normandy during June and July, 1944. It was one of the nine infantry battalions of the 29th Infantry Division which landed on Omaha Beach on D-Day, June 6th, 1944. The story is built around a battalion command post and the individuals in the platoons and companies composing the battalion. It is *real* drama—"suspense, excitement, elation, disappointment, fear, sorrow and chagrin."

A war correspondent who saw the unit capture St. Lo dubbed the 1st Battalion, 115th Infantry, "The Indestructible Clay Pigeons" and described it as being typical of American units that fought in World War II. To its commander and its officers and men, it was the "finest fighting unit in the whole Army."

It is unusual and rare when one can find a true story of actual combat of an echelon the size of an infantry battalion, but here it is, in plain words, without heroics, and with amazing frankness. What is more to the point, it is most interesting and readable. The principal character, whose actions and spirit animates the whole story is the young battalion commander.

If you want a graphic account of thirty days of exciting and victorious combat—of the indomitable fighting spirit—of well led and disciplined enlisted men who had been civilians only months before and the people who fight our battles, this book will please you. Their dogged determination to carry the fight to the enemy, in spite of rough odds and high casualties, resulted in the capture of assigned objectives.

From Omaha Beach to the Elbe, this battalion sustained a loss in killed and wounded of 2,384 officers and men—almost three times its strength. Of these, 454 were killed in action. And its commander was commended for taking objectives with minimum losses.

The story unfolds a fast moving action, with powerful emotionalism, and a leader who loved and was loved by his men—who lived for and with his men—who shared their sorrows and joys. It tells of the inevitable friction between upper and lower units, engendered by tense situations—what it is like to be in battle for the first time—the ever present tragedy and comedy —the devotion to duty—the desire of the wounded man to return later to *his* unit—the relationship between subordinate and senior, and the psychology of leadership in battle.

These things I know to be true, because *I was there.*

The author has portrayed war as it really is, and has provided the inexperienced young leader of the future with grassroot instruction on what to expect in combat on the small unit level, and the valuable lessons to be learned. At the same time, the author has not lost sight of the fact that "the story's the thing," for it grips you from the start, and places the reader mentally in the front lines with the Battalion Commander, a leader who knew that no one in the battalion would be more optimistic than he appeared to be.

There has been no attempt to paint anyone as a hero, and no attempt to cover mistakes and faults. It is above all a story of doughboys who "took everything the enemy could throw at them" and pushed on to victory.

If you were to break down the history of all battles from the Battle of Arbela—October 1, 331 B.C. to the Meuse-Argonne of World War I, in the hope of determining what contributes to victory, you would find that success in battle can be measured by the leadership, efficiency, and esprit of the small fighting units. The "Clay Pigeons of St. Lo" is definite proof of this fact.

WILLIAM H. SANDS
Major General, AUS-Ret
(1941-1946—Brigadier General, Comd'g
29th Infantry Division Artillery)

Acknowledgments /

NO BATTLE ever looked the same to any two people. This story is told the way that fellow, Major Johns, saw it. Some people and some units are mentioned only in passing, or not at all. I have no desire to slight anyone, but those not dwelt upon just didn't register through that well-known fog of war. It was right thick, sometimes.

Incidentally, in the narrative I have used the third person for two reasons: First, I just don't like the first person singular. To me it limits things too much. Second, people who fight wars up close to the enemy are not the same while they are fighting as they were before and after. "Major Johns" to me is a character who was observed closely and carefully for a somewhat confused and confusing period. His life during that time has always seemed that of another person.

In doing my best to broaden the view and report accurately on the thoughts and actions of others I have drawn on the memories of many others who were there. The battalion log has been used to confirm times, dates, and places; boundaries; and a gain or loss of yardage. The Regimental and Division histories were used, although in one or two places we do not agree in detail. The Department of the Army publication, "St. Lo," also confirms the general course of action.

I wish particularly to thank Captain Arthur C. Chadwick for the numerous detailed letters he wrote in response to my many questions. Chad is now living in Concord, New Hampshire, after recovering almost completely from a near-fatal head wound he received later in the war. Others who helped were: Captain Bill Kenney, Captain Leroy Weddle, Captain Julian Stoen, Captain David Mentzer, and the redoubtable First Sergeant Alton Shaff.

Captain Kenneth E. Murphy and Lieutenant Colonel Russell J. Manzolillo have been instrumental in assisting me to gain certain information needed during the final preparation for the publisher.

Mr. T. K. Massey prepared the excellent map.

—G. S. J., Jr.

Contents

Death in the Hedgerows / 1

THE SUN'S RAYS were warm on the peaceful Normandy field and a single cow grazed unconcernedly near the far hedgerow. The only sound that broke the late afternoon stillness was the uncertain rustle of men moving through heavy woods, and that died away to nothing as the two companies reached the edge of the trees and stood looking out into the open.

Major Johns, nervous with his first battlefield command, paced the trail that ran along the edge of the woods, impatient for the company commanders to step out and signal that they were ready. He looked repeatedly at his watch—they were already five minutes late. At length he sighed with relief as the two officers moved out into the road, raised their right arms over their heads, and stood looking at him. He stiffened, raised his own arm, then brought it down sharply in the direction of St. Lo.

Weddle and Sadler echoed the motion, whereupon little groups of wooden-faced men, carrying their rifles at the high port, moved out of the trees, across the narrow lane, down into the shallow ditch, and up the other side into the bright sunshine of the meadows beyond. Baker Company, on the left, slipped over a low hedgerow and disappeared. Charlie Company also moved easily across the empty field, reaching the middle without drawing fire. The squad leaders then began to look around to check the formation of their half-squad columns. The new battalion commander watched the grim parade-ground precision with deep admiration.

The men held up for only a moment at the big hedgerow where the cow was. The Major thought he saw a man give her a playful jab in the rump with a bayonet. Then they climbed the long mound of earth and in a moment the field was empty again. Still not a shot.

Puzzled, he turned to see if A Company, in reserve, had come up yet. Lieutenant Ryan, the company commander, was standing quietly just behind him. Major Johns could see Ryan's men leaning against trees as they waited for the signal to move out. The Major's own command post group was scattered along the road, too, so he raised his arm again and let it fall, moving forward into the deceptively peaceful pasture as he did so.

They walked about a hundred yards. There was no sound except the muffled clump of boots on grass. Two hundred yards . . . still no fire. Judas, he thought, Charlie Company must be nearly to that second hedgerow by now. Have the enemy really pulled out? Or are they waiting behind that readymade earthwork, letting the companies get within murderous range before they cut loose? He wished again that there'd been time to send out a patrol or two, so the companies would have an idea of what they were getting into and wouldn't be attacking blind this way.

Not a man said a word, but the tension grew with every step.

Then it came. It was almost a relief to hear the dozen German machine guns that ripped through the silence together. Rifle fire cracked between the long bursts. The crumping, flat crash of mortar shells came from the field ahead. Somewhere a man screamed. The cow, startled, galloped awkwardly back toward her ruined shed.

By the time the Major reached the hedgerow—in perhaps thirty seconds—his mouth was dry, his forehead and the palms of his hands were moist, and every nerve in his body was screaming like a ricochet. He lay forward against the earth wall of the hedgerow, peering over it to see what was happening and to hide his wild excitement.

He saw little. A few men darted here and there without apparent reason or direction; mortar shells shocked squat columns of black smoke into instant being; dust and dirty grey smoke drifted slowly with the light breeze. But that was all.

One seldom sees much on a modern battlefield.

He watched long enough for his heart to slow down, his nerves to relax a little, and the excitement of commanding men in battle for the first time to drift away. It didn't take long. He realized, suddenly, that all the fire he could hear was coming from the enemy. He was just wondering how close the Krauts had let them get when he heard a yell from Barbeaux, his orderly, "Major! Captain Nabb is down!"

He looked around to see the Weapons Company commander lying on his face fifty yards back in the field. An aid man from Able Company was already running toward the wounded officer. The Major pushed himself away from the hedgerow and trotted out to see what had happened. No shells had landed in the field behind them. The hedgerow* that stood between them and the enemy was nearly five feet high and a good four feet thick, all solid dirt. So how could a man get hit back there? Major Johns found Nabb not seriously hurt, just a single bullet hole in his upper thigh. But he didn't find the answer to how a bullet could get back there; and he had lost a man he had been counting on.

Nabb was furiously, fluently conscious, "Those bastards . . . Those damned sons of bitches . . . But I'll be back, Major, I'll be—."

A blast of machine gun fire from the hedgerow cut Nabb short and startled the Major so badly that he jumped and then ran back, almost forgetting to wave to the aid man to take over. He could see one of his own light machine guns firing into the tops of the trees that bordered the field on the right. Before he could get to the hedgerow a Browning automatic rifle (BAR) joined in.

"What the hell goes on here, anyway?" he yelled.

---

*The "hedgerows" of Normandy were earthen dikes from two to six feet high and as much as four feet thick, on top of which were growing hedges or trees. These hedgerows separated the individual pastures and apple orchards and made a virtual redoubt of each successive field.—Editor.

"I think there must be a sniper up one of those high trees, sir," answered Captain Newcomb, the S3. "He got your radio operator before you got to Nabb. I figure he must have shot Nabb too so I ordered these guns to clean up those trees."

"All right. But stop that shooting; it'll worry the boys up ahead if they think there's something back here."

Newcomb called to the two gunners and the firing stopped. Major Johns went over to look at his radio operator, who had been hit in precisely the same part of the body as Nabb. He had been lying flat on the ground, not ten feet from where the Major had been leaning against the hedgerow. Apparently Newcomb was right. The Major hoped the automatic weapon fire would at least scare the sniper off. But nothing had fallen out of any of the trees. He shook his head as he went back to his place on the hedgerow, hoping he might be able to see something up ahead this time.

He couldn't. There wasn't a man in sight. The top of the next hedgerow was still shrouded in smoke and dust, tracers ricocheted crazily, and mortar shells crumped steadily where Sadler's company was supposed to be. But the battlefield looked deserted.

Then the sound of new rifle fire began to come from well out to the left. It spread along the front until the Major knew that both companies had gotten themselves together and were beginning to fight back. An American light machine gun opened up over in Baker's zone, its slower, deeper tone making it stand out clearly from the ripping, tearing sound of the German guns. Another one from Charlie joined it. He heard the cough of a mortar, firing from not far away, and saw one of these little 60-mm weapons firing steadily from a position fifty yards down the hedgerow. Then the heavier grunt of the battalion 81-mm mortars began to come from farther to the rear. The Major thought he could distinguish the long sustained bursts of fire from heavy machine guns. Things were looking up.

A German mortar shell hit thirty yards to the front. The Major came off the hedgerow to sit again, trying to wait patiently for reports.

In a few minutes the fire in front began to slack off, then died away almost entirely except on the far left. That meant that Weddle, with Baker Company, was still after something. Or something was after Weddle. Only spasmodic bursts came from Charlie Company. It was time he was getting some news.

He waited ten more minutes, but nothing came over the radio and no runners came in. Impatient, he reached for the handset of the SCR 300 where it lay beside him, untended since the operator had been hit. Pressing the butterfly switch he called, "Hello Peter 4, Peter 4. Hello Peter 4. Over."

That was Charlie's call sign for the day, but though they were not more than 300 yards away there was no answer. He called Peter 3—Baker—and got the same result. He was about to give up and go forward to see for himself when a weak call came from Peter 4, "Hello, Peter 4, Peter 4. Over."

He grabbed the handset again, "Hello Peter 4. Go ahead. Over."

"Red 6? This is Charlie 6," It was Sadler himself. "Sir, we have the second hedgerow, but they stopped us cold in a little orchard up ahead. We're getting fire from the woods across the road on the right. I think they're forming up in there for a counterattack. Over."

"Hello Peter 4; yes, this is Red 6. I understand. Stay with 'em! We'll give you some help. Out."

He dropped the handset and turned to Lieutenant Martin, the artillery liaison officer. "Can you put some fire in those woods to the right?"

"Sir," Martin drawled in a rich Virginia accent, "that's out of our zone. I couldn't bring fire in close to the flank anyway because the tree bursts would spray over into C Company."

"Out of our zone? The hell with that! There isn't a soul in those woods except the enemy, and won't be until I send somebody. Now you shoot something in there and be damned soon about it."

Martin looked startled, but he got busy on his own radio and in a few minutes a flight of shells screamed over to burst deep in the woods. The artilleryman spoke into his radio again whereupon the next volley crashed closer to Charlie's right flank. They could see great limbs fly up from the trees. Martin made another correction.

While they watched the artillery fire the battalion radio stopped its sizzling noise again. Weddle's voice, weak but unmistakable, came through, "Red 6, this is Baker 6. Sir, we heard you calling a minute ago but couldn't answer right then. We're in a helluva mess over here. This damn country is so cut up I don't know where I am except I can tell I'm about a hundred yards ahead of Charlie. Enemy paratroopers* are all over the place and my left flank is hanging out in the breeze like an old sock. We're pinned down plumb complete. Can you do something about it?"

"Okay, boy," answered the Major, forgetting the precious radio "procedure" as he did most of the time. "I'll do what I can."

He thought Weddle was getting pretty careless with radio security, but hoped the Germans had been kicked around by the 116th Infantry enough that morning so they wouldn't be monitoring anything as small as a battalion SCR 300 radio net. He wasn't very worried about the enemy, but Division might be doing a little listening-in. He'd have to speak to the Baker company commander about it later.

The situation was becoming somewhat more clearly confused. At least that was the way the battalion commander felt about it right then. He was up against the problem he had been expecting ever since he had got the hurry-up-and-attack order earlier that afternoon. The right half of the battalion zone of action was pretty much open fields, but it was bounded on that side by a hard-topped road and there was a large triangular-shaped patch of heavy woods running for about 500 yards along the other side of the road. As artilleryman Martin had said, that put the woods "out of our zone." The only trouble was that it didn't belong to anyone else either. Nobody, that is, except the Germans. The nearest friendly troops, at least 800 yards farther

*Part of the German 2d Parachute Division, a crack unit.

to the right, might as well have been in Berlin for all the help they were going to be. It had been obvious from the start that those woods were a wonderful place for the enemy to use in any way they wanted to. Probably they were doing just what Sadler thought they were doing at the moment—forming up for a counterattack that could hit him in the flank and rear if they had the guts and the people to try it. And they probably had.

The left was just as bad. It was a rats' nest of tiny meadows, orchards, hedgerows, and sunken roads that extended to infinity as far as the battalion was concerned, because there was no help there either. The Major had given the maze of bad ground to his best and most experienced company commander. But nobody, no matter how good or experienced, could cover it all or keep hostile paratroopers from finding and hitting a flank that had no choice but to dangle "like an old sock."

And now, just as he had expected, both flanks were in trouble; or probably would be before long.

He still had all of his reserve company, but he'd been hoping to find a soft spot where he could use it to shove through where it would do the most good. Now there didn't seem to be any soft spots. If he merely wanted to hold what he had he was going to have to do something about those flanks.

The sun was still well above the horizon despite the fact that it was 1730 hours on the 17th of June. Still plenty of daylight. He was damned if he'd fold up that easy in his first fight. He knew the Germans had had a rough fight already that day and had probably used most of their reserves. But maybe they'd brought in more by now. The hell with it . . . you've got to take a chance once in a while . . . . He'd hit the Germans on the right, try to get back of the ones in front of Sadler, jar loose the whole front . . . Weddle could worry about his own flank for a while.

"Ryan!" he snapped.

"Yes, sir." The reserve company commander was close by his side.

"Take two platoons and cross over into those woods. Clear

them right down to the far end of the triangle, then hit those people in front of Sadler. Send to me the leader of the platoon you leave here."

"Yes, sir."

Ryan moved away. In a few minutes a young second lieutenant trotted up, saluted, and reported that he was the platoon leader of Able 3. The Major told him to stick around. Then he turned to the artillery liaison officer. "Martin, tell your people I'm sending two platoons into the woods, so they don't shoot in there except when we ask for it."

"Roger."

Ryan moved fast. His two platoons streamed across the road into the trees without trouble, but in a few minutes firing began about halfway to a point opposite C Company. Johns was glad he'd decided to clear the woods because it looked as if maybe the enemy had been forming up in there. In this way he would break up any counterattack and maybe get at the Germans in front of Sadler. It all depended on how many there were.

As the sound of the firing swelled, Johns listened carefully, trying to judge his chances for success. It seemed that the German fire was just as heavy as Ryan's, but he didn't want to give up hope too soon.

He was still listening when the B Company runner came pounding down the hedgerow from the left. "Sir," he panted, "Captain Weddle says tell you they are hitting us on the left. The Jerries are coming in from behind and we can't cover all the ground. He says he can't get his left platoon back; they've already kicked off one attack."

He looked anxiously up at the Major who smiled and said, "Okay son, we'll look into the matter."

From this slightly garbled message it was pretty obvious that Weddle was in some sort of trouble. Major Johns didn't think he would have sent a runner if it hadn't been fairly serious. Weddle had a reputation for being as calm in a fight as the next man.

He turned to the lieutenant commanding Ryan's remaining platoon, "Follow this man back to B Company and cover their left flank. You will take orders from Captain Weddle but do anything you think you need to do to secure that flank if you don't see him right away."

The lieutenant saluted and ran back to get his platoon as the Major turned to the runner, "Lead this platoon to Captain Weddle. Tell him to use it to protect his left flank."

The runner nodded and rushed after the lieutenant.

Now the command post group was left alone behind the hedgerow. Johns was beginning to get a little panicky down deep inside. His unit had been stopped, he had committed his reserves, there was one hell of a lot of shooting going on again, and he couldn't think of another thing he could do—except wait.

But he was a poor waiter. He fidgeted with his pipe, with his .45, and even with his helmet, which had suddenly become uncomfortable. He tried the radio again. No answer. Trying to look calm and unperturbed, he casually got up to try to see something over the hedgerow, couldn't see any more than he already had, sat down and started the whole process over again. The rest of the staff, of which only Newcomb, the operations officer, and Grimsehl, the intelligence officer, were left beside the artillery liaison detachment, the runners, and wiremen, sat quietly against the hedgerow. His two staff officers and most of the men watched him covertly, now and then, trying to get a line on their new commander.

The firing on the right continued. It was more intense than that from either Charlie or Baker company now, but all had picked up volume considerably since the last lull. The whole front was alive—crackling. Then, for the first time, he could hear the characteristic hollow, clumping roar of hand grenades from Ryan's woods. He tensed. That meant they were getting in close.

The sound of the grenades kept on interminably. He wondered who was throwing the most. You couldn't tell from the sound they made. The volume of small-arms fire was still about the same on both sides.

Such intense fire couldn't last long, and it didn't. It began to die out again until it was almost silent in front and only sporadic on both flanks. Then the German fire came back with a rush and a roar from the front and left. Their mortars crashed like a gargantuan surf, the Major thought to himself, only sharper and louder than any surf could ever be.

At least two batteries of friendly artillery switched their fire suddenly to in front of Charlie Company. Their shells whined close overhead. Oddly enough, there was still no German artillery fire falling close, although quite a bit had gone well over to land in the trees that had marked the Line of Departure.

The 300 came to sudden, squawking life as the C Company operator screamed something that sounded like "Counterattack —counterattack—they're coming through the orchard."

It was too much for the battalion commander. He could not sit behind that hedgerow and not know what was going on while all three of his companies were in close and bitter fighting. He barked at the nearest man, "Take that radio and follow me."

The man looked at the set as if it were something alive and horrible. He shrank away from it and stammered, "N-n-not me, sir, I ain't no radio man."

Johns was speechless with surprise. Before he could recover, a calm voice at his elbow said, "I'll go with you, sir."

It was Jimmy, the pint-sized operator from A Company, who had lugged his heavy set so cheerfully during the hot speed-march that had brought them to the woods earlier that afternoon. The Major did not stop to ask why the man was not with the reserve commander, nor to take action against the other man, who had refused his order. He just nodded, calling to Newcomb, "Come on. We're gonna see what is happening at C Company."

He turned to the hedgerow and started to climb over. Just then a long burst of machine-gun fire clipped the top from a bush a few feet to his left. He changed his mind and moved toward the road on the right.

The road ran at right angles to the front line, straight into enemy territory. If Major Johns stopped to think at all, he must have thought that Ryan had had time to clear the woods and should be in control of both sides of the road. It did occur to him that perhaps it was Ryan's flank attack on the Germans in front of Sadler that had made the C Company radio operator, or even Sadler himself, think they were receiving a counterattack. He cursed himself for not sending a runner forward to tell Sadler what Ryan was doing. He hoped the Able commander had had presence of mind enough to yell across the road and tell somebody in Charlie Company what was going on before he slanted across their front. He decided that Ryan would surely have enough sense to do that much without orders.

Anyway, use of the road was the quickest way to get forward. Nobody had said anything about seeing any fire coming down it.

He pulled himself across the low hedgerow that separated field and road, and looked over into the woods. No movement. He looked forward. Still no movement. He dropped into the shallow ditch along the road and lay quiet for a moment. No fire. He got to his feet and walked forward. Newcomb, brushing past him, took the lead.

They walked rapidly for a hundred yards. The firing began to die away. Then it stopped all along the whole front. The Major slowed a bit. These sudden changes in the tempo of the action puzzled him. He wondered if C Company had repulsed the attack, if A Company had driven in from the flank and forced the enemy to retreat, or if Ryan had been stopped and had pulled back into the woods to re-form and try it again.

While these questions passed through his mind a nasty feeling of failure grew inside him. Night was closing in. He had not succeeded in taking his first objective as a battalion commander. His stomach was knotting slowly but tightly with that overpowering fear, not fear of death or injury, but of failure. He kept moving forward.

They were only a few yards behind the hedgerow that Sadler was holding when a half dozen men ran across the road at least 300 yards ahead, just where a bend in the road carried it out of sight to the right. A voice from behind cried, "Ryan's men! They're behind the Germans!"

Newcomb was still in front. The voice, which was definitely

not Jimmie's, startled the CO.* He stopped to look back. Lieutenant Grimsehl almost bumped into him and he could see men scattered back along the ditch for a hundred yards. The whole command post group was following him, though he had wanted only Newcomb and Jimmie!

"What in hell are all these people doing out here?" he demanded.

Newcomb and Grimsehl both looked as surprised as Johns. They hadn't looked back either and no one had ordered the advance of the command post group as a whole. But since the Major hadn't told any of the officers not to follow him, the runners, seeing the officers going, came along too. Even the telephone men were patiently laying their wire although it had been cut by shell fire behind them ever since early in the fight.

None of that was clear at the moment. Major Johns, seeing the group, let them stay. As he turned to move on he was struck with the realization that he had not reported to Regiment since the attack had been launched, over an hour ago. That wouldn't do at all! Colonel Ordway would be wondering what was going on. He sat down in the shallow ditch with his back against the hedgerow. The others did the same except for Newcomb, who remained standing with his back to the enemy. Jimmie went down on one knee at the Major's feet, half in half out of the ditch.

Major Johns reached for the handset of the 300, intending to call Major Morris, his Executive, back at the rear command post, to tell him to call Regiment and report that they were held up, were in a little trouble, and could see no immediate prospect of further advance without help. Then he remembered you were supposed to write down all messages—that's what they had taught at Leavenworth, anyway. He guessed maybe he'd better write this one, just for the record.

Absent-mindedly clinging to the handset, he reached into a pocket for pencil and message book to write the first combat message he had ever written outside a classroom. Holding the

---

*Unless they are speaking formally, military men invariably refer to the commanding officer as the "CO" or the "Old Man."

book against his left knee, along with the handset, he began to fill in the blanks:

"To: CO, 115th Inf"

No, he remembered, that wasn't right. You had to use code names. Carefully he scratched that out and substituted "Lagoon 6." He ignored the other blanks, went straight to the message itself, "Stopped at second hedgerow. Both flanks in trouble. Cannot get ahead without help."

He looked at what he had written, but didn't like it. He was damned if he would squall for help so soon in the first fight.

He was drawing a line through the last sentence when the world suddenly exploded all around him. Sharp ballistic cracks pounded his eardrums so rapidly they seemed like one impossibly prolonged rifle shot. He was instantly paralyzed with overwhelming fright.

The radio operator, Jimmie, slumped forward at his feet, another man stumbled past to fall into the ditch ahead, and Newcomb cleared the eight-foot hedgerow apparently with one jump. But the Major was too shocked to move. His stomach knotted itself into a tight ball. It jammed against his pounding heart while his breathing stopped completely for an instant, then came in jerky gasps. The hair on his head felt as if it were rising like the hair on a cat's back. His skin prickled all over. But the most awful thing was the cold, empty feeling in his guts.

The burst of German machine gun fire lasted only seconds. But it seemed a lifetime before he could reach up and snatch a grenade from his pistol belt. He'd never heard a bullet crack by, inches from his head. He didn't know they sounded like that. He thought there was a German with a burp pistol behind the nearest tree on top of the hedgerow. He grabbed the pin on the grenade, but before he could throw it something made him stop and yell, "Anybody on the other side?"

He got a quick answer, "Hell yes!"

Before he could lower his arm the blast of a rifle right in his lap made him flinch. He squirmed back even closer against the hedgerow as Martin and Grimsehl went into action. They'd been at the front all the eleven days since a continuous line had been established in Normandy. The crack of bullets was nothing new to them. Almost side by side, lying flat in the ditch, they fired methodically across him and over Jimmie's head. Mechanically, he checked the pin in the grenade then, still a little dazed, hooked it back onto his belt harness.

He sat there for ten heartbeats before he realized just what had happened: the men they had seen run across the road ahead weren't Ryan's! They belonged to A. Hitler and Company and had undoubtedly been a machine-gun crew getting the hell out of the woods ahead of Able Company. They might have been scared too, but not too much to know a good target when they saw one; and the command post group, strung out down the ditch, was about as good a one as any machine gunner could ever expect to find. So they'd stopped at least long enough to let loose that one blast.

Even when he had it all figured out there was nothing he could do. He couldn't move without making Jimmie get up and disturbing the two officer's aim, and he didn't have a rifle himself.

He looked at the man who had fallen into the ditch and now was trying weakly to push himself up. It was Lieutenant Sadler, his face already greenish-grey with shock. He had been hit five or six times—in the head, chest, and both arms. Major Johns knew instinctively that Sadler was as good as dead. He called to him to lie still and take it easy, but the Charlie Company commander was already beyond hearing.

Johns felt that he ought to do something constructive—something to get their minds off the tragedy that had just struck. But he was without inspiration. Merely numb. Then, as often happens in times of crisis, inconsequential thoughts intervened—trivialities. Perhaps that was the best antidote. He found himself staring at a ring on Lieutenant Martin's finger, half under his M1 rifle. It jerked every time Martin fired, but it was a big ring and Johns was able to spell out the inscription: "V I R-G I N I A   M I L I-".

"Well I'll be damned," he said, "You from VMI?"

The artilleryman was so surprised at such a fool question in the middle of a firefight, that he paused in mid-squeeze. But he answered, "Yeah, why?"

"Me too. Class of '31. What class were you in?"

Martin grinned as he completed the trigger squeeze and the Major shuddered again as the rifle blast hit his battered eardrums. "'38," he answered. "You must have known—."

That was too much for Grimsehl. "Hey, you guys," he yelled. "Break up this alumni meeting. Let's scram out of here."

That brought the commander out of the daze he had been in ever since the deafening burst of enemy fire, perhaps two minutes before. He leaned forward and shook Jimmie's shoulder. "Come on, Jim. It's all over now. You can get up."

But Jimmie didn't move. Major Johns shook him again. Then he saw blood oozing slowly, thickly, brightly across his own shoe. Gently, he pulled at Jimmie's far shoulder. A neat, clean little bullet hole in the boy's helmet came into view, so the Major knew that Jimmie was dead. Something impelled him to pull Jimmie over until he could look into his face. The eyes were closed and an odd little half-smile made Jimmie look as if he were asleep, dreaming pleasant dreams. Slowly, the Major lowered him back to the ground and for a fleeting instant watched Jimmie's lifeblood continue to flow across his shoe.

But the emergency had to be met. Jimmie had now become a problem. They needed his carbine and radio, both of which were strapped to his small back. "Dead weight" took on a new meaning as they tried to get the carbine out from under him. Major Johns was afraid to lean too far forward, while neither Martin nor Grimsehl could even kneel without making good targets, so Jimmie's 120-odd pounds were hard to handle. Somehow they got the gun loose after Martin stopped firing long enough to cut the strap, but it was so choked with dirt and blood that the Major wondered if it would fire. He aimed it in the general direction of the woods where the Germans had disappeared, and pulled the trigger. It fired but failed to throw a new cartridge into the chamber. He worked the bolt by hand and fired again. It was okay for single shots.

Next came the radio. It took all three of them to get it off, and again Martin had to cut the carrying straps.

"You two take the radio with you. I'll cover you with fire while you make a run for the woods. Then you can cover me." The Major rolled over into firing position without waiting for an answer, put an elbow in the pool of the radio operator's blood, and began to work the bolt on the carbine as fast as he could. Martin and Grimsehl ran together across the narrow road into the cover of the trees, then took up the fire. Johns followed. The Germans didn't fire another shot.

Together on the edge of the woods they looked back at Sadler. He was quiet now, his eyes open to the blue sky.

"No use sending a medic for him now." Martin shook his head.

"Maybe not, but I'm going to anyhow. The Doc said they do some wonderful things sometimes."

Sadler had been his friend, but Grimsehl had seen more men die than either of the others. He shook his head. "No use, Major. Ol' Sad never knew what hit him. But he was a mighty brave guy, and never would quit. I guess he kept trying to go on even after he was struck."

Division Wants La Forge Tonight! / 2

NOTHING SEEMED to be happening anywhere on the front, but Major Johns wasn't anxious to get to C Company any more. In the few minutes they had been tied up in their own little fight it seemed as if all the rest of the battalion, as well as the Germans, had stopped shooting to see how the command post group would make out. If there had been a counterattack on the center it couldn't have been very serious or Sadler wouldn't have been able to leave his company and come looking for the Major; and as Ryan wasn't firing any more he must have the woods in hand. But what about Weddle? Johns decided to go back to the point he had left and send runners if he couldn't get reports by radio. He tried the set they had salvaged from Jimmie's back, but got no answer.

They looked for the last time at Sadler and Jimmie. Then the Major got another shock when he saw a third man, well back of where they had been, also lying on his face in the ditch, in the stillness of death. They made their way through the woods and crossed over to the hedgerow corner they had left not more than fifteen minutes before. All the rest of the command post group was there, except for two men who had been slightly wounded by the same burst of fire that had killed the three. Newcomb was fingering a hole in his field jacket where a bullet had passed between his left arm and body without touching him. He was shaken by the experience but he had already sent messengers to all three rifle companies, calling for a report, and had sent the wiremen to look for the break in the wire to the rear.

The commander sat alone against the hedgerow thinking things over. He had gotten over his fright, except that his innards seemed sore from their recent acrobatics. Regiment was only some 800 yards behind them on the far edge of the main woods. He decided to go back himself, which he could probably do before the wire was fixed, give a report to Colonel Ordway, and find out what the units on the flanks of the battalion were doing. Then he would come back and make a determined effort to get that little dump called La Forge, which was the battalion objective, by picking up the attack again just at dusk. He looked at the sun, which was nearing the horizon. He might barely have time to do all this if he hurried like mad. He wanted very badly to capture that village.

He told Newcomb and Grimsehl that he intended to renew the attack. He directed Newcomb to plan the details in light of what he should learn from the companies, and instructed Grimsehl to see if anybody had taken any prisoners who could tell them anything about the enemy strength. Then he started briskly to the rear.

As he walked he couldn't keep his thoughts away from the hot spot he had been in a few minutes before, and the lessons he had learned so quickly but at such a price. In little more than an hour of his first fight he had lost two company commanders, two radio operators, and three other men, besides just escaping death himself. As he thought about the crack of those machine gun bullets his stomach began to squirm again until by a conscious effort he forced it to behave.

He couldn't understand why he hadn't been hit too. Jimmie's head had been not more than two feet from his own. Newcomb, in front, and Sadler, directly behind him, had been hit. The whole burst must have missed him by scant inches, he decided, and he very seriously thanked God for his safety. At the same time he promised never again to risk the lives of others if he could avoid it. It was a bitter lesson, repeated every time the eyes of his mind focused on Jimmie's bright blood oozing over his shoe or on Sadler's sudden death. He looked down at the shoe, shuddered at the still-red stain, and tried to scuff it off on the grass.

He thought some more about the way those bullets had cracked. The sound had been as sharp as the crack of a bull-whip, yet vastly louder. He had heard more distant snapping sounds in action before, but he had never known what they were and had been too busy then to ask. Now he knew—after learning the hard way. He wondered if the infiltration courses he had heard about were teaching the new soldiers what that snapping sound meant.

He also wondered how many of the fiction writers who wrote of a bullet "whizzing" or "singing" or "zipping" had ever heard one.

On his way to the regimental command post the Major passed a knocked-out Sherman tank. What distinguished this smoking brown hulk from others he had seen that day was the single blackened, claw-like hand and forearm that was thrust out of the turret toward the sky. The fingers were separate and more than half curled, like the talon of a striking eagle. But this hand was not striking. It seemed, rather, to be calling down an imprecation on the fate that had let it die there in agony.

The Major found Colonel Ordway, telephone in hand, standing at the foot of the big tree he had noticed when the battalion had moved forward past that spot earlier in the day. Colonel Ordway was a big distinguished-looking man. He had been chief of staff at division headquarters until a few days before, where Major Johns had known him. He liked Colonel Ordway and was very pleased to serve under him. The Colonel was a gentleman as well as a splendid officer. In the field you couldn't always tell who was a gentleman—not that it mattered much.

"Well," boomed the regimental commander, "what's going on? I've just been trying to get you."

Johns saluted as he answered, "Sir, we're stuck at the second hedgerow and I had to use my reserves to protect my flanks. It doesn't look as if we'll get to La Forge today unless we have better luck later."

"Have many casualties?"

"I don't know about the companies yet, because I haven't any reports from them except yells about their flanks and counterattacks, but Nabb was wounded early, Sadler is dead, and I've lost two radio operators, besides three other men out of my CP group." He was still too full of his experience not to want to tell about it.

The Colonel listened sympathetically.

"Well," he said when the Major was through, "we've got to keep going regardless. Division wants us to get La Forge tonight. And by the way, I saw your jump-off. It was mighty fine."

The battalion commander smiled weakly. He was beginning to appreciate how tired he was after marching and skirmishing all the night before, making a forced march forward during the early afternoon, and undergoing the nerve-racking ordeal of taking a unit into combat for the first time. He was, he realized, also extremely thirsty. He took a pull on his canteen.

"Sir," he answered, "I feel we can take that next hedgerow and keep going, all right, but before we try it I've got to get forward to see my company commanders and lay on a few plans. I figure we can try it right at dusk and, if we make it, go as far as we can in the dark before we have to quit and hole up. It's bad country, damned bad for night work, but it'll have to be that or nothing now."

He glanced at the sinking sun and went on, "If we could push the 3d Battalion through those woods to the right of the road—we've got the woods clear right down to the end now— that battalion could get behind the Germans in front of us and we could make it easy."

Ordway took no offense at Johns' suggestion as to how he should fight his regiment, but he shook his head.

"That's out. Division has nailed the 3d Battalion down tight. They're the only reserve left in the whole outfit."

The Major looked disconsolate. "Yes sir. Shall I go ahead on my own then?"

The Colonel had a look at the sun, now barely visible

through the tops of the trees. "Yes, you go ahead and do the best you can. Keep me informed; the wire is in again."

Johns saluted, moved away a bit, paused long enough to take another drink from his canteen, then struck out at a fast walk, head up and shoulders back. No use letting the regimental staff think he was whipped down. Or licked, either.

It didn't take him long to get back to the little knot of men behind the hedgerow. He was surprised and pleased to find Weddle and Ryan both waiting for him. With them was another lieutenant, slight of build and unprepossessing in appearance, whom he did not know. As he looked at this officer for the first time he was struck by a resemblance to pictures he had seen of the young Abraham Lincoln.

Captain Weddle performed the introduction. "Sir, this is Lieutenant Kenney. He just got back a few minutes ago. Newcomb gave him Charlie Company."

The Major remembered what he had heard about Kenney and his outstanding leadership in the ill-fated attack at St. Clair a few days before he himself had been sent down to take the battalion.

"Glad to see you, Kenney," he said. "I've heard a lot about you, all good. You picked a good time to get back." He remembered that the lieutenant had collapsed from exhaustion after an earlier fight and had been sent to the rear for a rest. "How do you feel?"

Kenney smiled. "Fine, sir," he replied. "And I'm mighty glad to be with the company again. But I sure hated to hear that ol' Sadler had got it."

The battalion commander nodded sadly and turned to the others. There was work to be done. "How're we doing, fellows?"

Weddle answered first, "Well, sir, it's rough over in those little fields. I still don't know where some of my people are, but we can hold what we have, I think."

He looked in the direction of his company as a single shot reverberated. Then he continued, "My right flank got separated from C Company when they had to pull back out of that orchard and now I figure we're about a hundred yards or so ahead of them, with our left flank on a sunken road. Much obliged for sending that platoon from Able over to help us. They ran right into a gang of Germans who were tearing into us over there. Stopped 'em just in time, too."

The Major nodded approval. "What's the chances of making some more progress?"

Weddle looked up quickly. "Now?"

"Sure."

"I dunno. What about Ryan?"

Ryan picked up the report. "Well, we got the woods clear without any trouble. Didn't lose but a few men. But then when we got to the end of the cover it was a different story. There are Krauts all over the country around that little triangular tip of woods, and we're holding it in a sort of V with people looking in every direction but up. We tried to get across the road to help Sadler, but the enemy were right there waiting for us so that every time one of our men would stick his head over a hedgerow he'd get a half dozen hand grenades and sixteen burp pistols fired at him. There's a little orchard on our right, with another hedgerow on the far side, complete with Heinies and guns."

He thought a moment, then added, "We might make it across the road if we pour a lot of smoke and mortars into 'em and then rush 'em, but it's getting awfully late to be beating around in this kind of country."

Ryan stopped and looked at Kenney. It was Kenney's turn.

"Sir, I only had a few minutes to look things over before Weddle came along and invited me back here to see you, but that orchard is a terrible place. No cover anywhere. Machine guns covering every inch of it. We lost a lot of men in there the first time." He paused. "But we'll do the best we can."

"Well, rough or not, we're going ahead," the Major stated flatly. He spread his map on the ground, looked at it for a minute, then pointed to a lateral road that ran between the hardtop road on their right and the sunken road where Weddle had put his flank. "If we get to this road we'll at least have the battalion all in one piece, instead of scattered all over hell and gone the way it is now."

The company commanders nodded. The battalion lay in the shape of a rough, winged U, with C Company to the rear and B Company so far forward they seemed to be on a line with where the Germans faced C. There was a vertical gap of over a hundred yards between B and C and almost as much between C and A. Not a very desirable situation.

The battalion commander looked at his watch and glanced at the shadows that told him the sun was almost on the horizon.

"Let's try this—it's getting on toward 2100 hours but it'll be light for about an hour yet. At 2125 we'll put smoke from all our mortars on the enemy in front of C Company, concentrating on the corner near the road; and the artillery will smoke your front, Weddle. Then at exactly 2130 all the mortars and the artillery will fire one round of high explosive from each gun. When you hear the HE hit, you take off like hell for the next hedgerow—all except Ryan.

"I figure the enemy will think you're going to try to come across the road," he went on, speaking to Ryan, "and will be looking for you there. You fire up a storm, throw grenades, and make 'em think you've got a whole army rarin' to get at 'em. If they fall for it Kenney ought to be able to get across the orchard. Weddle ought to be able to make the little way he's got to go anyway, and once we get on that road we can have a quick look around and maybe keep right on going into La Forge. I'll go with Kenney. Any questions?"

"Yes sir. Who's going to make the arrangements with the artillery? You want my forward observer to do it, or will you?" Weddle asked.

Martin broke in, "I'll get it laid on, but you tell your FO about it and have him keep on adjusting fire wherever you want it, as soon as the smoke stops."

"That reminds me," said the Major, "who's taking Nabb's place?"

"Sergeant Wiskamp. He's right here," answered Newcomb,

nodding at a husky noncom who stood on the edge of the little group of officers, notebook in hand.

"Can you get this fixed up with the mortars?" asked the Major.

"Yes sir. Consider it done—easy, sir," grinned the sergeant.

The meeting was about to break up when Johns looked again at his watch and grunted, "Whup—timing's going to be damned important. Let's do a little watch synchronizing. You, Martin, and you, Wiskamp, be sure you do the same with your gun people."

After they had gone through the ritual of synchronizing their watches, the company commanders took off at a dead run for their companies. They had a lot to do and little time in which to do it. Martin took up his phone, which had arrived a few minutes before. Sergeant Wiskamp ran in the direction of the nearest mortar forward observer, who he knew had sound-powered telephone communication back to his mortar section.

The CO looked around to check on his own group. He saw a new man sitting against the hedgerow. A 300 radio sat on top of the hedgerow itself, its long slender aerial concealed beside a sapling that grew atop the 'row. Newcomb followed the commander's eyes and answered the unspoken question. "Major Morris* heard we were out of radios and operators so he sent us a whole new set, complete with operator. I don't know where he got it, but it works and we're in with all companies for the first time this afternoon."

"Well, Allah be praised for small favors," Johns breathed. He turned to see what Grimsehl, who had been quivering by his side for some moments, wanted to say.

The S2 was pale as he saluted, stiffly and unnecessarily. Then he blurted between trembling lips, "Sir, they got Doc Carter."

"What do you mean, 'They got Doc Carter'?"

"Yes sir, they got him; he's dead. Sniper shot him through the head early this afternoon."

"A sniper? For God's sake what was the Doc doing where

---

*The battalion executive.

a sniper could get him? And why would a sniper be shooting a medic? He had his armband on, didn't he?"

"Yes sir. He had it on all right, but they shot him just the same. From a range of not more than 150 yards. He was prowling around up front—maybe you didn't know he was a psychiatrist. He was up watching how the men acted under fire. Some bird caught it in the leg through a gap in a hedgerow and Doc, naturally, stopped to fix him up. Then the sniper got Doc too."

Grimsehl swallowed painfully. Then continued, "Ryan didn't want to tell you, but that was one of the things that slowed him up going through the woods. His boys heard about it as soon as it happened. They were all so mad they wanted to go after the sniper. Some of 'em even started over the hedgerow before Ryan went back there himself and finally managed to get 'em back on the main job."

Major Johns bowed his head and stared at the ground for just an instant. Sadler, Jimmie, and now Doc—the fine, sensitive man who was far more interested in others than in himself; who had shared his last half bottle of wine with the new major the night he had taken over the battalion, just three days before. I guess that's the way it goes, he thought. The best men always catch it first.

He looked up at Grimsehl, "Thank you, George, I know how you feel. Did you get any more information about the enemy?"

"No sir," answered the S2. "We haven't had a thing since this afternoon when we first got here."

The Major turned to Newcomb. "Look, Newc, I'm going forward to C Company to see how they're getting along. I'll probably go with them when they move forward in the attack. I do NOT want anyone to go with me, not even you or the radio man. You stay right here until we attack. Then as soon as you hear we have that road up there you move the whole works straight ahead until you find me. I'll be looking for you and I'll stick close to the Charlie radio so we can keep in touch."

The S3 said "Yes sir," whereupon the commander scrambled

over the hedgerow into the field ahead. He slanted to the right until he found a shallow ditch running along the hedgerow that bounded both pasture and road—the same one he had followed before, but on the field side this time. He trotted toward Charlie Company, hoping his plan would work. There had been no firing, except occasional single shots, for a long time.

Reaching the second hedgerow he turned left, looking for Kenney. The men, who were spread out well, seemed in good shape in spite of their trouble in the orchard ahead. He missed Kenney but ran into a tall young second lieutenant whom he did not recognize. The officer introduced himself, "Sir, I'm Lieutenant Iperian, Section Leader for the Dog Company* mortars. Got my observation post right here."

"Good," answered the Major, "Mind if I have a look?"

Without waiting for an answer, he stepped up into a hole cut into the side of the hedgerow. From there he peered into the dusky orchard that separated his own lines from the Germans. He saw no enemy but he could make out a number of still forms scattered on the grass beneath the apple trees. They marked the high water line of Charlie's first try across the orchard. Something about a cluster of four made him look again at them. He stepped down.

"Those men out there—they aren't all dead, are they? I thought I saw a couple of them move."

"No sir, there's at least four in one bunch that aren't dead. We're going to get 'em out in a few minutes, as soon as it gets a little darker or we attack."

Major Johns stepped up for another long look at the men. He was thinking about going after them himself. It would be a good thing for him to do in his first fight. It ought to prove to the men that he had enough guts. He looked again, trying hard to see the far hedgerow. He couldn't. As he stepped down he thought of Doc Carter and discarded the idea. Dead battalion commanders didn't do their men any good, or themselves either.

He nodded at Iperian, then went on looking for Kenney. He

---

*The Battalion Weapons Company.

finally found him at his command post, holding the radio handset, obviously waiting for his commander. It was 2120. The show would start in five minutes.

Kenney drawled, "Sir, Captain Newcomb wants to talk to you. He's about to have a fit."

The Major got his S3 at once. "Sir," yelled the S3 so loud he hardly needed the radio, "The Colonel just called to say no show. D'you get it? No show."

"Sure, I get it," answered Johns, trying not to display his own relief at the recall from what might have been a very messy affair. "No show. Have you told the companies yet?"

"No sir."

"All right. Tell 'em. I'll listen."

Newcomb made the cancellation official with some formal double talk, but he could have saved himself the trouble, as every operator had already heard the original talk between the S3 and the battalion commander.

By the time the last "Roger" came through, Kenney had sent messengers to each of his platoons, just in case the word didn't reach them via the little SCR 536 radios used for intra-company communications. It was well that he did. One platoon leader, whose set was not working, was getting nervous because the promised mortar barrage hadn't started on time.

The Major then sat down for a little chat with Kenney. They talked over the condition of the men, the ammunition supply, the chances for success in the morning, and a dozen other things. They were interrupted by a burst of hostile fire from the far left. Simultaneously a long string of tracers flew across the field, waist high, twenty feet behind the hedgerow. Their crack was vicious even at that distance, causing Major Johns to flinch a little in spite of himself.

Then things began to happen fast. Kenney jumped up and ran toward the left. There was some yelling in that direction; it was pretty obvious that Weddle was having trouble again.

The Major slid forward onto his belly and edged his way ten feet out from the hedgerow, facing left. Pushing Jimmie's carbine forward he pulled the bolt back to make sure there was a shell in the chamber. Then he snapped it back and let it fly forward of itself, to see if it would feed. It did. The man back at Regiment who had cleaned it while he talked with the Colonel had done a good job.

His object in moving out into the field was self-protection, hard as it was to force himself away from the solid earth hedgerow. He knew that if an attack should come through the vertical gap between Charlie and Able Companies the line of men in their holes behind the hedgerow would be enfiladed. He did not propose to be caught in any such fire again.

On the extreme right a voice barked, "God damn you, stay the hell up on that hedgerow and watch that road! There's a whole company between you and them bastards over there, but there ain't nobody on that road. Now WATCH it!"

A squad leader was tending the right flank.

In every squad there were men assigned the job of watching toward the front. Most of them kept their posts. But one or two dropped down into the holes they had dug, only to be ordered back by sergeants and platoon leaders. Charlie Company was not going to be caught by the same ruse they had planned to try on the Germans. The battalion commander watched the by-play with approval.

The firing on the left swelled. The cough of mortars joined the crack of rifles while the thin "burrrrrrp, burrrrrrrrp, burrrrrrrrrrrrrrp" of the German machine pistols made a sort of obligato to the heavier tones of other weapons. It was incessant while the fight was at its height. Tracers flew over the hedgerow. Occasionally another stream of machine gun bullets crackled across the field, safely high.

The Major got to his feet. He started a crouching run to the left. He had nearly reached the end of the field when four or five men, yelling, "Don't shoot, don't shoot," piled over the hedgerow that separated Charlie and Baker Companies. He stopped, carbine alert. It could be a trick. But it wasn't; the men were GI's all right.

As he lowered his gun, wondering what this was all about, a figure stepped out from the hedgerow and voiced the same question, "What's going on here anyway? Just what's this all about?"

It was Lieutenant Iperian, arms spread wide to catch the running men, carbine slung over his shoulder, the picture of calm.

He caught the leading man by his jacket, which piled the others up in a tight little knot. The man panted, "Krauts! Paratroopers! They're right behind us! Run!"

Iperian glanced over the man's shoulder, unmoved. "Well, now, I don't see any Krauts. Just look."

The men looked back. All they could see were several Charlie Company men, standing quietly, rifles ready. The leader of the runaways relaxed then shuddered violently. Iperian went on, "I don't think there're any Krauts chasing you at all. Let's just go see about this."

The man tried to pull away from him. "But there were," he cried, "There were, I tell you! They came right over the hedgerow and shot right down the whole squad. They got the sergeant and all the rest. We're the only ones left. They nearly got me. Look!"

He poked a finger through a hole in his jacket. But Iperian, unimpressed, moved in the direction of Baker Company even as the man protested, dragging him along while the others followed meekly.

"Well," Iperian went on, "let's just go and see what Captain Weddle has to say about all this."

He called softly to the men guarding the company flank, "See anything?"

"No sir." The answer came back quickly and calmly.

The mortar observer and his little group of panic-stricken men disappeared over the hedgerow.

The Major knew he had just seen a wonderful example of leadership at its very finest. Iperian, quickly, calmly, and efficiently, had stopped what could have been a rout. He made a mental note to see that the young officer was recommended for a Bronze Star.

He moved to where the men were watching the left flank,

but in a few more minutes the firing died away. He started back
to Kenney's command post, then remembered the men in the
orchard. Iperian's observation post being almost beside him,
he stepped up to have a look. He couldn't see the men, because
by then it was very dark under the trees.

He turned to the nearest man. "Will you go out with me to
bring those men in from the orchard?"

The man answered, grinning, "Oh, we got 'em out of there
about fifteen minutes ago. An aid man came by and Lieutenant
Iperian and a couple of us went out and brought 'em in. They're
all back at the aid station by now."

The Major thanked the man and walked on, wondering how
many more young officers like Iperian he might have under
his command. He hoped that there would be a lot.

Kenney was at the command post when he got there. He had
news.

"Sir, Captain Weddle just called back to Battalion to tell you
a platoon of German paratroopers hit his left flank again but
his company ran 'em off after they got into one squad and did
some damage. I think from what he said that it was one of his
squads that he had lost on the way up and hadn't found yet."

The Major merely nodded. He walked slowly back across
the field to his own command post in the corner of the hedgerow by the road.

You Don't Say "No" to the General / 3

THE PHONE was in. The Major called Colonel Ordway, getting him at once.

"Hello Johns," said Ordway, "still want to make that attack?"

"No sir, not now any more. It's too dark."

The regimental commander chuckled briefly. "Well, you won't have to tonight. Division says hold what we have but expect orders later tonight. So you go ahead and dig in where you are. Try to let your men get a little rest. They may need it for tomorrow. I don't think we'll have any trouble with the Germans tonight but we'll run contact patrols anyway, of course. You'll send one every hour to the 116th, on your left, and the 2d Battalion will come over and visit your right."

"Yes sir. May I send my S2 back to you to get a line on the 116th?" As he spoke he remembered that he had forgotten to ask how the other units had done earlier in the afternoon.

"Yes, Johns. Certainly; furthermore you'd better come back here yourself as soon as you get your companies straightened out so I can give you anything that comes down from Division later on tonight."

"Very well sir, I'll be there in a half hour or so." Ringing off, he nodded to Grimsehl to indicate that the S2 could go back to Regiment at once.

Then he turned to Newcomb. "Newc, tell the companies to dig in where they are for the night. Tell Weddle he will run contact patrols to the 116th every hour. I want him to take a route well to the rear of his left flank so that his patrols will run into anything that might be trying to cut in from behind. At the same time the patrols will stay clear of any outposts the Krauts may have out there. Also tell him that Grimsehl will be over in a little while to show his first patrol where the 116th is.

"Find out for me exactly where Ryan's right flank is and mark it on my map. I want to take this information back to Regiment. The 2d Battalion is going to run patrols to us but they won't have the foggiest idea——."

The phone rang. The operator handed the handset to Captain Newcomb, saying, "It's Captain Warfield, in Regimental S3, sir."

Newcomb took the phone. "Yeah Al; okay Al. Right away."

Handing the phone back to the operator he looked up at the Major. "Warfield wants an overlay of our positions. He always does, of course."

The Major stared at his map, a light blob in the dark. "Now just how the hell does he think we're going to make an overlay in the middle of the night with Germans all over the place?"

The S3's teeth shone in a grin. "Major, that's strictly our problem. All he has to do is tell us he wants one so he can tell the Colonel we didn't give him any when the time comes to send the regimental positions back to Division."

"All right. I'll give him something when I go back there in a few minutes. Weddle doesn't know where his left flank is, 'cause he never has had a chance to go see, I guess. By the time he can find out it'll be too late for me to take the coordinates to Regiment. But I think I know about where the flank is and by the time it gets on that big picture map at Division it won't make much difference anyway. Have we got a line to Ryan yet?"

"Yes sir."

"Then call him and ask him how far his right flank extends back along those woods. That's going to be important to the 2d Battalion."

"Right." Newcomb turned to the phone while Major Johns

started for Regiment, flinging over his shoulder, "I'll call you as soon as I get there."

Suddenly he was conscious of the fact that he was very cold. He called softly, "Barbeaux?"

No answer. He called again, cursing his orderly, whose sole mission in life was to be available at all times. Someone in the dark nearby smothered a giggle and volunteered, "I saw him down the 'row a while back, digging a hole."

"Thanks," said the Major, moving cautiously along the hedgerow until he found his coat lying folded beside a shallow hole in which Barbeaux snored gently. He wanted to prod the man with his foot and give him a dressing down for not being on hand when he was wanted. But for some reason he did not. Instead he unslung his carbine, belted the heavy coat around him, picked up the little gun again, and struck off across the field.

It was an eerie feeling, walking alone across the pastures, thence down the narrow, hard-topped road that led under the trees of the Bois de Bretel. His heels rang out much too loudly. He tried to tiptoe, but felt silly. Stepping off the road, he tripped over branches. He moved back onto the road, thinking, "The hell with it. If the Krauts are that close it won't make much difference where I walk."

The distinctive smell of burned metal and rubber, flavored with a suggestion of charred flesh, told him he was approaching the knocked-out tank near Regiment. He was passing it somewhat gingerly when a sharp. "Halt! Who's there?" brought him up short.

He jerked his carbine half up before he realized it was part of the guard around the Regimental command post. He answered in a stage whisper, "Lagoon Red 6," giving his code name.

"What's your name?" The guard matched his whisper.

"Major Johns."

"What's the password?"

Password? He had forgotten there was such a thing. "That's

a good question, soldier, but I don't have the faintest idea what it is tonight—it was 'roof' last night."

The voice did not answer immediately. The Major became mildly amused at the ghostly interrogation.

Then it came again. "You sound okay, but put your hands up over your head high and walk straight ahead so I can get a look at you."

Johns did as he was told, holding his carbine in one hand. He jumped just a little when a form loomed up beside him to peer at his face as a bayonet pressed against his side.

"Okay, Major, go ahead, but you better get the word before you come back. Some of the guys got itchy trigger fingers tonight."

He breathed more easily, thanked the guard, and fumbled his way to the big tree where he found Colonel Ordway in exactly the same position he had left him earlier. He said, "Good evening, sir."

The colonel's booming voice was subdued somewhat as a courtesy to the situation, "Hello, Johns, how do you feel?"

"Pretty well, sir. Any word from Division yet?"

"No, not a thing. I doubt now that we'll hear anything much before midnight. Why don't you lie down over there and catch a little rest while we're waiting?"

"Thanks, Colonel, I've got to give Warfield our positions first, but I'll probably do that as soon as I get through. May I use the phone, please?"

The Colonel, pointing to the telephone operator at his feet, moved away.

"Get me Red," said the Major to the operator, "and don't ring either loud or long. It's neither necessary nor desirable."

In a moment he had the information he wanted about Ryan's flank. He asked the nearest form where he might find Captain Warfield. The man offered to lead him to the jeep where the Regimental S3 had last been seen. Johns accepted the offer with thanks.

Warfield was still there. The Major was very tired and his temper was definitely showing signs of wear. He launched his attack without preliminaries, "Warfield, I'm Major Johns. Just how the hell did you expect my company commanders and my S3 to make you an overlay in the middle of this black night when there's Krauts all over the place and no more shelter for light than the palm of my hand?"

If the S3 was taken aback he failed to show it. He hesitated only a moment before he answered, "Why, I didn't know what you have for shelter up there. But we've got to know where your lines are. Newcomb knows we always ask for an overlay as soon as we can."

This was logical enough. But Johns was in a stubborn, unreasonable mood. A more conciliatory reply from Warfield, showing appreciation for what the battalion had been through in the last few hours, might have calmed the Major down somewhat and made him realize how unreasonable he was being. As it was he snapped back, "Well, in the future before you go asking for impossible things you better make it your business to find out what the situation is. What the hell would you do with an overlay if I gave you one?"

"Put it on my map."

"How?"

"In the jeep, here, under a blanket."

"All right. Show me your map and I'll show you where our lines are."

They got into the jeep, heads together in the small area of the back seat, while two men arranged a blanket over them. Warfield turned on a flashlight with a bit of blue cellophane over the lens. It gave a sickly light that was barely adequate for the job. The map lay on the back seat and the Major took the Regimental S3's pencil and carefully marked the locations of the companies on it. He did not hesitate to show Weddle's line drawn back down the sunken road. He was sure it must be that way.

Warfield looked at the line. "Any outposts?"

Johns answered, "No," quite flatly, without offering to explain.

"What are you doing about those big gaps on both sides of C Company?"

"Damn it," the Major flared again, "They're my gaps and I'll damn well look after them."

"Okay, sir," There was an unnecessary emphasis on the "sir." "But they're the Colonel's gaps too. He'll want to know about them."

"Tell him I said not to worry about 'em. I have men covering the far side of each hedgerow and we're running patrols back and forth."

This was not entirely true at the moment, but Major Johns had not thought much about the gaps since the attack had been cancelled. He would set up the patrols as soon as he got back to his own command post. He did know that Weddle and Kenney had men on the far side of their flanking hedgerows to keep out any attempts at infiltration during the night.

"All right, Major, I'll tell him."

Warfield switched off the light and threw back the blanket.

Johns looked around blindly in the darkness. He had temporarily lost his night vision in the dim light of the flash.

"Have you seen my S2, Lieutenant Grimsehl?"

"Yes, he got the dope on the location of the 116th and the 2d Battalion and left here about 10 minutes ago. But I don't know where he went."

"Thanks." The Major crawled carefully out of the jeep. He, too, wanted to know about the 116th and the 2d Battalion, not only where they were but how they'd done that afternoon. But he'd rather have it from the Colonel.

He found the Colonel and asked what had happened on the flanks. Ordway replied, "We haven't heard much from the 116th, but from their position it doesn't look to me as if they got off the LD; 2d Battalion hit a big chateau over there and spent the whole afternoon scrapping around it. At dark they had the stables but the Germans still had the house.

"I think you got farther from where you started than anyone else. In fact, I believe that's why Division cancelled your attack. If you'd made La Forge you'd have been way out on a limb and stood a good chance of being cut off."

Major Johns, elated at their comparative success, was thankful that he had not renewed the attack and perhaps made another 500 or 1,000 yards. They would have been out in front like clay pigeons, for anyone to knock down. It was the first time he had seen a practical application of what was popularly known as "the big picture," supposedly concocted for the edification of high brass and war correspondents yet sufficiently vague to cover a certain amount of error on the ground. His mind jumped quickly to the enormous classroom at the Command and General Staff College at Fort Leavenworth where just such problems had been shown on huge maps or worked out by the student officers in practical exercises. He smiled to himself as he hoped that Bill Witte, the Division G3, was a graduate.

The Colonel, standing by the big tree, nodded smiling assent when the Major said quietly that he thought maybe he would take a little nap.

But sleep would not come, tired as he was. His mind would not relax, but insisted on reviewing nearly everything that had happened since he had taken charge of the battalion. He lived again the scene when General Gerhardt had called him in and asked abruptly, "Johns, can you command an infantry battalion?"

Having served under the General back in the old 56th Cavalry Brigade, down on the Mexican border, he had learned then that no junior officer ever said "No" to General Gerhardt.

"Yes sir," had slipped out before he could think. But the answer would have been the same if he'd had a week to study about it.

"All right. You've got the 1st Battalion of the 115th. Ordway just called up and asked for you, although I can't imagine why." The General had a twinkle in his eye when he added that last phrase.

"Yes sir. There's just one thing, sir."

"What's that?" The General frowned.

"Sir, I don't know a thing about the administration of an infantry outfit."

Gerhardt laughed. "You've got a staff for that. All you have to do is fight 'em."

So, in a proud daze he had bundled his bedroll into a jeep and gone down to take over a unit he had never seen.

He had found a dispirited battalion that had lost its longtime commander, Lieutenant Colonel Blatt, the day after they hit the beach. The unit had had a very rough six days culminating in a bloody repulse at St. Clair sur Elle. But it was basically a fine battalion. Two days' rest, out of the fighting line, had been enough to bring it back to normal. He'd cracked down hard on loose chin straps, flopping trouser legs, and other signs of low morale, thus earning for himself the title of "That red-headed garrison sonuvabitch with the little mustache." But the outfit was a going concern again and he was mighty proud of it already.

He flinched a bit when he thought of how he had fouled things up the night before on the march that had brought them from their reserve position to the Line of Departure in the Bois de Bretel. Then he'd done the same thing that very day. He'd have to get over this business of rushing up front every time a shot or two was fired. Or at least he must remember to tell other people not to come along. Last night he'd jammed half the battalion on top of the other half just because Weddle's point had gotten into a little scrap and he'd been impatient to find out what it was all about.

Then, irrelevantly, the fact that he had done nothing about getting more food and ammunition up to the companies struck him with the force of a blow.

He jumped up, looking for Colonel Ordway. The Colonel's big form was sitting against the tree. He called softly, "Colonel?"

But the Colonel was not asleep. He answered instantly, "Yes, Johns?"

"Sir, if you don't mind I'd like to go back to my CP. It isn't

far and I can always come back for orders, or I could send
Newcomb back here."

"Certainly. Go right ahead. Never mind about Newcomb.
I'll call if I want you."

The Major saluted absent-mindedly. It was a habit to salute
colonels, even in the dark. He started back to his battalion, remembered to ask the password of the operations sergeant, then
hit the hard road.

Passing the sentry in good order he made excellent time by
paying no attention to the noise of his heels on the pavement.
Then he moved out into the meadow, staying well to the right
in the pitch-black shadow of the trees. There was no moon but
it was a clear, starlit night. Finding the stillness oppressive in
the open, he began to feel something like a little boy going
upstairs to bed alone in the dark of a great house. He hunched
his carbine up to a ready position, surprised and a little abashed
to find that he was trying to tiptoe again.

Halfway to the command post he heard a slight scuffling
noise out on the road. Instantly his heart began to pound. He
sank slowly to one knee, swinging his carbine toward the sound.
It was not repeated. He was about to relax when a quick,
scurrying rustle sent his heart into new paroxysms while his
hands began to sweat though his mouth was dry again. Then
he recognized the sound for what it was—a rabbit breaking
cover—and laughed at himself as he stood up and resumed
his quiet walk.

His own command post sentry stopped him this time, whispering the challenge as softly as he could. The Major obeyed it
instantly. The sentry, recognizing his voice, let him pass at once.

As soon as he got to the scattered group of sleeping men
that marked the command post he grabbed the nearest shoulder
and shook it hard.

"Where's Captain Newcomb?"

"You've got him, Major. What's up?" The S3 had either
been awake or had a remarkable ability to snap out of sleep.

"What about ammo and chow?"

"Oh hell, Major, Jim Morris and I took care of that an hour

ago. Every man in the outfit has a full supply of ammo and three more C-rations by now. I've got yours around here somewhere."

An hour ago! What time was it then? He looked at his watch and was amazed to see that it was 0130. He hadn't known it, but he must have been sound asleep for at least two hours while he'd been at Regiment.

To Newcomb he said, "Thanks. I'd forgotten all about it. Any news?"

"Nope, everything's quiet as a church." The S3 looked at the battalion commander in the starlight and grinned as he went on, "Now, Major, you don't have to concern yourself with everything up here. You just leave the details to us. We're used to looking after them."

"All right, Newc, I'll do that," he answered, thinking that the General had known what he was talking about when he'd said 'You've got a staff for that.' Then he remembered Grimsehl.

"Where's George? Did he get back?"

Before Newcomb could answer, the S2's voice came from close by, "Right here, sir."

"Oh—good. Did you get all the dope you wanted? Are the patrols moving okay?"

"Yes sir to everything. The 116th is a good 600 yards to our left. I came to Baker Company as soon as I found out where they were, and took the first patrol over myself.

"Hell, Major, the Krauts could filter a regiment through that hole if they knew it was there and wanted to try it. I told Weddle to have the patrols go very slowly and take a full hour to make the trip, so there would be somebody along the way all the time. But I needn't have bothered. That country's so rough it'll take 'em an hour anyway, if they don't get lost.

"I sent a sergeant who went with me to take the second patrol over. They'll keep that up from one patrol to the next."

"How about White—, the 2d Battalion? Have they been over to see Ryan yet?"

"Oh, yes. They've got an easy route to follow, but they're almost a thousand yards over to our right, all mixed up with

the Jerries in a big chateau over there. I heard they had an
unholy row, trying to get the place. The 116th didn't get anywhere at all. They're still on their LD."

"Yeah, Colonel Ordway told me. Well, guess I'll fold up.
Goodnight."

A laggard dawn touched the trees and hedgerows with cold,
grey light before Johns was able to outmaneuver a root in the
only hole he could find. But he rose with the rest, stiff, sore,
red-eyed, and very weary.

Barbeaux, bright and almost cheerful after a sound night's
sleep in his commander's commodious foxhole, brought the
Major a cold C-ration which the latter dug into with small
appetite. It seemed that he always drew corned beef hash,
morning, noon, and night. At the moment he couldn't think
of a single dish he liked less, particularly out of a can.

Nothing had come down from Regiment about an attack.
Therefore as the sun began to show through the trees Johns
reached for the phone to ask for news. It rang before he could
touch it, the operator answering, "Lagoon Red."

He listened for a moment, then handed it to Captain Newcomb, saying, "Captain Warfield, sir."

Newcomb said, "Yeah, Al." And then he listened for a long
time before saying, "Okay, Al. See you later."

Handing the phone back to the operator, Newcomb looked
up at the Major. "Al says Division says to hold what we got
until further orders. They don't know when that'll be or if we'll
attack at all or not."

"All right. If that's the way it's going to be we'd better call
the companies and tell 'em to relax a little. There's no use
keeping 'em on edge, thinking they're going to attack any
minute. But don't let 'em turn loose completely. And see if you
can get a strength report while you're at it."

He was anxious to know the cost of the fighting the day
before.

Within a few minutes all three rifle company commanders
came in to give their reports in person. They were glad for the

chance to let down for a few minutes and to come back to Battalion and compare notes.

Weddle was not very cheerful. He had to admit that the attacks on his left flank had cost him almost a whole platoon, including the platoon leader, Lieutenant Harris, who had been killed in the first advance. There were only five men left in that platoon now, while Lieutenant Chadwick's 3d Platoon had been reduced to twelve men and the 2d had about twenty. The weapons platoon was better off, but Baker Company was in pretty bad shape.

The other two companies had not suffered as much the day before, but not one had more than ninety men in the line. The total casualties were an even fifty. Of those, fifteen were dead, most of them from Weddle's mauled 1st Platoon.

Neuritis / 4

AROUND 1000 the Germans shelled the battalion heavily but they didn't follow this up with an attack; by 1100 the wounded had all been evacuated and the wire lines had been re-laid to Regiment. The first message over the new line was for Major Johns to report back to the regimental commander.

The orders he got there were welcome yet, paradoxically, disappointing: There would be no further attack. The battalion would pull out of the fields at once and take up a defensive position around the Bois de Bretel and the little orchard where the battalion mortars were.

Johns called for Newcomb but got Grimsehl instead. The S3, it seemed, had gone over to see Lieutenant Ryan just after the Major had left for Regiment. The Major instructed Grimsehl to collect all five of the company commanders and meet him as soon as possible at the crossroads on the edge of the woods from which they had first attacked.

It was only a little way from the regimental command post to the edge of the woods. He got there well before the others. When they came up a few minutes later he missed Newcomb before he caught the meaning of their odd manner. Grimsehl's set face should have given him a hint as the S2 stepped forward, saluted very stiffly, and said with visible effort to keep his emotions under control, "Sir, I must report that Captain Newcomb is dead."

The others looked silently at the ground and tears began to stream down the gentle Grimsehl's face. The news struck the

Major with the force of a physical blow. Of all the fine men he had met since taking command of the battalion, Newcomb had been one of the very best. He was quick, willing, and intelligent—wise far beyond his twenty-four or -five years.

He also stared at the ground for a moment and then asked quietly, "How did it happen?"

Ryan spoke up. "Same sniper, same place as the Doc. One of my men warned Newc to stay out of that gap in the hedgerow but he took the steel part of his helmet off and sat down on it, right square in the gap itself. The sergeant, who thought the captain must have gone nuts all of a sudden, was coming after him to drag him away. But too late. The sniper got him right in the temple."

Johns felt numb inside. But to dwell on his sorrow wouldn't help. Nodding solemnly, he leveled his finger at Captain Weddle. "You are now Lagoon Red 3; but you will retain command of your company until we complete the move into these woods."

Weddle, equally grave, replied, "Yes, sir. I have a little bad news, too. Lieutenant Chadwick got half his helmet knocked off by a burp gun during all that shooting awhile ago. He caught either a part of the helmet or some of the slugs in his arm. He's out, but he isn't hurt badly. He'll be back."

Major Johns, who had never met Chadwick, merely nodded again. It didn't hurt so much when you didn't know the man. Furthermore, a wound, regardless of its severity, lacked the awful finality of death. Chadwick's temporary loss meant one less officer, whereas Newcomb's death left a hole in his heart. Although he knew Weddle would probably be a good S3, too, Newcomb, in the four short days he had known him, had become a friend.

Grimsehl had moved a little away from the others. He was leaning against a tree, his head down in the curve of his arms, sobs shaking his body. He and Newcomb had been close friends for years and had worked together daily. The Major spoke to Captain Mentzer, the Headquarters Company commander, "See that Lieutenant Grimsehl is pulled off somewhere where it's quiet and given a chance to lie down and get some rest. If he objects, tell him it's an order. I don't want to see him around any more today."

Mentzer, small and dapper, saluted sharply. "Yes sir, I'll look after George all right."

By mid-afternoon the move had been completed. One man in each forward squad kept watch while the others dug foxholes and gun positions, both for themselves and for those who had drawn outpost duty. Later the men from Able Company, which the battalion commander had put around the rear, would come forward and dig alternate positions all along the line so each man would know exactly where he was to go if they had to move up to meet an attack.

Johns drew a sketch of his idea of what a semi-permanent battalion command post should be like. Part of the Ammunition and Pioneer Platoon was directed to work on it. They dug a hole seven feet square and five feet deep with the top raised another foot for headroom. It was covered with logs and earth to keep out fragments from tree bursts. On the side opposite the entrance a section of earth was left untouched, two and a half feet wide and about chair height. This would be a bench during the day and the Major's bed at night, thus serving two useful purposes while saving a lot of digging. That left just enough room for a folding table and a chair. The space would accommodate the rifle company commanders, the S3, the S2, the artillery liaison officer, and the battalion commander during a conference, briefing, or issuance of orders.

By nightfall "The Hole," as it was promptly named, was complete. Most of the men had deep foxholes, also with overhead cover if they were anywhere near trees. Shells bursting in the branches would hurl fragments into the deepest holes unless the latter were well covered.

There was room for Martin and Weddle to sleep in The Hole. The artillery and battalion telephones were brought in, the operators staying within easy reach in nearby foxholes outside, as they were not normally needed at night. The radio operators were also close, the idea being that from this shellproof nerve center the battalion could be fought and supported as long as either wire or radio communications was working.

The telephone net was such that every company and the regimental switchboard could be reached over the battalion phone, while the artillery liaison officer could get any of his forward observers and the division artillery fire direction center from his. It was theoretically possible for the two phones to be connected with one another by going all the way back to Division and over to divarty*, as the regimental switchboard had connections that led to Division and from there into the stratosphere of Corps. Not that any battalion-level people were ever apt to call anything beyond Division!

Major Morris, Captain Mentzer, and Lieutenant Grimsehl each had separate holes nearby, but sufficiently separated that one shell could not get them all at once. It was necessary for the battalion commander, his operations officer, and the artillery liaison officer to be together almost constantly as they did the active work of directing and controlling the fighting or defending of the unit. The executive, the intelligence officer, and the artilleryman's sergeant formed a second team that could take over on a moment's notice; it was their business to know what was going on at all times. The S2 and S3 were almost interchangeable anyway.

The next evening, just after they had eaten another C-ration supper, Colonel Ordway came by to see them. When he left he took Major Morris with him, because the Exec had developed serious foot trouble of some kind and could no longer keep up with the outfit when it was on the move. Morris had reluctantly asked to be relieved. The officers of the staff were equally sorry to see him go.

Before Jim Morris left, Major Johns managed to talk him out of a little triangular-shaped French bayonet one of the men had taken away from a prisoner and given to Morris a few days before. It made a wonderful pointer, which Johns had been coveting ever since Morris had obtained it. Just as Jim

---

*Division Artillery headquarters.

was about to leave, Johns said "And say—what about the little bayonet? I'm gonna need that thing up here to prod the boys along with, or fight the Krauts off. What'll you take for it?"

Morris obviously didn't want to part with the souvenir, but he said, impulsively, "Okay. It's yours. You want it so damn bad, you can have it with my best wishes that it'll bring you a lot of luck. In return you can give me the first Jerry pistol you get."

"That's a deal, boy. I'll go on patrol every night myself until I get you a good one."

"No, I wouldn't do that if I were you. Your feet are too damned big and clumsy. But you'll get one sooner or later and I'll be around."

He offered his hand. They shook, and went off in opposite directions.

That night it rained. It came down in sheets. In a few minutes nearly every man in the outfit was soaked. The water ran down the entrance to The Hole and nothing Barbeaux could do would keep it out. He rigged raincoats in all manner of positions, but it always came through. He dug a sump at the bottom of the entrance which caught much of it there to be dipped out with a helmet. But some still seeped in, so that the floor was soon soggy with heavy mud.

Around midnight the commander and the two officers got ready to turn in, leaving Barbeaux on sump duty with one of the unemployed telephone operators to relieve him. At 0200 the rain stopped. There was no sound except the drip of water from the trees and the snores of the officers in The Hole.

At 0202 the drip of water outside was joined by the drip of water inside. The earth and logs of the roof had finally been soaked through.

Martin caught the first drop squarely in a tight-closed eye. He squirmed and moved his head. The next drop hit him on the neck. He pulled the blanket over his head.

Weddle's bare foot received several drops before he was sufficiently awake to realize what was going on. He jerked his foot under the blanket. Then, getting one in the ear, he pulled his blanket over his head. His foot stuck out in time to catch the next drop.

Johns went through the same process. It was maddening. The water came in slow dribbles from dozens of places in the timbered roof. There was no way to stop it or catch it or avoid it. And it was cold.

By 0230 they were all awake. Weddle lit the single candle, after which they surveyed the situation sorrowfully and silently. Barbeaux sat damply on his log by the entrance, grinning sardonically in the shadows.

Between the three of them they could command men to go out to die, or they could bring down tons of screaming metal on the enemy. But they couldn't stop the drip, drip, drip from that damned roof.

Finally they admitted defeat, pulled their raincoats over them, and tried to get back to sleep. No one said a word except to curse the rain, the Germans, the war, France, and the Ammunition and Pioneer Platoon.

The raincoats did all right for about a half hour. By that time the water had gathered in the folds of the garments to such an extent that the least movement precipitated a tiny deluge that would run inevitably to the bottom and soak blanket, clothing and, ultimately, skin.

By dawn all three officers were out, thoroughly sick of The Hole. They had had almost no sleep and were in no humor to be trifled with. The Major, his rumpled uniform splotched with wet spots, sat on a damp log under a dripping tree, refusing to speak to anyone. He tried to heat a cup of coffee over a K-ration box but even the waxed container was too wet to burn properly. He had to gulp down the muddy fluid while it was only lukewarm.

The rest of the battalion was in pretty much the same shape. It was a good thing for the Germans that they did not try an attack that morning as the collective American temper was definitely at an explosive pitch.

By noon the sun was out. Blankets and clothing were strung wherever the rays came through the trees. But in The Hole it was still raining. Barbeaux was sent down to retrieve the sodden blankets. Before he went below, with a straight face and elaborate care he put on a raincoat whereat the officers in the command post group had a hard time to keep from laughing.

At dark Johns ordered extra raincoats rigged under the roof in such a way that they would catch all the drippings and funnel them to a few holes dug in the floor around the edges of The Hole. That helped, but it was a long way from being perfect. Every time anyone stood up his head or helmet was sure to upset a pocket of water which never failed to run down someone's neck, onto a map, or into some bedding.

The nerve center of the battalion was having a bad attack of neuritis.

The night was not quite so bad as the one before, but it was still rough. Johns crawled out at dawn feeling as if he had gone through another battle. His first words were to the A and P sergeant, "Dig me another hole. Be damn sure this one is shell-proof AND waterproof."

That night they slept well—and dry.

Early next morning a jeep rolled up on the road near the command post. A large stranger dismounted, lugging a bedroll and musette bag. It was obvious he had come to stay. He saw the Major, halted, saluted, and said, "Sir, Major Hoffman reporting for duty as your new executive officer."

Major Johns had been expecting a replacement for Morris, but he sized up the new arrival with some surprise. Hoffman looked to be at least ten years older than the 32-year-old Johns, who was instantly certain that he was considerably outranked. Of course that rarely made any difference in combat but the commander had expected some bright young man from Regiment or Division, out to win his spurs. He looked appraisingly at Hoffman as he returned the salute, shook hands, and said, "Glad to see you, Major. Had your breakfast?"

"Yes sir. I had mine at Division before I came down to Regiment this morning."

Having introduced the new exec to the rest of the staff, the

Major went back to finish heating his coffee before his box burned out. He was too late. Again he had to swallow the stuff lukewarm, wondering why in the world the great U. S. Army couldn't figure out a way to give its fighting men something reliable with which to heat coffee.

Hoffman gave them all the latest rumors from up the line and filled in the big picture while Johns rinsed his canteen cup from a five-gallon can of water and drank a little to get the taste of the coffee out of his mouth. Then he motioned to the new exec to follow him into The Hole. He wanted to learn more about this man and make up his mind what he might expect from him.

When they came out he was well satisfied. He felt sure that Hoffman had been carefully selected to give him help where he needed it—with administration. The new officer, having had seventeen years' experience in the Infantry, knew everything he needed to know about the things on which Major Johns was hazy or completely at a loss. Those things did not include tactics or handling men. But there is a great deal more to fighting a war than the actual combat; and paperwork had always been a mystery to Johns. Mentzer was a capable enough adjutant, hence with Hoffman to back him up the commander felt he would have no more worries on that score.

Ten days dragged by while the battalion sat in the Bois de Bretel. If the days were sometimes dull they were rarely uneventful. Men were wounded or killed nearly every day by artillery, mortars, or the fire from self-propelled 88's that could move unseen into positions from which they could fire into the tops of the trees of the Bois, and then pull back before the artillerymen could bring fire on them.

Those casualties were bad enough, but they were to be expected. There was one incident that the battalion commander thought they could have got along very nicely without. Regiment had directed that the battalions erect barbed wire along their whole front, which they did cheerfully. But when a truckload of antipersonnel mines came down the Major looked at them with misgivings. Those things were as dangerous to the people who laid them as they were to the enemy, he thought. So he supervised the mine laying carefully, meticulously noting the location of each mine on a large-scale sketch of the area being mined.

The day after all the mines were laid he heard the flat, muffled roar of a land mine. At once he ran toward the sound. He got there with the aid men, to watch with sorrow and anger while they evacuated three men from the middle of their own minefield. One of the men was dead. The last litter carried Iperian, who, badly hit in the legs with several fragments, did not know how severely he was hurt.

Iperian and his mortar forward observer group had been up ahead of the field doing some adjusting of fire. On the way back, their guide—one of the men who had helped lay the field —had been clowning, and stepped on a mine.

Iperian, seeing Major Johns, roused himself from his state of semiconsciousness and lifted himself on the litter as he saw the look of concern on his commander's face. He cried, "I'll be back, Major. I'll be back in a couple of days. It's just a scratch, Major. Don't you worry about me, now. I'll be back."

That was the last Johns ever saw of the young lieutenant, for whom he had had such high hopes.

The other wounded man, unconscious, was being placed on the medical jeep when still another litter came around the corner of the little farmhouse that stood on the edge of the woods. The man on this litter had his eyes closed. His face was twisting horribly. He jerked all over, bringing his legs up so hard the aid men had to hold him on the litter. The Major, looking at the man in wonder, asked, "What is the matter with him?"

The aid men were contemptuous. "Ah," said one, "this guy never got hit by nothing. He was in a hole fifty yards from where it happened, but he started screaming and yelling and carrying on something awful. We thought he was hit but he ain't got a hole in him. He was like this when we got to him."

Johns realized he had just seen his first case of neuropsychosis, commonly called combat exhaustion, or CE. It wasn't the only one he was to see.

Combat has its rewards too. One day the Major was returning from a round of inspection when he saw the immaculate jeep with two stars on the front that meant the division commander was in the area. He broke into a run and found the General at the command post.

Johns reported and the commanding general flipped a half-salute at him in answer. The characteristic gesture told the Major that the General was in a good mood.

"Hi there, boy, how're you doing?"

"Fine, sir," Johns grinned back, happy to see the man he admired so much.

"Well, stand up close here a minute. I've got something for you."

The major did as he was told, puzzled. The General reached into a pocket and brought out a little bar of red and white ribbon. It was the Bronze Star!

He pinned it on Johns' left shirt-pocket flap and shook his hand. "That's for doing a mighty fine job for me back at Division."

The Major tried to salute and shake hands at the same time. He was completely dumbfounded at the suddenness of this unexpected decoration.

The General went on to add compliments about the battalion and before Johns could answer he waved another half-salute and was gone.

The little show was typical of the General's gay, light, enthusiastic manner when pleased. He went away leaving Johns, who knew his other moods as well, walking three feet off the ground. The rest of the officers and men, who were standing around in awe, grinned and rushed forward to shake his hand and congratulate him.

The Major could only look in the direction where the general had disappeared, shake his head, and mumble, "There goes the grandest little guy that ever lived. I love him."

Eight Days Ago /5

THAT NIGHT things were pretty quiet. The inevitable bull session was going on down in The Hole, when Hoffman asked the Major just what he'd done to get the Bronze Star.

Johns thought for a minute. Then he said, "Well, I guess it was mostly for running around and getting shot at once in a while but not hit. That first week after we hit the beach was right hectic, of course. But even so there weren't a lot of people in division headquarters that ever got into any fighting like the regiments were in all the time; and the Old Man was pretty good to the people who got into the most trouble. That meant mostly the liaison officers at Division who were under my control. There were lots of times when Division couldn't reach some regiment. Then they'd have me send out an LO with a message, or to check on positions or something like that. I found out about the second day that being Liaison Control Officer meant that when nobody else could find an outfit I got sent. I guess that was just so I'd keep working on the boys to keep 'em good, because I didn't find any more than my share of 'lost' outfits.

"Anyway, we had a lot of fun that way. I got behind the German lines three times in three days because we never knew where anybody—including the enemy—was for sure. A little major used to go with me sometimes. Cole, I think his name was. I hear he got captured right after I left. Then there was a real nice young captain who did a lot of good work. I hear he caught a mortar shell right in his lap a couple of days ago. The point I'm making is that this liaison work wasn't the soft snap that a lot of people seemed to think it was. It may be better now but during that first week you never knew what was going to happen next.

"Twice out of the three times I got into trouble I got out again before the Jerries even knew I had been back among 'em. But the third time was kinda funny and I think maybe that's what the Old Man had in mind, mostly, when he gave me this." He paused a moment and fingered the little ribbon which was still pinned to his shirt.

"It was a helluva lot of fun, really. Here's what happened: On D plus three the 115th was lost—or at least nobody back at Division knew where it was and they couldn't get the CP on the radio. The regiment had cleared Colombieres, which was on the other side of the inundated area from Division then. That was the last that had been heard from them. The Old Man began to get worried about the outfit after a few hours because the engineers who were working on the causeway over the inundated area were getting quite a bit of fire from the far side even though that whole area was supposed to have been cleared. It began to look as if the 115th was cut off, but nobody knew if they were in trouble or not so the Old Man got the usual bright idea, send Johns over to see.

"It was late in the afternoon when they called me into the War Room, where they told me all this long tale of woe. Of course I saw what was coming right away and I don't mind telling you I didn't hear half of what the little man said. I was too damned scared. Then I guess I got resigned to my fate, so to speak, and decided to make the most of it.

"The General gave me a lot of instructions and when he got all through you could have heard a pin hit that big rug they keep on the War Room floor. I could just see what they were thinking, 'Well, it's been nice knowing you, old boy.' But I was feeling pretty important by then, so I stuck out my chest as far as I could, took a deep breath, gave the Old Man one of my very best salutes, and staggered out the door.

"Colonel Ordway, who was Chief of Staff then, came along.

Outside he put his arm around my shoulders, then shook my hand, and said. 'Good luck, boy.' Cripes—I could already see my folks getting that telegram, 'The War Department regrets to inform you . . .' But I tried to carry it off big, thanked the Colonel, and went looking for the headquarters commandant who was supposed to give me what I wanted for the trip.

"He shows up finally and asks what can he do for me. Reminded me of the warden and the condemned man, the way Major Marr was so solemn about it. I told him I wanted a jeep with a good driver who wasn't afraid to go where I told him to go, and two good men who could and would shoot tommy guns just in case the opportunity should arise. Marr had one hell of a time getting the men and guns together because we were still awful short of everything, but he finally made it. I crawled into the front seat carrying a carbine with lots of extra clips and enough grenades to blow up the Empire State building.

"When we were all set I told the three boys what we were going to do."

The Major paused and laughed out loud. "You should have seen those kids. Their eyes got big as dollars and they couldn't talk right for ten minutes. None of 'em had been anywhere near any real shooting up to that time. But they were dead game. By the time we got going we were all feeling as if we were going on a picnic. Half tight, I guess, just from smelling the cork on a bottle of danger.

"We drove on down to the causeway easy enough. Then I put the tommy gunners to sitting up on the rear seat so they could shoot over our heads if they had to, and we moved out onto the causeway itself after I told the driver not to stop for anything except a roadblock that he couldn't get around. I also told 'em all that if we did run into such a block to be ready to hit the ditch in a hurry and keep going on foot.

"About halfway across the causeway we started seeing engineers lying in water up to their necks yelling, 'Don't go any farther, there's Krauts up there.'

"We tried to look big and bold and yelled back, 'We know

that,' then kept going. We just barely made it over the causeway because the engineers hadn't anywhere near finished fixing it yet. But we made it. We went on for about three miles into what was supposed to be enemy-held territory.

"For the first mile or so we didn't see a thing, but I'll tell you for sure we were looking. My heart was putting out a lot more horsepower than that jeep. As we started down a long hill I told the driver that the map showed a hard-top road at the bottom where we were supposed to make a sharp left turn.

"We were drifting down the hill with the clutch out, not making a sound, when we got to the bottom and saw the road. There was a house on the left corner with a low stone wall around it, and a higher wall on the other side of the road. Just beyond the house there was a little lane that came in from the far side. Out of that lane was coming a whole damn platoon of Krauts, wandering across the road like they were all going out for a cup of coffee.

"My little driver had guts. He never batted an eye, but turned right into the middle of those birds just as though they were crossing the wrong way against a traffic light. None of us said anything while we were making that turn. The Krauts didn't even see us until our tires began to squeal. Then they were staring us right in the face at a range of about forty yards. Hollering 'Fire!' I cut loose with my carbine.

"Hot damn! You should have seen it. We all opened up together, while the driver gunned that jeep until it sounded like it was shooting too. Our tommy guns were ripping like nothing you ever heard, one of 'em right over my head. The Krauts started running in all directions just like chickens. I guess they thought we were leading an armored division, because they only had one idea in mind right then, which was to get the hell out of that road and our field of fire.

"One big German turned and ran right up the road in front of us. Some of 'em fell down, others hit the ditch, and others just ran. I was so excited I didn't have sense enough to aim right, although I saw what I think was four of 'em fall. Actually I still don't know if I ever hit more'n one.

"We were still right in the middle of 'em when my carbine stopped shooting. You can empty a clip right fast, I found out. So what do I do? Put in a new clip? Hell no, not me—I'm an old Cavalryman and I cut my teeth on a .45. So I forget all about that neat little carbine with all the extra clips lying around. I whups out my trusty automatic and starts blazing away with it like I was in the wild, wild west. If you'd seen it in a movie you'd have laughed at the silly things they do. But by damn that's exactly what I did. Just goes to show you what training will do for—or to—a man.

"I used to be a crack shot with a .45, both mounted and dismounted. But I never tried out on any live targets before, except a few rabbits and coyotes, who don't shoot back. I honestly don't think I even came close to a single one of those nice, ripe, juicy Krauts until something told me I was about to get off my last shot. By that time we had almost run over the big guy who had been pounding along in front of us. I had missed him at least six times with the carbine. He cut off the road to the right. As we were just passing him at a range of not more than about seven feet, I leveled on him real careful and squeezed off that last shot. I think it was my only bull's eye too, because I saw the dust fly out of the back of his jacket as he threw up his arms and went on his face in the ditch.

"That really was the last round in my pistol. So do I drop it and start tossing hand grenades over my shoulder? Hell no! I grab for a fresh .45 clip out of my pouch but find the damn thing all wrapped up tight in that waterproof plastic stuff we used on the landing. Me and my one-track mind! I still don't think about the carbine or the grenades, but fumble with that damn clip like it was a red-hot rivet, while we make tracks up the road.

"In the meantime, the Krauts have got a rifle or two to working. But they're also so scared they can't shoot right. They never came near us. Before we got around a bend about 600 yards up the road they finally got a machine gun going too. But it wasn't any better, and we came out of the show without even a hole in the jeep.

"We kept right on going until we ran into some of our Division 29th Reconnaissance Troop in armored cars, which I didn't even know was over there. We tell them all about our little scrap, whereupon they look wise as a tree full of owls, but don't act much as if they want to go check up. Not that I blame them. They tell us that part of the 115th is up ahead on the edge of Colombieres. We go on to find most of the regimental headquarters people there, but no CP and nobody that has any idea where the Colonel and the staff have got off to.

"By that time it's nearly dark but I ask for some more men to make up a patrol to go looking for the advance CP, and at the same time get all the radios in the area to working, calling anybody who'll answer to see if they know where the Colonel is. I can't find a soul who even has an idea in what direction they left. Therefore I have to give up the patrol idea because I don't know which way to start out, and they could be 'most anywhere. So could the Krauts. I hated to quit, but I didn't see how I could do any good out beating around in the hedgerows in the dark. Finally I crawled into a C and R car that was doing a lot of the radioing, and devoted the next few hours to some plain and fancy nail chewing.

"It must have been along about 0200 when somebody pulls my arm. It was Captain Whitehead, who was the General's aide at that time. I was so surprised I could hardly ask him if the Old Man is there too. When he says 'Yes, he is,' I thought I must be asleep, but I didn't take any chances. I piled out of the car and ran over to where the General was giving somebody hell about something.

"As soon as I report to him he naturally starts chewing me out, too. But I knew he was just going through the motions because he could see what the situation was and he knew I'd have been a damned fool to take off into the countryside in the dark with no idea where I was going.

"So when he calms down a little we start talking about other things. I tell him about our little shooting bee on the way in. He is very interested, getting real excited when I tell him I thought I saw some Krauts go down under our fire. The boys say there were forty Krauts, of which they maintained we got ten or twelve. But I'm more conservative, claiming only five or six out of about eighteen or twenty.

"Then we go over to the motor park to bed down for the rest of the night. Around 0400 we hear a lot of screaming and yelling over on the other side of the park. We all jump up and run over to see what's going on. It turns out to be a man from the 2d Battalion's Naval Shore Fire Control Party. He had been shot through the arm and is about two-thirds delirious from fright, shock, and pain. He tells us that the 2d Battalion had just been caught with its pants down, run over, and completely destroyed. He claims he is the only man left alive but that a lot of the men surrendered without a fight when they found they were surrounded. This makes the Old Man hopping mad. He all but calls the guy a liar right there. I was impressed with the whole story because it was the first 'sole survivor' report I'd heard. Not the Old Man. He wouldn't believe more'n about half the yarn in the first place and kept shaking the poor devil by the arm every time he'd pass out—or act like he'd passed out—to make him give more details about where they were, when it happened, what they were doing, and all that.

"The aid man finally took this bird off to an aid station, while the Old Man is about to have a fit. He just can't wait till it gets light enough to see, so we can go looking for what is left of the 2d Battalion.

"Now get this. Here's a two-star general up with an outfit that is supposed to be cut off. Furthermore he has come up through enemy-held territory in the middle of the night with no escort but his aide. Now he wants to go looking for a battalion that has been shot up by a superior enemy force, though he doesn't know where either the battalion or the enemy is!

"We take off before it's light enough to see very well. The General tells me to go back by where we had our fight, which is on the way to the area where he thinks the 2d Battalion got run over. I didn't even recognize the place at first, but went right on past because it looked so different, coming from the other direction and not shooting. He stops and yells for me to come the hell on back. Then he gets out and looks all over for signs of the fight. Do you know, we couldn't even find a drop of blood! I had expected to find bodies all over the place, but no—not even the big guy in the ditch.

"Boy! Does he take me apart then! 'You and your big do-ings,' he says, 'I don't think you even SAW a German.' I walked right under my jeep without even scraping my helmet, I felt so small.

"Then he starts in after me like a hound dog after a rabbit. I can't do anything right. When I run off the only map I have he won't even let me tell him I'm outa map. He just says, 'You go to the next damn corner and stop and wait until I tell you to go on.'

"After that I go to each road intersection, stop real easy short of it, and creep up to look things over, with the tommy gunners covering the flanks. Remember, we have no idea what to expect and the last people seen behind us less than ten hours before were enemy. But does the General creep around? He does not! He stomps up the middle of the road like he was in garrison.

"The first time this happens I try to get him to move off the road into the ditch until I can at least have a quick look around. But he, thinking I'm scared, won't do a thing but stand right in the middle of the intersection, with his map in his hand, wide open from four directions and asking to get shot at.

"The man nearly gave me heart failure. Of course I was scared anyway because I expected to run into half the German army any minute. Having a two-star general on my hands makes me even more nervous. In fact, I was twice as scared because I'm not only scared FOR him, because he won't stay down, but he makes so much noise that I'm scared BECAUSE of him too.

"Once he starts up after me before I got a chance to look over a house that was about 150 yards past the road junction I had halted for. Seeing him coming I go back, actually grab him by the arm and push him into the ditch while I point at the house which, in plain sight, could hold a platoon of Krauts easy. He's such a little guy, I think about sitting on him until one of the boys can go up and have a look. But he got so mad when I pushed him into the ditch that I finally got mad too and said to myself, 'Okay. So you want to get yourself shot. Go right ahead.' And after that I let him do what he wanted to. When I grabbed him by the arm I'm surprised Hitler didn't hear him, clear to Berlin, giving me hell.

"We keep this silly business up for about three hours until along about 0800 I see a column coming down the road toward us. It's still not good light yet, what with trees along the road and a little ground fog. They look an awful lot like the Krauts we had seen the day before, so we drift up on 'em real easy like, with our fingers on the triggers and the safeties off. They turn out to be what's left of the 2d Battalion, about 22 or 23 men. Were they glad to see us and surprised to see the General!

"He talked to them for quite a while, finding out where they'd been and what had happened. They said they'd been walking and fighting all day, until around midnight they hit a couple of fields where the orders went around to dig in for the night. But they were so exhausted, after three straight days of fighting, with no sleep at all, that nearly every man was asleep before he hit the ground. Then the next thing they know there're two 88's in the field with them, firing along the hedgerows. Krauts are running all over the place with burp guns, shooting at anything that moved. The whole staff and the battalion commander are killed early in the fight when some Kraut in a tank or SP gun calls on Colonel Warfield to surrender, and when Warfield tells the Kraut to go to hell, they cut the whole bunch down with a machine gun.

"We sent the survivors on to the rear, then kept going until we found the place. It was pretty much like they said. There were dead all around the two fields. One SP 88 was still smoldering, with the bazooka that must have knocked it out still lying by a gap in a hedgerow. Warfield and his staff, all except the S4, are lying in the road, headed toward where the Krauts were coming from. Warfield has his .45 still in his hand. We found the S4 over by the door of a house where he'd probably crawled after he was hit. Two old ladies were still in the house.

They had already come out and put flowers on his body before we got there.

"The General looked at the bodies, especially the Colonel's, and said that was the way to die if you had to.

"From the number of bodies we counted, 37 I think it was, we estimated there ought to be at least 300 more men left out of the battalion even after allowing for wounded and a guess at the number captured, because most battalions had about 600 men in them at that time. Then we took off for the rear. The Old Man was so mad at the 115th that he forgot to bitch at me any more.

"We found their regimental CP a little later. The General relieved the regimental commander on the spot. It was quite a shock to the old boy because I don't think he even knew, at that time, what had happened to his 2d Battalion. Anyway, the General sent the regimental exec off to round up what was left of the battalion and make a unit out of it again. I don't know how many they finally found but in a couple or three days they had it back in the line again."

The Major, having finished his story, looked around at his little audience which had sat silently through the long recital. He was somewhat embarrassed at having talked so long, but he made one more comment. "That's one reason why I think so much of the Old Man. He went where he could have sent scouts or part of the Recon Troop, but he went because he either thought he ought to or because he wanted to. Anyway, he wasn't afraid to go. And I think he must have found out something more about our own little shooting scrape because he has mentioned it two or three times since then and he always acts as if he thinks we shot up a few Krauts that day. Of course he hasn't said so yet, but I sort of figure that's what he had in mind when he gave me this thing today. Or maybe it was just to make up for chewing my tail so long that morning."

The Major grinned, the staff laughed; the bull session was over for the evening.

Ryan's War / 6

WHEN THE BATTALION moved to take over from a whole Combat Command of the 3d Armored Division it had received nearly 300 replacements. It had also acquired a vast feeling of superiority, which was donated by the 3d Armored itself. The tankers brought this esprit with them but they left it on the field after getting a very bloody nose in a one-day fight. So, naturally, the "veterans" of the battalion picked it up along with the stacks of machine gun and mortar ammunition that the armored boys had left behind with their cockiness. The Major himself was inclined to be tolerant, for he still knew what a first fight was like. And if his own men gained some of what the newcomers had lost, at least temporarily, then it wasn't a complete loss after all.

Since the new positions were not as simple as the tight little ring around the Bois de Bretel had been, he had to put all three companies on the line.

They all had their problems but Ryan seemed to be the most worried. Late in the afternoon of the first day after the move Ryan came in to Battalion. He was very unhappy about his company position. It seemed there was a hedgerow just about 150 yards beyond the one the 3d Armored had gained —the only one—and Ryan wanted his own men out there. The Germans who owned it were being very unreasonable about giving it up. The enemy seemed impervious to mortar and artillery fire. A fairly large and reasonably determined combat patrol that Ryan had sent out to persuade the Germans that they should go away and let him have their hedgerow had come back with two wounded and no hedgerow. He was quite put out about it. After all, he only wanted an outpost on it, not the whole damn thing. Furthermore, he had ideas about how he would get it yet.

Ryan, Weddle, Martin, and the Major put their heads together and came up with a plan. At 2130, which was just when dusk was turning to dark, the artillery would throw in everything Martin could talk them out of, just behind the German outpost. The battalion mortars would beat hell out of the post itself with white phosphorus shells, then two squads from Able Company would hit it from the right flank. This seemed to be a very reasonable, workable plan that ought to take almost any ordinary outpost. Everybody was very pleased with it.

At 2130 the artillery fire moaned overhead to crash comfortingly near the outpost. The mortars coughed in the rear and their shells splattered the target. The infantry squads started to move in from the right while Major Johns and the others watched for the yellow flare that was to be the signal that they were as close as they could get under their own fire and were ready to close as soon as the artillery and mortars ceased firing.

About 2138 the flare bloomed in the right spot. The Major yelled "Cease fire." The last rounds from the artillery screamed in, the mortars crashed once more, and all was quiet for long seconds.

Then came the first shots from the patrol. They were going in well and it looked for a few seconds as if Ryan were going to get his outpost. But a flare of three red-star clusters floated up from the German lines and all hell broke loose again.

Every Kraut gun that had been used to help stop the 3d Armored, plus probably a few that had come in late, opened up on about 150 yards of the Able Company front. It was concentrated, thunderous murder, such as no one in the battalion had ever seen before. Ryan's line was a mass of seething, leaping, flame that looked as if it were fed from below rather than from an inconceivable torrent of shells that came on and on and on.

Ryan called in, superfluously, to report the enemy fire. Frantically he asked permission to move his men out of the 150-yard stretch that was getting the brunt of the fire. At first the Major would not grant it, afraid that an attack would come in under the fire. But when it kept coming he knew that no man would keep his head up to look for an assault as long as those shells rained down like that. Consequently he called Ryan and told him he could move the men if there were any left who could get out of their holes with any degree of safety.

The barrage switched suddenly from the company to the battalion command post area itself. The battalion commander and his staff, hearing the first whine of the shells, dived for the new command post hole where they huddled while the walls shuddered and dirt rained down from the roof. Concussion blew the candles out but nobody was hurt. The German gunners switched to C Company for a few rounds, then went right back to their prime target—Able.

While they were pounding Kenney's company a single short call came in over the 300, "Able 6 is clipped." That meant Ryan had been hit. But there were no details.

Twenty minutes after that pretty red-star cluster went up all was quiet again except for some moans and cries for medics that floated back from Able Company. But at least no German infantry had come in under the fire.

In that twenty minutes the company lost 54 men plus its company commander. Almost every man in the patrol had been caught above ground and was killed or wounded while most of the other casualties came from tree and hedgerow bursts that sent fragments down into the holes.

The men of the command post group, gathered around The Hole, silently watched the parade of walking wounded that filed slowly by on their way to the aid station. Occasionally a man would stumble or waiver whereupon a messenger or wireman would jump to help him. Every aid man and litter in the battalion was already up at the Able line and the first litters were not far behind the walking wounded. Some of the victims moaned and a few cried out a little now and then, but most were very quiet. Johns was glad he could not see their faces in the dark.

The last litter went by with no word from Ryan. Johns was beginning to hope he hadn't been hurt badly, when four men loomed out of the darkness, each carrying a corner of a blanket. Ryan was half sitting, half lying in the makeshift litter, gritting his teeth at the pain of wounds in an arm and a leg.

They laid the blanket gently down in front of the Major, who stripped off his coat and laid it over the company commander. Ryan managed to work up a feeble grin. "It didn't work too good, did it, Boss?"

And before Major Johns could answer he added, "But if they want that hedgerow so bad they can damn well keep it."

The Major admired Ryan's courage but it was later before he could afford to smile at the remark. Instead he said, "How're you feeling, boy? Are you hit bad?"

He turned and snapped at Mentzer, "Get a litter quick."

But Ryan interceded. "Don't bother, Mentzer, I'm okay. The aid station isn't far and I'm not hit in the guts and nothing is busted so far as I know. I'll make it all right."

He beckoned with his good arm to the men who carried him. They picked him up again. As they started to the rear he waved feebly. "Don't worry, Major, I'll be back."

He smiled again and was swallowed up in the dark.

Even a war has a little comic relief. Johns got a good belly laugh one day while in this area. He was sitting quietly in the shade of a big tree, his back against the wide bole, trying to figure out a way to pull something in the way of a reserve out of the line.

Voices from the other side of the tree disturbed his thoughts.

"Well, damn me," said the first, "What the hell are you doin' up here? I thought you guys was all back somewhere taking it easy."

"Yeah, we were," answered another, "but I heard something the other day made me want to come back up here and have a look around."

The man, obviously from the 2d Battalion, paused a moment to look cautiously around to make sure nobody was near. He didn't look on the far side of the tree. "Now don't you go and tell anybody this," he went on, "but I heard there was a helluva lot of whiskey and stuff in the old shatto."

The Major's ears pricked up at that. His men had inherited the beautiful old building along with the rest of 2d Battalion's area, but he hadn't heard of any whiskey and hadn't been down in the cellar.

The first man drew in his breath sharply. "The hell you say! Do you know where it is?"

"Naw, not exactly, but I got a good idea."

"Why didn't you say so sooner? I'll help you look. But wait a minute—just how do you know it's in there at all after you guys was all over the place and the 3d Armored was through here too?"

"Cripes, I don't know for sure there's any left, but I do know there was a damned big pot full of it before. I heard some F Company guys talkin'. They said the first night they hit the place, while the Krauts was still in it, they sent a patrol over to try to run 'em out in the dark. The patrol crawls in a basement window and finds a whole room full of liquor, so they forget all about the enemy until a gang of Krauts comes bustin' down the steps to get some of it for theirselves. Then everybody starts shootin' in all directions and the F Company guys get the hell out of there the best way they can, carryin' liquor in one hand and shootin' with the other.

"After that they run patrols in there every night, volunteer patrols every time. At first they used to run into the Krauts all the time and a lot of guys got hurt. But then they got smart. So did the Krauts. So help me, they started runnin' them patrols on a schedule—our guys and the Krauts—they had it all figured out. The F Company gang would go in at 2100, get their stuff and come out. Then the Krauts would come in around 2200 for theirs; and E Company—they'd heard about it too—would get there about 2300. And so on all night. It worked fine until some damn officer heard about it and pulled an ambush on the

Krauts. That made 'em mad again. It wasn't safe any more after a lot of guys got shot, so they quit goin'."

"What makes you think there's any left now?"

"Cripes, the F Company guys said the shatto was a Luft-waffy headquarters and there was enough stuff in there to float a battleship. Said a company couldn't carry it all out in a day."

"Well, what're we waitin' for? Let's get goin'."

They took off at a fast walk for the chateau itself. The Major, laughing, let them go. He never learned if they found anything, but by the time he got to the fabulous cellar there was nothing left but a mass of broken bottles plus a strong alcoholic odor.*

When the order came down to prepare to move to a rest area nobody in the command post group believed it at first. If Major Johns hadn't heard it straight from Colonel Ordway he probably wouldn't have either. It wasn't really a rest area they were going to, actually, but it was just as good as one be-cause it wasn't in the front line. Anywhere back of the second hedgerow from the front itself was a rest area to the weary men. They were to go to Les Foulons, the very settlement from which they had started their speed march to the Bois de Bretel. If this wasn't out of artillery range at least you didn't have to keep your head below a hedgerow all the time to save it from being shot off.

The news was so good that the Major went forward to visit all the companies and carry it himself. In the C Company line he climbed over a hedgerow and almost stumbled over the body of an officer. The man lay on his side with his knees drawn up to his stomach, almost as if asleep. But his face told another story. Contorted and grey, it showed that he had not died an easy death.

The battalion commander was annoyed. Not recognizing the officer, he thought he must be one of the replacements who had

---

*A German commander described this same incident to American officers after the war, so it is not apocryphal. The German claimed that he sent a note to the Americans when he pulled out, offering them the remains of the liquor, with his compliments, and hoped that they would enjoy it as much as the Germans had.—Editor.

come in only a few days before. But he had long ago issued orders that dead officers were to be evacuated at once regardless of the circumstances, and that he was to be informed as soon as possible. It was bad enough to have dead riflemen lying around, but too often they died in tight positions where it would have endangered other lives to have removed them right away. A dead officer was another matter. It was not that an officer was different from the men just because he was an officer. He was a dead *leader;* experience had already shown that the effect on the men of having a dead platoon leader lying for hours where they could see him was far worse than having a dead buddy or two around. A dead buddy was bad, there was no question about that. But when a man lost a friend it often made him a more bitter fighter whereas the sight of a dead officer frequently left the man with an uncertain feeling, his confidence shaken. True, if the officer had been well liked, his death might make the whole platoon fight harder. More often it had an adverse effect.

He called for Kenney as he stood looking down at the shredded leggings, shoes, and trousers and the shallow hole just behind the officer's back.

Kenney came trotting down the hedgerow.

"Why wasn't the death of this officer reported? Who is he, anyway?" snapped the Major.

Kenney had to think a moment. "Sir, he was one of the new officers." He gave the Major a name and went on, "He caught a 50-mm mortar almost in his hip pocket. It hit right at his feet."

"I can see that. Why haven't I been told about it?"

"Well, sir, it only happened a couple of hours ago. I've been a little busy and just haven't got around to calling you before now."

"All right. But get him out of here."

Kenney called to some men nearby, who left their rifles leaning against the hedgerow as they came forward to pick up what was left of a young officer who had had about 48 hours of experience in the line.

Major Johns watched as they pushed the body over the

hedgerow, then turned back to Kenney to tell him about the relief order. As he talked he moved to the corner of the hedgerow and looked cautiously toward the German lines. Another hedgerow, not more than fifty yards away, blocked the view. He broke off suddenly in the middle of a sentence, motioned to Kenney and the ever-present Weddle not to follow. Then he slipped over the hedgerow.

He had seen the outpost Kenney had stationed on that far hedgerow and it didn't seem to him that the men out there were very alert. He walked slowly and carefully up behind them, crouching low so that his helmet would not show over the hedgerow. The three men did not hear or see him until he purposely kicked a branch just behind them. Then they gasped and whirled, guns level.

"What the hell do you think you're having out here—a picnic?" Johns snapped.

The sergeant in charge of the outpost was so relieved to see anyone besides a German that he ignored the sharp question. "Jeez, Major, you hadn't ought to crawl up on us like that. It's jumpy as hell out here, with them Krauts right over there."

He jerked a thumb toward the next hedgerow less than a hundred yards across an open field. A burned-out tank in the middle of the field marked the farthest advance of the 3d Armored attack in that sector. The sergeant went on, "They get in that tank sometimes and give us hell."

The Major was not amused. He had noted that another hedgerow ran perpendicularly from a point near the outpost to the German lines. It was obviously the main reason for placing the post there in the first place. But the men had let the tank distract them, because not a man was nearer than ten feet to the hedgerow junction.

Johns pointed to the corner. "Does it take all three of you to watch that tank while the whole German army could crawl up to within ten feet of you without you knowing it?"

The sergeant's mouth dropped open. "God, Major, I never even thought about it after they shot at us from the tank last time."

"Well you'd better by a damn sight start thinking about your flanks if you want to go on being able to think at all. I wouldn't give a damn if they knocked off all three of you stupid bastards. But if they got you they'd have a good chance of getting into the middle of your company—and I wouldn't like that. Now, damn you, START THINKING!"

The sergeant stammered something but the Major, ignoring him, stalked back to the company line. He slipped over the hedgerow again, and started lecturing the apprehensive Kenney before he hit the ground: ". . . Furthermore, the carelessness of that one sergeant is endangering his own life and the entire battalion position. If he let something get past him . . ."

The commanding officer's surprise attack over the sergeant's outpost had just about penetrated to Division, when a head popped up on the other side of the lateral hedgerow. It belonged to a squad leader, who remarked casually, with a grin that indicated that he had heard and appreciated the hiding Kenney was getting, "Sir, you hadn't ought to stand in that corner so long. There's some German over there with a grenade launcher who likes to drop one in there every so often."

The head disappeared and the Major wound up his lecture, ". . . Now don't ever let me find another outpost like THAT one." He nodded toward the front, then crawled over the hedgerow onto the path that led to the rear.

Kenney nodded dazedly, even forgetting to salute. He hadn't known the Old Man could get so hot, even about outposts.

Weddle grinned broadly at the hapless company commander. "Guess that'll hold you for a while," he said as he put one foot against the hedgerow and started to follow the battalion commander.

Kenney grinned weakly as he turned to trot toward his own command post. Twenty seconds later there was a small explosion in the now empty corner. It came from a rifle grenade lobbed in by "that German over there with a grenade launcher." It hit between the footprints left by Kenney and the Major as they had stood talking.

Both heard the little flat crump of the grenade but paid no attention. They didn't know, just then, that an alert squad leader had probably saved their lives.

Close Order Drill-- 30 Minutes / 7

IN THE DUSK of that evening, a couple of miles to the rear, the Major saw his command post tent for the first time. In fact, he hadn't even known he owned one until Mentzer had come looking for him and escorted him with a little swagger of pride to the neat dark-green tent. It was about seven by ten feet in size, with a sort of L-shaped, lightproof entrance so you could keep a lantern going in it at night. In fact, it even had a lantern, the first regular Coleman gasoline job that the commander had ever seen forward of a regimental command post. He was as pleased with that lantern as he was with the tent; he was getting weary of nothing but candles, and not enough of them.

That night was blissful and the distant sounds of firing that drifted back once in awhile only made the men sleep more soundly. They were perfectly satisfied to let other guys fight the war for a while. Next morning when the kitchens came up they got the first hot food they'd had in a month. They sat around on the grassy fields, leaning comfortably against the hedgerows while they stowed away great quantities of hot cakes and scrambled dried eggs and bacon. The few men who had been in on the D-day landing and were still around were comparing the quiet of that morning of 6 July with the hell at Omaha Beach on 6 June, while the new replacements listened with proper awe.

Regiment's schedule for the day called for nothing but cleaning up in the morning. That included everything—men, weapons, and all equipment. The weapons came first, then the equipment, and finally the men themselves. It was ordered that way, but there was no need for the order. Nobody has to tell an infantryman who has been for a month or even a week in the line that he has to clean his gun before he brushes his teeth.

There weren't any showers. But there was plenty of water, and a helmet makes as good a basin as anything you'll find. The Red Cross sent up soap, new toothbrushes, razors, anything the men might need for cleaning up. By noon every man had cleaned everything he owned and was positively resplendent, at least by comparison with his condition the day before, in a fresh uniform over a clean hide and under a freshly shaven face.

When they got around to looking at the next item on the schedule there were a large number of assorted comments. The schedule read, very simply, so you couldn't possibly take it for a typographical error or interpret it any way but just the way it stood: "Close-Order Drill—30 minutes." There wasn't even an exclamation point after it.

The staff was incredulous. After all, they were still within artillery range. You can't have close-order drill without getting people close to each other. And, besides, they had those 300 replacements who needed to know a lot more about attacking hedgerows than they did about drilling. Weddle even called Warfield to ask if somebody was getting funny. For once the regimental S3 was sympathetic, but he stood his ground. The schedule meant just what it said, "Close-Order Drill—30 minutes."

The Major, Hoffman, and Weddle carefully split up the area between the squads and platoons of the companies so that no two squads would ever be any closer together than they could help, just in case some Jerry gunner should happen to crank his gun around in that direction and throw one in.

Actually, the drill proved to be beneficial. You have to form up a company before you can really know who's in it, and you don't form up companies in combat or to clean guns, or even to go to chow in an area that is likely to be shot into. So when the squads fell in for the drill it was the first time a lot of the men had ever lined up together in close formation. Sure, they knew each other, but it put a different slant on things when they could look around and see every man in the squad at one time. The platoon leaders, the company commanders, and even the first sergeants discovered men they hadn't been able to tie up with a name on a list before. The replacements had a good look around, too. Hence the formation served a good purpose, even though it brought some sad recollections to the few National Guardsmen from the original companies. Most of these found themselves standing next to men they hardly knew, where buddies had stood beside them for years, back in Maryland or Virginia or Pennsylvania or maybe in England.

Even the drill itself went prettty well. The men probably didn't realize that it was doing them good to see the "team" in close formation but they knew how to drill and they did it with a sort of "Well, if that's what they want me to do I'll humor 'em" attitude.

That is, the drill went well until there was an unexpected diversion. American planes began to come over from all directions, high up in the clear blue sky. A few minutes after the first squadron passed, the rumbling concussion of the bombs they dropped on St. Lo pressed gently against shirts and trousers and shook the leaves on the trees. The General had come down to watch the drill. He and the Major sat side by side on a hedgerow silently watching the big planes as they came on and on, drawn to the air above St. Lo like bees to nectar. As the vapor trails streamed back, little puffs of black ack-ack began to blossom around the formations. But they bored on in relentlessly.

When the first plane was hit and started to fall, school was out. The drill broke up but no one knew or cared, not even the General. Every man watched that fascinating high-air drama as the Flying Forts streamed in endlessly and the little black puffs multiplied until the ships seemed to be flying through a black-mackerel sky. A plane exploded in mid-air. Then another was hit, white parachutes blooming sharp against the dark field of the antiaircraft bursts. Another and still another was hit. Once there were six planes falling simultaneously.

But the bombs kept falling too, while the thunderous roll of the explosions was constant. There were more bombs than there were guns; eventually the black puffs in the sky slackened until there were only a few when the last planes came over, dumped their loads, and turned wide to go back to England, still trailing their proud streamers of mist.

It was an awe-inspiring spectacle, which the men watched silently except to draw in a sharp breath when a plane was hit. If such a craft started down they watched it, counting parachutes. If ten snapped open a sigh of relief ran down the hedgerows. If all ten didn't show and the plane fell far beyond the trees, sometimes to send up a small, distant cloud of smoke, the sigh was different. That sigh was for the buddies, unknown airmen, but still buddies, who wouldn't be dropping any more bombs to help the slogging infantry.

No one knew what time it was when the last plane had come and gone. But drill was long over and chow was ready. The men were too excited over what they had seen to remember for long the planes that had gone down. They were remembering instead the booming thunder of the bombs and the tugging at their clothes that told them what fierce hell the Germans were catching. And the men gloried in it.

Orders came down during the night directing that Lagoon Red, Major Johns' 1st Battalion of the 115th Infantry Regiment, would relieve Lemon Red by midnight of the following day. Lemon was the code name for the 116th, whose Red (1st) Battalion was holding the line to the left of where Lagoon Red had hopped off from the Bois de Bretel nearly three weeks before.

It was rough country, a continuation of the tiny, hedgerow-bounded fields, sunken roads, and apple orchards that Baker Company had been in that first day. But by that time everyone was pretty used to that sort of thing. If you ever found a place where you could see for over a hundred yards you just considered yourself lucky.

The Major and his staff, with most of the company officers, rode in jeeps on their way forward for a look-see. At least they rode until they came to a big sign that said, "DANGER— ENEMY AHEAD. Dismount here." Nobody questioned the sign. There was no argument about dismounting.

A guide was sitting on the ground, his back against the sign and his helmet over his eyes, sleeping so soundly that Johns had to take him by the shoulder and shake him gently before he woke up. He blinked a couple of times, grinned broadly at the welcome relief force, and jumped to his feet. Before he would lead them to the lines he had to give them a little speech, warning them that they had to be cautious and mustn't bunch up on the way in because anything was apt to happen and frequently did. Then he showed them the route to a point a little way back of the command post where they met Lemon Red 6, Major Dallas.

Dallas was a big man. He was close to six feet tall and would weigh in at better than 200 pounds. He looked a bit on the chubby side, but his men, who were loyal, contended it was all solid muscle. Like most big men, he was pleasant and affable. He had been a salesman in civil life and the Major decided he was probably a good one. His line of talk was fast enough, anyway.

The big commander, introducing himself, shook hands all around. Then he took a deep breath and started in on a careful, detailed briefing. "Fellows," he said, "this is a hot spot. I know you've all been in lots of them before, but please take my word for it, this one is REALLY hot."

He paused and looked at the officers, as if to make sure they were going to take his word for it. Then he went on, "We've got Nazi paratroopers on the other side of the hedgerows. They're the best that Hitler has and they know it. They don't give us much rest. We don't give them any."

He stopped again, to let that sink in. Then he repeated what the guide had said, "Anything can happen here, anywhere, anytime. And frequently does. We don't move around any more than we have to. I don't mind telling you that I'm worried about this relief. I'd almost—but not quite—rather stay here than take the chances we'll run while you look the ground over and then move in. Whoever is running that bunch over there is smart. He moves fast. If he gets an idea we're being relieved tonight he'll hit us, as sure as God made little green apples. You can depend on him to do it just when we're half out and you're half in."

He stopped a third time, shoved his helmet back on his head, and waited to see if anyone had any comments. Nobody had. He went on, "If you will please do what I ask you to, we'll probably be okay. I don't want more than two men together at any time. That means one guide and one new man. And at least a hundred yards between pairs when you have to go over the same paths, which you will have to do in some places. Stay well down behind the hedgerows and don't let your helmet show; they'll fire a half dozen mortar rounds at one quick glimpse. They know right where to put them because they know where you're going. Having been here a long time before we were, they've got this place zero'd better than any rifle range you were ever on."

This time he looked directly at the Major and Weddle. "You're going to find this the screwiest setup you ever saw. I can't tell you exactly why, because you have to see it to appreciate it, but take my word for it, there's an orchard that sticks in between the two right companies that can't be covered any way you try it.

"That orchard is the hottest place I've seen yet, including Omaha Beach. They send patrols in there every night and sometimes even in daylight. They're big, tough, fighting patrols that cause trouble every time they come in. Hell, they sent a whole company in there once and we damned near couldn't hold 'em."

The big officer seemed to pause involuntarily this time, to look off toward the hot orchard. Then he shoved his helmet forward again and picked up his long speech. "We have casualties every day, so please do your best not to cause any more than we have to take anyway. My boys have been in here for two weeks now and they're getting right touchy, so if any of you get snapped at, don't pay any attention; just let it go and they'll get over it.

"I've got a guide here from every platoon and a couple from the Weapons Company. You can sort yourselves out; and please, for heaven's sake, be careful. You can get anywhere on the front without being seen if you do what you're told; there isn't any reason for anybody to get hurt.

"Now. Are there any questions?" Dallas seemed relieved to get it all off his chest.

Major Johns thought it was a good talk. He grinned and said, "Looks as if you covered it all."

In fact, it was such a good talk that there was only one casualty and that one came from a stray mortar shell that was thrown in apparently just for the hell of it.

At dusk the battalion was strung out along the road back of the 116th, waiting to go in. The mortars were able to get into position before dark, trading precious, carefully counted ammunition in their trailers for the same amount on the ground. No mortar outfit ever gave away ammo. They moved in one gun at a time and there were always five tubes ready to shoot, which was just as well because they fired three short missions before the move was completed.

As soon as it was dark the rifle platoons started in, one squad to each company at a time. The units moved slowly and carefully, well spaced along the line until they reached a point near their position. Then the squad leaders got together and traded man for man. In this way no one spot on the front was left unguarded for more than a few seconds and no more than two or three men were moving about above ground at one time in a small area. It was a long, tedious process, but a necessary one.

While the relief was progressing, the two battalion commanders found a sheltered spot near Dallas' command post, where they sat quietly, talking about people they knew in the division, then swapping stories about the things that had happened to their outfits. Even so, the time passed slowly. It seemed ages before Kenney called in to say that he was "home" and had taken charge of the company area. A few minutes later

Dallas' company commander called to report that they were all out and had turned over to Kenney. So the relief was officially one-third complete. Able and Baker companies had the tough sector on the right; they wouldn't say anything except that they were getting along, but slowly.

Around 0130 Julian Stoen, the new Baker company commander, said he was settled.

Then Able's new commander reported that he had two platoons in place. He paused a long time after making the report. Then, very reluctantly, he admitted that he was afraid his 3d Platoon was lost. No one had seen or heard from any part of it in more than an hour. He hadn't been able to get an answer on the 536.

Johns was furious. He had put the officer in command because he was senior lieutenant in the battalion, which was reason enough, but he decided that about one more stunt like that and there would be a new Able Company commander.

At 0200 the platoon was still lost and Dallas had ribbed Johns about it until it wasn't funny any more. They were both nervous about it because if the platoon happened to move a little too far in the wrong direction, lost as it was, and ran into the enemy, things could get right serious.

The two majors sat silent for a while. At length Dallas remarked, "Boy, it's quiet; I wonder what those paratroopers are cooking up now?"

Johns didn't answer. The Lemon Red CO went on, "You know, those Germans are the best soldiers I ever saw. I wish I had a battalion of 'em."

Johns sat bolt upright. This was heresy! "What the hell do you mean, they're the 'best'? You don't mean to sit there on that big butt of yours and tell me you think they're better than our own people?"

"I damn sure do. I don't take my helmet off to any battalion in this whole army of ours, either. But those paratroopers are the damnedest people you ever saw. You just wait—you'll see for yourself. They're smart and they don't know what the word 'fear' means. They come in and they keep coming until they get their job done or you kill 'em."

"Well, if they're so all-fired good why haven't they run you out of here by now?"

"Just one reason, bud, just one reason—there just ain't enough of 'em. If they had as many people as we have they could come right through us any time they made up their minds to do it."

"I don't believe it! I know our people have to take a little shoving sometimes, but I'll be damned if I'll admit any paratrooping SOB, especially a German one, is better than my gang."

Dallas smiled. He had got under Johns' skin, whether he really meant what he had said or not, and for some perverse reason he seemed to get a kick out of it. He answered very quietly, "Okay, bud, just stick around. You've got lots of time. You'll see what I mean before you get out of here."

Major Johns was annoyed. In fact, he was quite huffy about it. His faith in his men was so colossal that he would not sit still and let them be attacked even indirectly by anyone. It was probably just as well that the phone rang at that moment.

It was Able 6, reporting with considerable relief in his voice that the lost platoon had been found and was getting into position. It seemed they had taken a wrong turn somewhere and had been wandering around for an hour and a half in empty fields all of which, fortunately, were well behind the lines.

By 0240, two and a half hours late, the relief was complete. The two majors shook hands and said goodnight. But Dallas couldn't resist a final dig. As he left he whispered over his shoulder, "You'll see, bud, you'll see!"

Pigs or Paratroopers? / 8

MAJOR JOHNS talked again to each company commander, then decided it was time to hit the sack. He walked over to where he thought Dallas' hedgerow hole should be, felt around with his hands until he located it, then looked for his musette bag and blanket. As usual, Barbeaux had managed to put them just far enough away so they weren't where they really should be, but near enough so that he could look hurt if the Major said anything about it. He found them by the elementary process of stumbling over them, propped the bag just outside the entrance to the hole, and threw the blanket inside. Then he knelt and started to crawl in, head first.

It didn't take long to discover that that was not the way things had been planned, if they had been planned at all. One shoulder hit a root which stuck out of one side, and the other shoulder hit the other side of the hole. His helmet bumped the top, dislodging dirt which fell down the back of his neck. In addition, he had a sudden and severe attack of claustrophobia. Backing out hastily he sat down for a moment, reflecting briefly on the terrors of war. Then he tried it again, feet first. That worked better. The large end of the hole was toward the entrance and he found that there really was adequate room inside for him to lie down provided he didn't overdo it and try to stretch out full length.

Now Johns was one of those unfortunate souls who can't sleep on their backs. In fact, he had a lot of trouble sleeping at all unless he was exhausted, which he usually was these days. However, having had a good rest the night before, he was pretty well caught up. Therefore he wasn't tired enough yet to ignore the root and the damp, musty earth that pressed so close to him all around. He tried to lie on one side, but the root caught him just in the small of the back. If he so much as took a deep breath it jabbed him in a kidney or some tender spot. He tried lying on his back, but this wasn't comfortable; Dallas had not scooped out a place for his hips and shoulders. The hard ground made him feel as if he were suspended between two chairs, like the girl in the magician's act. He tried to turn over, whereupon the root caught him on a hip bone. He tried to lie on his stomach but found that to be worse. And at every move the confounded root jabbed him somewhere.

He attacked it with his little souvenir bayonet, thinking to shred it and then hack off the shreds. It didn't shred. He wormed his trench knife out of the sheath on his right hip and tried to work on the root with that. But to put any strength into it, he had to sit up. That, of course, was quite impossible because the hole was not over two feet wide or deep anywhere. He hacked feebly for a while then gave up. The hell with it. He'd have a new 6-hole dug in the morning.

He pulled his musette bag in for a pillow, kicked his blanket around his legs, spat wet dirt out of his mouth, and tried to sleep any-old-how.

By 0400 he was dozing nicely when machine gun and rifle fire broke out strongly on the right. He sat up quickly—as far as he could. His head hit the top of the hole, dirt cascaded into his hair and down his shirt in front and back. The hole had taken the offensive and it was far stronger than the Major. He scratched and scrambled in a near panic to get out of the blasted den once and for all.

The phone rang. It was Able 6. "Sir," he reported, "we think a German patrol may be coming through the orchard. The outpost heard something and beat it in here. We started firing, just to be on the safe side. I've asked for a flare from my 60's. There it goes now."

The Major, hearing the cough of the little mortar, instinctively looked up in time to see the flare burst into brilliant white light, making eerie dark shadows dance across the trees and hedgerows. He heard the pop a second or two after it opened. The small-arms firing was still going on.

He waited a moment or two, then asked, "See anything?"

"Can't from here, sir, but I'll give you the dope in a minute. Hang on."

Major Johns held the phone, watching a lone tracer streak crazily over the trees. The firing dwindled, then died out entirely. Suddenly a single M1 rifle cracked flatly, eight times—a full clip.

He spoke sharply into the phone. "Find out who did that last firing. Get him straightened out if he didn't have a good reason. You know damned well that trigger-happy stuff doesn't go around here."

Able 6 replied meekly, "Yes, sir."

The phone went dead for a few moments, then opened again. The company commander said, "Sir, Sergeant Clinton says they just killed another pig. This country is lousy with 'em. That orchard stinks with dead pigs, dead Krauts, and dead Yanks. I'll be mighty glad when we get out of here."

"Okay on the pig. But you can sure count on staying there awhile, stink or no stink. Out."

He dropped the phone into the hole and heard it clank on the operator's helmet, but didn't care. A Company's wild firing had almost surely told the Germans that a new outfit had moved in. He doubted that Dallas' company, after two weeks in there, would have thrown so much lead before they could see what they were shooting at. But then—he paused and collected his thoughts more tightly—you never knew. Dallas' outfit might have been even more trigger happy after losing men out there. He wondered if the Germans shoved the pigs over the hedgerow, just to cause excitement in the American lines. If they weren't doing it, they were missing a bet because this little show had waked every man in the battalion. Then he had to laugh a little to himself. You couldn't really blame the boys for cutting loose into the dark, but the idea of half a company shooting up a thousand rounds of ammunition to kill one pig was either funny or ridiculous. He wasn't sure which.

He started back for Dallas' hole, took one look at where it crouched, waiting for him, then decided that he wanted no part of it. If the Germans dropped something on the command post that night he would just sit there and take it. He dragged his blanket and musette bag out of the hole, thumbed his nose at it, shook the dirt out of the blanket, and rolled up in it next to the hedgerow. He slept soundly until dawn.

An unusual odor awoke him. He yawned, stretched, and sniffed. It smelled just like frying bacon. But that was preposterous! He rose, washed sketchily in a little water from his canteen, making mud pies behind his ears where the dirt from the hole still clung, and walked purposefully in the direction from which the unique aroma was coming. He wondered if the Germans had a new secret weapon calculated to lure GI's into their lines.

It *was* frying bacon! Mentzer and Grimsehl had a meat can full sizzling away over a small fire. Mentzer looked up. "Morning, Major, breakfast coming up. How d'ya want yours, crisp or juicy?"

"Where in hell did you get that stuff?" was all Johns could answer. He hadn't seen real bacon in months.

Mentzer, laughing, pointed to a large can. "10-in-1 ration from the artillery. I went back there last night before we came up here."

Weddle and Hoffman were pulled in by the second batch. As they arrived Mentzer put more wood on the fire. The wood, which was green, made a fair amount of heavy smoke for two or three minutes before it caught well. The five officers watched the smoke as it curled upward in the still air, ascending well above a big tree nearby.

"The bacon was good, but you're liable to get something hotter than that fire if you're not more careful," observed the Old Man a bit acidly. "Come on, Grimsehl, let's you and me go visit Kenney while these chow hounds invite the German Army to drop something in for breakfast."

Turning, Johns walked rapidly down the hedgerow. He knew that he need say no more. But he was somewhat annoyed with himself for permitting the wonderful aroma of frying bacon to make him forget even for a moment that building smoky fires within 300 or 400 yards of the enemy was not really a very intelligent thing to do.

Before they got to Kenney's command post they heard the flat crashing of several mortar rounds behind them. The Major grinned at Grimsehl. "I guess that'll teach Mentzer to fry his bacon somewhere else."

Grimsehl didn't think it was funny.

They found Kenney's command post, but a well-indoctrinated guard would not let Grimsehl go forward unless the battalion commander said it was essential, which it wasn't. So Johns crawled along the few yards to better shelter, leaving the S2 to wait behind the hedgerow.

Kenney stuck his head out of a hole and crawled out as soon as he saw his visitor. Johns spoke first. "Hello, Bill," he said, "how d'ya like your new home?"

Kenney, serious though cheerful as ever, answered quickly, "Good morning, Major, glad to see you. I guess it's all right, but I think we'd better go inside because the Germans seem to have an idea we have something back here. They drop a shell in every once in a while."

He pointed at a little crater almost under the CO's feet. "They just sent us that one a couple of minutes ago."

Johns glanced down briefly and answered, quickly, "Thanks, but I don't think I'll stay more than a minute; sort of thought you and I might have a look at your line."

Kenney was obviously concerned at the idea of having his battalion commander standing around in the open. He walked a few steps closer to a screen of leafy young trees that effectively blocked the Germans' view of the command post area. Here he peered through a small gap in the foliage. Johns followed and did the same. Kenney said, "Sure, Major, glad to show you what we've got."

"You know," he went on, "I think maybe they've got some observers in those high trees you can just barely see over there about 400 yards because every time anybody gets out of that covered route you came down, or stands up a little farther back, we get a couple of mortar rounds in here. That's why I've got that man up on the hedgerow back there."

Major Johns could see the tops of the high trees Kenney was talking about. They dominated the smaller growth along the C Company line. "Why don't you have your forward observer throw a few tree bursts in there every once in a while? That ought to discourage 'em if that's where they are."

Kenney brightened up. "Say, that's a helluva fine idea."

Moving to the hole, he called down, "Joe. Get Lieutenant Dettman on the soundpower. Tell him to have the FO throw a few rounds into the tops of the taller trees all along our front. Tell him I said do it every once in awhile all day at irregular intervals."

Kenney listened until he was sure Dettman had understood what was wanted. Then he turned back to the Major. "Now if you'll just follow me, sir, we'll take a route by which we can get all the way down to the front lines without being seen."

He moved around to the right and along a hedgerow that ended in a clump of trees. Major Johns followed, not too closely, and thus they made the rounds.

When Johns got back to the hedgerow where he had left Grimsehl, he found the latter sound asleep. I'll let him rest, he thought as he picked up the A Company runner and went on.

The Able Company command post was in a sunken road, right in the middle of the line itself. It wasn't a good place for a company command post but there wasn't a better spot available. Also, the line looked good as it was. The Major and the new Able 6 followed the road to the point where it made a sharp bend. Beyond that was the no-man's land that was part of the cause of all the trouble, the orchard. The road was untenable on either side for a distance of about a hundred yards. Beyond that, it belonged to the enemy.

A dead paratrooper lay a few feet past the turn. He had been there for days but Johns could see the tops of some papers sticking out of a jacket pocket. His old G2 training asserting itself, he instinctively started forward to search the body. An alert sergeant grabbed his arm before he could take the step that would put him in full view of an enemy machine gun, saying, " 'Tain't healthy to be going out there, sir. Like as not you wouldn't get back in one piece."

Johns tensed, then instantly relaxed again as he turned to the sergeant. "Thanks, Sarge, guess I'm a little absent-minded sometimes." He looked at the dead man with the intriguing papers, not more than ten feet from where he stood, but as unreachable as if he had been in Berlin.

He turned back to the noncom. "Sergeant, I'd like to know what those papers are. Will you get them, and anything else he has on him, and bring them to me tonight as soon as it gets dark?"

The sergeant looked at the dead German before he answered. He was thinking that paratroopers have very big ears. He was remembering, too, the hail of fire that thudded into the back of the curve, just above the body, periodically during the night. But he didn't hesitate long. "Sure, Major, I'll get you everything he's got, just as soon as it gets dark."

Able Company looked good. The Major could find nothing to complain about. Able 6 was showing improvement.

On the way back he picked up Grimsehl, who probably never knew that he had missed the trip to A Company. Together they walked slowly back to Battalion. It was nearly noon. The Major remembered that he had forgotten to tell Mentzer to have a new CP hole dug before night. He'd have to do that right away. Stoen and Baker Company could wait until tomorrow, or possibly later that evening.

When they reached the command post they went directly to the spot where the bacon-fry had been in full swing when they left. Mentzer's meat can lay against the hedgerow, a hole ripped across the bottom. Bacon was strewn over the ground, and even the fire looked as though it had been kicked around by shell fragments! The commander's eyebrows went up. "Mentzer! Weddle!" he snapped.

They both popped out of a low clump of brush almost beside him, grinning. Johns was relieved but a little annoyed. He knew they had been waiting for him and had probably been amused when they saw his concern.

"Anybody hurt?" he asked.

"Nothing but Major Hoffman's dignity," Weddle replied. "I didn't know that the old boy could move so fast." He laughed and went on, "We were sitting here licking our chops over that bacon just after you left, when we heard those Kraut mortars go off. Nobody had to tell us who they was shootin' at. We took off like those well-known birds. Major Hoffman made fifty yards in nothing flat and hit a nice big deep hole while he was still going full speed ahead. He slid into the hole like a rabbit. By the time those shells got here there wasn't a soul above ground for a hundred yards in either direction." Weddle laughed again before going on.

"They dropped an even ten rounds, with a one-turn traverse between rounds, right down the hedgerow. Every damn shell hit either on the 'row or just on the other side. Except the one that messed up Mentzer's meat can. Those Germans are either lucky or good."

Major Johns looked until he saw a couple of the mortar craters. "They're good," he agreed. "Furthermore they know this ground like they do their own faces. They undoubtedly even know this is a nice spot in which to cook breakfast. That's why they could drop one right in your skillet." He turned to Mentzer. "Don't forget that they can do it again any time they have a mind to. Now stay away from this tree in the mornings. And NO MORE FIRES."

Mentzer looked hurt. But not very much. He grinned broadly as he answered, "Sir, you didn't have to tell me that. THEY already did."

Johns couldn't help smiling. Then he remembered the CP hole.

"Oh, I forgot to tell you before I left this morning that I wanted another hole dug up next to the hedgerow, just on the other side of where the phone hole is now." He pointed.

"I knew you would, sir, so I told the A and P gang to be ready to go to work as soon as you got back and would say where you wanted it. I'll have 'em start right away. Same size as before?"

"Yes, except make the steps a little longer, so they slant more. Sergeant Fischhaber almost broke his neck the other day when he slid in just in front of a close one. Knocked him cold for five minutes, which wouldn't have happened if the steps had been longer."

"Right, sir. Longer steps. You want the entrance to the rear, I guess?"

Johns nodded, yawning. He was tired, the sun was warm, and the front was very quiet; not a shot had been fired for a good half hour. He thought about B Company; he hadn't been down to see them yet. Well, he decided, Baker could wait until tomorrow. He had had practically no sleep and there was an excellent chance that he wouldn't get very much that night.

His eye lit on the big hole for the telephone operators. It was empty. The operator was lying back against the hedgerow, enjoying the warm sun. The Major walked up to him and motioned to him to remain sitting. "Look, Smitty, I'm going to crawl into your hole here and catch a nap. I don't want to be disturbed unless it's something mighty important. You can get Major Hoffman or Captain Weddle for almost anything that comes in short of an attack, or a call from Colonel Ordway. Otherwise, I want to sleep."

Smitty grinned widely. "Okay, Major, I'll keep 'em off you for a while, and if I have to come in there in a hurry I'll try to keep my feet out of your face."

Johns lowered himself into the big, deep hole, stretched luxuriously, and squirmed into his best sleeping position.

He slept soundly for two or three hours. Not a shot or explosion disturbed him. Then the sound of picks and shovels, grunts, and bits of talk penetrated his consciousness. The noise dragged him slowly out of the deep well of sleep. A new voice broke in loudly. He could hear and understand everything it said.

"——got to keep the Major's tail dry again, do we? Hell, you'd think we didn't have nothin' to do but dig these damn super deluxe foxholes for that guy."

One or two other voices chorused agreement, as the griping went on. The Old Man lay back and listened. He really didn't mind a little good, honest griping. Also, in spite of his rising ire he was still logy with sleep. He didn't want to get up and bawl the A and P gang out, but it was beginning to look as if he were going to have to explain a few things about "super deluxe foxholes" to them. Then a particularly vicious, profane remark by the new voice sent his temper flaring. He popped out of the phone hole and stood over the men.

"Now listen to me, you birds," he barked, with an edge to his voice that cut through the other sounds and brought them up sharply. "So you think you're digging that hole to keep the Major's rear end dry, do you? Well, you're damn right you are! And while you keep that dry you're keeping his maps and his orders and his phones and his radios dry; and you're making a place where his 3 and and his 2 and his company commanders can look at things in the dark, and where his artillerymen can work and where they can all move around and think and get messages and give orders when the shooting is going on instead of hugging the ground in a bunch of little holes scattered from hell to breakfast without any cover or any way of getting to one another. And don't you ever forget for a minute that every one of those things that is 'his' is yours and the battalion's too. You dig that hole so he can fight this battalion and fight it right."

He paused for a deep breath. "Furthermore, my tail has been a damn sight wetter and a damn sight colder a damn sight more often than any of yours, and it probably will be plenty more. Now dig, dammit, and don't you let me hear any more griping out of you. Any time you have anything you think you ought to gripe about, you bring it to me. If it's legitimate I'll do something about it. But don't you go griping when you don't know what you're talking about."

The men stood for a moment silent, abashed. One of them, Private First Class Champagne, obviously older than the others, nodded and smiled at the Major, then swung his pick in a blow that had lots of willing strength behind it. The rest followed suit. There was no more griping after the Old Man, still piqued, swung off down the hedgerow toward Baker.

The firing had resumed and it was rare for five minutes to pass without a burst of machine gun fire, the cough of a mortar, or the explosion of a shell on one side or the other. Artillery went over both ways, but less frequently.

At Lieutenant Stoen's command post he learned why he had been able to sleep so soundly during the early part of the afternoon. Just after lunch, one of the Baker outposts had been startled to see a German medic climb nonchalantly over a hedgerow and make his way calmly across the field directly toward them. He wore the fore-and-aft garment common to all German medical personnel, a white smock bearing a very large Red Cross. Furthermore, he seemed to have complete confidence in the immunity it was supposed to give him.

He approached within a couple of paces of the outpost, saluted stiffly, and handed a note to the nonplussed sergeant in charge. It requested a truce while the medics of both sides went out to retrieve the dead and wounded who still lay in the fields. It authorized the bearer, a captain, to make detailed arrangements for the German command.

The sergeant called Lieutenant Stoen who in turn called Battalion. Major Johns was not to be found, so Grimsehl accepted the call and went forward to the Baker Company outpost where he met the German medic and agreed to the truce. For some reason that was never made clear, it had been impossible, apparently, to reach the Major, Hoffman, or Weddle. Johns was annoyed with Grimsehl for taking so much on himself, but said nothing to Stoen. Then he remembered that the incident must have occurred while he was having his "Do Not Disturb" nap. He made a mental note not to indulge himself in any such luxury again.

In any event, the truce had been called. For two hours the medics of both sides had worked along the front, gathering in their dead and wounded. Most were found in the orchard, with only a very few along the rest of the line. The effort seemed to be worthwhile because one of the men from the 116th who was brought in from the orchard still showed some signs of life and the Doc said he might pull through even though he was badly shot up and had been in the orchard without food, water, or attention for at least two days and nights.

When Stoen finished the story, he and his battalion commander made the rounds of the Baker lines. As usual, Major Johns asked a number of men how they were getting along. He got one answer that surprised him. A sergeant said, "Well, sir, everything's okay. It's a tough spot but I figure we're as good as any other outfit to hold it down and somebody's got to do it. But I sure wish the Major would get around and see us more often. It does the men a world of good to see you down here in the lines."

The Major, who had thought he was getting around about as often as any battalion commander should, was seriously concerned because this sergeant didn't seem to think so. Instead of being annoyed, he was pleased that the man had the uncommon guts to say what he thought, whether or not he was right. He answered, "Okay, Sarge, you'll see me around a lot more in the future."

The sergeant saluted sharply, whereupon Stoen and the Major went on, Stoen trying to stammer out an apology for the brash sergeant. Johns cut him off, but not before Stoen had volunteered the statement that he himself thought the Major got around more than any battalion commander he had ever seen. The fact that Stoen had not seen many battalion commanders did not escape Johns, who smiled to himself as the company commander lapsed into an embarrassed silence.

On the way back to Battalion he reviewed his own approach to the problem of leadership. He knew that he must prove himself—especially his courage—to every man in the outfit if he expected to get the maximum from them. He felt that he had done so fairly effectively as far as C Company was concerned because he stayed with them the night the counterattack had threatened their left flank at the Bois de Bretel. Also his personal intelligence service told him that A Company had approved the little battle he and Grimsehl and Martin had had with the machine gun that killed Jimmie and Sadler. But it was apparent that this was going to be a company-by-company proposition. Baker Company didn't seem to be impressed. He'd have to do something about that.

Sounds in the Night / 9

THE NEW CP hole was ready by dark, so the battalion CO moved in, taking Weddle and Martin with him. The battalion and artillery phones were installed inside. The radio operators with their sets were in holes nearby where they could be reached by a whisper if needed. The telephone operators likewise had holes in the immediate vicinity, as did the Message Center Chief who was responsible for keeping track of the company runners. The gasoline lantern didn't work, but somebody stuck a candle in a bottle, lit it, and the command post was all set for another night in a defensive position. It was a typical evening.

Each of the three officers took turns heating, over the single candle, his little can of meat that came out of the supper K-ration. He did this by opening the lid most of the way with the key that came with the ration, bending it back and holding the can over the candle flame by grasping the bent-back lid with a pair of pliers. The meat simmered and the grease melted and spit, but if it was a bit messy it was still the best available way to get a hot meal. The bouillon powder, which nobody ever used to make soup, made an excellent flavoring agent and with it the meat wasn't bad at all.

Weddle, finishing his portion, set the inevitable chocolate bar on the table alongside the little packet of toilet paper, the stick of chewing gum, and the four cigarettes, that also came with the "supper" ration. The chocolate was either sickeningly sweet, if you happened to have the new K-ration, or consisted of the hard, nondescript D-bar if you had the old ration. Few men would eat the D-bar unless they were on the verge of starvation, or thought they were. Weddle looked at the two objects, remarking, "You know, they've really got this thing figured out. They stop you up for the night with that damn chocolate and then open you up for the day with that fig-bar thing in the breakfast ration. Only thing is, they ought to have some more of this," he held up the toilet paper, "in the other rations, especially the dinner one."

The others nodded in solemn agreement. But the Major reached for his helmet. "If you'd just store enough of it in here," he pointed to the inside of his helmet to show two thick flat rolls of white paper stuck between the fabric straps and the plastic liner, "you wouldn't have to worry about that piddling bit in the ration."

"Oh, hell, Major," Weddle protested, "I got enough of that stuff stuck around inside my helmet to last me a month and keep out anything short of an 88. But you got to have something to gripe about . . ."

The phone rang briskly. Major Johns picked it up. "Red 6."

It was Kenney. "Charlie 6, sir. Fire mission for you."

Johns nodded to Martin, but the artilleryman had caught the words "Fire mission" and had alerted like a bird dog. "Okay, let's have it."

"My outpost number 2 says they can hear movement out to their left front about 600 yards. They say it sounds like trucks. I figure maybe the Krauts are bringing up stuff on the main road over there as far forward as they can, maybe to that road junction at 563-653. Can you put something out there to worry 'em?"

"Sure, just a minute." Johns bent over the map, located the Charlie outpost, moved out 600 yards, and found a road junction. He checked the coordinates on the map to be sure it was the right one. Then he turned to Martin, keeping his finger on the road junction.

"This is between our flank and the 116th Infantry, but Regiment said they weren't putting any patrols out that way tonight. Let's shoot it."

Martin looked at his own map for a moment, then replied, "Okay, we'll give her a try."

He cranked the artillery phone which, as usual, had its own line directly to the artillery Fire Direction Center. "This is Nighthawk 1. Fire mission." He stopped and looked carefully at his map again. "Concentration 196 is 100 left, 600 short. Enemy trucks on highway."

The FDC operator answered, "Roger. Wait."

Major Johns spoke to Kenney over the other phone. "Looks as if we'll get it. Hang on."

Dead silence for a few minutes. Then the sound of four cannon firing together came clearly and sharply over the artillery phone. With the report came the always-electrifying phrase from the Fire Direction Center, "On the w-a-a-a-ay."

In a few seconds the distant rumble of the guns rolled in the entrance to the command post. Johns repeated to Kenney, "On the w-a-a-a-ay," and heard him pass it on to the outpost by the soundpower phone he held in his other hand.

Then came the gathering whine of the shells coming over from the rear. They would pass only a little to the left of the command post. The sound of their passing swelled to a modest scream, then began to diminish. Artillery fire always sounded so good when it was going out. The Major knew how menacing it would sound to the Germans on the receiving end. He could imagine that the enemy truck drivers, as they heard that noisy death approaching, would realize they couldn't get out of their trucks before it would hit. Always provided, of course, that the educated guessing which the battalion's observers were doing would place the shells within a hundred yards or less of the target. Shooting at night, at sounds several hundreds yards away, was largely a matter of luck. If you had reason to believe the enemy were doing a certain thing at a certain spot you had a fair chance of dropping something on them, or at least scaring them and harassing them in their work. The artillery could fire with amazing accuracy, even from a map. But when you could not observe the strike and make corrections, Lady Luck had a very large hand in the game. Still, amazing things happened.

The mortar round in the frying pan that morning had been unobserved fire too.

The rustling whine of the shells still hung in the air when the hollow roar of their impact came back across the lines.

The Fire Direction Center came to life. "What was the result?"

Martin looked pained. "Now how the hell would I know? You know perfectly well we can't SEE out there. I'll try to find out something, though, and let you know. Out."

Kenney was already asking the outpost more or less the same thing. He spoke to the Major. "They say it sounded pretty good but they want to try it again another hundred yards out with no change in deflection."

This went to Martin, who nodded, cranked for the Fire Direction Center again, and said, "Nighthawk 1 again. Same mission, 100 short. Outpost says it sounded good."

It took a little longer this time before the sound of the guns and the "On the w-a-a-a-ay" came back. Fire Direction Center added, "Can't give you any more on this mission unless you can tell more about the result."

Apparently there had been some discussion in the artillery Fire Direction Center about whether they could afford to throw any more shells at vague sounds in the night.

The shells burst almost imperceptibly farther away. Kenney's voice, talking to the outpost, came indistinctly over the battalion wire, then he reported to Major Johns. "They say that was right in there! Wait a minute."

He came back in a moment. "They say they can hear trucks moving out up the road, fast. Looks as if we drove 'em away, whether we hurt 'em or not. Many thanks. Everything else is right quiet. Out."

Once more Major Johns relayed the information to Martin, who told the Fire Direction Center, "Mission complete. Enemy vehicles withdrawing hastily to the rear with burned tails."

FDC laughed and said, "Okay. Call us again sometime."

They laid the phones on the table and Johns swung his feet up onto his sleeping shelf. But before he could lie back, the battalion phone rang again. Weddle took it. "Red 3." Pause. "Yeah, Stoen." Pause. Then, to Johns, "Stoen says they can hear movement in that orchard again. He wants us to lay a battery on concentration 180—that's on the hedgerow at the far end of the orchard—but not to fire it until he says so. He thinks maybe he can catch something in the open if we work it right."

A burst of German machine gun fire from the A Company front punctuated the pause. An awed voice outside exclaimed, "Boy, look at them tracers!"

Major Johns nodded to Martin, who called the Fire Direction Center. "Nighthawk 1. Look, we got a stunt on this time. Lay Battery A on concentration 180, but don't fire until I say so. C Company up here thinks they can catch a patrol in the open if we work it right."

There was quite a wait while Fire Direction Center kicked the idea around. Then the answer came, "Okay, we'll wait for the word, but if anybody else has a fire mission, we'll have to shoot it."

Weddle told Stoen, "The deal is on. We'll keep the lines open and you say when."

The operator at the battalion switchboard took advantage of the pause to tell Weddle, "Sir, Able Company wants to talk to you."

Weddle shook his head at the phone. "Tell 'em we can't break our connection with Baker, but you can put 'em on too."

In a moment Able 6's voice came over, sharp and tinged with excitement. "Tell the Major we got that patrol started on time but they didn't get over the hedgerow good before the Krauts caught 'em with a machine gun, getting one man in the arm. So they all came back."

He was referring to a patrol that had been briefed to go out and attack a known German outpost with the mission of bringing back a prisoner. Regiment, or maybe it was Division, had an idea that the enemy paratroopers were running a fresh outfit into the line. Only interrogation of a prisoner could verify these suspicions. Paratrooper prisoners were hard to come by but

Johns knew he would have no peace from Regiment until a concerted effort was made to get one; so, although he was not the least bit optimistic about the chances for success, he would have to push it as hard as he could.

He said to Weddle, "Tell him to wait about two hours, then send them out again on the first alternate route we planned."

"Roger. Hmmm. What do you say we send Grimsehl down to needle 'em a little. He may have some ideas by the time he gets down there."

The CO nodded agreement whereupon Weddle said into the phone, "Look, I'm going to send Grimsehl down with some orders for you on that job. Regiment wants that prisoner right bad and we aim to please."

He moved the crank a quarter turn. The operator answered instantly, "Yes, sir?"

"Cut Able off, but leave Baker on." He handed the phone to Johns. "I'll get George on the way."

Major Johns took the telephone. "Okay, but remind him that he is not to go on any patrols."

Weddle, nodding, drew back the blackout blanket. There was a Division order prohibiting intelligence officers or their personnel from going out on patrols, but George Grimsehl was forever wanting to violate it when an important job came up. This one was important.

Stoen cut in, over the still open line to Baker. "If Able can't get you a Kraut maybe we can snag one out of that patrol we're getting ready to squash."

Johns had his mouth open to answer when Stoen called sharply, "FIRE." The command was relayed—the Major to Martin to the Fire Direction Center to the guns—to the patrol. The sound of the guns came over the phone and the shells whined overhead seconds later, on the right. The roar of their explosion was much closer than the other had been, near enough to have a little crack to it, rather than the rolling boom of the more distant bursts.

An instant after the shells hit, the sound of rifle fire came from the same direction. Then a German machine gun ripped out a long burst, joined by the heavy stuttering of their own machine guns covering the orchard. The sound of firing ripped and snapped for maybe two minutes, while ricochet tracers yowled their fiery way over the trees, just as they had done the night before. Then all firing stopped. A tense silence settled over the front.

Johns spoke into the phone, "Hey, what's going on over there?"

No answer.

"Stoen, dammit, what's happening?"

No answer.

Weddle came back down the steps. "What's the matter? The orchard acting up again?"

"Yeah, but Stoen doesn't answer any more. You reckon they got into the CP?"

Weddle smiled. "Naw, Major. No grenades. Stoen's just gone out to see for himself. He never sticks around the CP when there's any excitement going on. He'll be back and tell you about it in a little bit."

Weddle, as usual, was right. Ten long minutes passed, during which the commander wished he could run out and see for himself too. But he knew very well that before he could get a tenth of the way to Baker, through fields and over hedgerows, the excitement there would be over. Meanwhile, something would be happening over at Charlie Company. He was doomed to wait until somebody told him.

The minutes were not quiet. The row in the orchard had stirred up both sides. Artillery fire was both coming and going, while the German mortar shells were marching deliberately across the Charlie and Able fronts, their crunching reports clear in the night. The men who had been lounging around outside the command post, in case they were needed, had scuttled to their holes.

A volley of heavy projectiles passed high overhead, whispering and muttering on the way to the Regiment's rear. It hit far back and the sound of the big shells was lost in the noise nearer the command post.

Martin grinned. "That was headed for my people. Just to let 'em know they're in the war. Do 'em good."

Weddle nodded. "Yeah, or Regiment. Some day I'm damned if I don't hand the Krauts an overlay showing where Regiment is, just so they can shake that gang up a little back there and let that damned Warfield—and Whittington—know they're in the war too."

Whittington was Warfield's assistant and there was an eternal bickering between the S3 sections of Battalion and Regiment. The men nearer the front contended that the Regimental people didn't know what a war was all about. When their reports were questioned or remarks passed about their inability to get prisoners, the battalion officers always had a standard answer, "If you don't believe us, then come down here and see for yourself."

The invitation was practically never accepted.

Johns paid little attention. He was anxious to hear from Stoen who, he was beginning to hope, was actually doing something about getting a prisoner. Finally, the phone rang.

"Red 6."

"Baker 6, Major. Well, we had a little fun up here. I thought for a minute I was gonna be able to scoop Able on that prisoner deal, but no soap."

Johns relaxed. He was glad to hear Stoen's voice, but disappointed that he hadn't got the prisoner even though it would have been a miracle if he had. Stoen went on, "We were right about the patrol and I believe Regiment may be right about that new outfit. This gang made a lot of noise just getting ready to come over the hedgerow. We heard 'em talking. They made so much racket I was beginning to suspect a trick but we were ready for anything so we just sat and waited. Then when they did come over they made so much noise I think one of 'em musta fallen off the hedgerow. Sergeant Clinton saw 'em and gave the word. We fired a flare same time the artillery came in and we saw the shells hit behind about a 12-man patrol. Couldn't tell if it got any of 'em, but some of my riflemen cut down on 'em. The nearest man went down and the others ran.

Then Clinton went over the hedgerow after the guy that was down. But the flare was still burning and the Germans had a covering gang on the hedgerow that saw him and cut down on him. Clinton got back okay, but his jacket is pretty well ventilated in a couple of places. Then everybody cut loose with everything in a regular shooting match. We fired more flares in the light of which we could see two or three of 'em down out there. But the rest must have made it back."

Major Johns interrupted. "Do you think you can get to any of them?"

"I doubt it, Major. We don't know if they're dead or not but I'd bet they are because we put enough lead out there to kill a whole herd of hogs, or Germans. We don't expect to give them a chance to get the bodies back but I don't think we can get to them either because the nearest one to us is still nearer the Krauts. Dragging people makes a lot of unhealthy noise."

"All right, Stoeny, nice try anyway. Tell Clinton I said so." He laid the phone on the table and looked at the roof in disgust. The phone rang before anyone could say anything. Johns picked it up, barking, "Red 6."

The operator's voice came through clearly, "ARE you finished?"

"Yes, I am." He slammed it back on the table.

Weddle shook his head. "You forgot to ring off, Major. Sergeant Wilson gives the operators hell if they don't make sure the lines are clear."

Sergeant Wilson was the Acting Communications Officer. The original man had been killed and Wilson was doing a fine job. He had been in for a commission for quite a while.

Johns picked up the phone and twisted the crank on the leather case. The operator answered instantly, "Yes, sir?"

"What's your name, operator?"

"Private Henderson, sir." The voice was a little uncertain.

"Okay, Private Henderson, you keep on doing your job the way you're supposed to. Don't mind me if I snap at you once in a while. I'm sorry." He started to lay the phone down, smiled, picked it up and added, "Finished."

Henderson said, "Yes, sir," relief clear in his voice.

It was nearly 0200 before quiet settled over the front. Grimsehl came back with the story of another unsuccessful patrol, a dozen fire missions came in from the companies besides those fired by the forward observers, and a runner came in to deliver to the Major the papers he had seen in the dead paratrooper's pocket that afternoon. They were valueless, but Johns got a kick out of seeing them and knowing that the sergeant had been as good as his word.

During the short periods of quiet inside the command post Major Johns thought about the communications system. He decided it was wonderful. Any man in the outfit who could get to a phone or a radio could call for any kind of support he might want. He could adjust both artillery and mortar fire, through company and battalion, or he could report the presence of an enemy patrol. Every platoon and every outpost had a soundpower phone with field wire leading back to their company command post; from there the channel went on up the line. Communication was infinitely better as long as the wire stayed in; but even if it went out, the radios could still function except that there weren't quite so many 536's as there were soundpower phones. It was easier to scrounge soundpower phones than 536 radios, the battalion having several times its allotted number of the former.

The biggest advantage of this extensive network was in the artillery and mortar work. Each company had an artillery and a battalion mortar forward observer besides their own 60-mm mortar people. But those men couldn't be awake always, nor could they cover all of an 800- or 1000-yard front where visibility was frequently limited to a hundred yards and never exceeded two hundred. At night, of course, the situation was worse; but with lots of phones available, every outpost was its own forward observer. There was nothing about the war that Johns enjoyed so much as the fire missions that came through the command post.

This network of communications enabled three men to keep accurate, minute-by-minute track of all that was going on over the entire front, covered by nearly 600 men. From this one spot they could direct the lives of all those men, actors in the most thrilling and awful drama of all time. He himself, as battalion commander, made the decisions; but there were few, during the course of an ordinary day, that were not mostly automatic, cut and dried. His general assistant, Operations Officer Weddle, could make most of them and seldom be wrong. It was only when something special occurred that the Old Man had to exert himself and be prepared to take the responsibility for what he did. If he made a wrong decision, he could cause men to lose their lives needlessly; or if he was clever or lucky he might, by moving a single squad or platoon, or calling for fire support, defeat the enemy and gain additional glory for the unit, all without moving from his communications when in a defensive position such as this.

His artillery liaison officer, Lieutenant Martin, was a specialist in charge of the battalion's most powerful support. With a word into the phone, or over his radio, he could call for and direct the fire of a single 105-mm howitzer or a battery. Or, if the need were great, he might get the entire support of most of the division and corps artillery, dozens and dozens of cannon up to 155-mm in caliber and even greater. It was amazing how quickly this deadly support could be had.

The details of the action in the command post were what made the whole thing so dramatic. Anything could happen, and you never knew for sure what was occurring until a report came in. A single rifle shot could mean the death of a company commander, or it could mean nothing. A mortar round might wipe out an outpost and lay a company open to a surprise attack, or it might only kick up a little dust and scar a few trees. A volley of artillery fire could come through the roof over their heads, or it could burst harmlessly in the fields outside. A burst of firing from the orchard could mean another pig or a full-scale German attack. Each sound built up a certain amount of suspense, to greater or lesser degree. The ring of the phone itself built the tension higher and higher, until the first words that came in would perhaps screw it even tighter or dispel it entirely.

A battalion command post was one hell of an interesting place in which to be.

Johns had just reached this conclusion, and decided he'd rather be where he was than back at Division, when the first sound of incoming artillery came in through the blanket over the entrance. It swelled in volume and pitch. It was coming close. The three officers reached simultaneously for their helmets as Johns rolled off the shelf onto the floor.

Four shells hit just on the other side of the hedgerow, perhaps ten steps away. They were big shells, probably 150-mm or better. The concussion of their crashing explosions shook the entire hole. Dirt rained down from the roof and the candle flickered but did not go out.

Everybody sat up. Weddle shook dirt off the map. Martin carefully brushed more of it away from the back of his neck before it had a chance to work down farther. Johns removed his helmet to do the same.

Weddle must have sensed something of the Major's thoughts about the drama of the command post. He said, "I'm damned if this doesn't remind me somewhat of that play that came out after the last war—play, book, movie—maybe all three. What was it, anyway? Something about 'Glory'?"

"You mean 'What Price Glory'? That's not it." Johns thought he could remember some other play having a number of men in a dugout under fire. One had gone mad or something. "No, I believe you're thinking of 'Journey's End,' the scene of which was a British dugout near St. Quentin."

"Yeah," Weddle said, reflectively, "only I don't think any of us are apt to go nuts like that guy in the play did."

They laughed.

"You know," put in the Major again, "if I could write I'd like to do a play based on a story built right around a battalion command post. You could lay every scene right here and you could get everything you'd need in a real drama—suspense, excitement, elation, disappointment, fear, sorrow, chagrin. What else could you want?"

"Babes," stated Martin, flatly.

"Yeah, I guess so. There was a babe in 'What Price Glory,' wasn't there? Hmm, don't know how we could get any love interest into this setup." He looked around at the earth walls and the dirty blankets, empty K-ration boxes and single flickering candle. "Guess we'll have to make our play different, with no babes in it."

"No good. Wouldn't sell."

Johns lay back on his blanket, visualizing a scene on a stage with a cutaway dugout like the CP hole. He could hear the telephone ringing, see messengers rushing in and out, the company commanders coming in for orders and a look at a map, a wounded staff officer staggering in with extra-dramatic gestures as he told of a flanking attack that had been beaten off by Charlie Company after all communications were out. The telephone in the stage command post rang while the staff officer was still telling his story. He could see himself, on the stage, reaching for the phone, but it was Weddle's voice that answered, "Yeah, Kenney, okay. I'll tell him."

Major Johns opened his eyes, surprised to find that it was after 0300. Weddle looked sleepy and Martin was stretched out on the floor, snoring softly. Weddle said, "Kenney spotted a small patrol on the left flank which he ran off with 60-mm fire. Couldn't tell if they got any of 'em."

The Old Man nodded very sagely, as if the information were of terrific importance and he would have to study it very carefully before giving an answer.

The sun was clear of the horizon before he woke again.

Counterattack! /10

AS THE SUN climbed higher the temperature rose with it. The day was going to be hot. And it was hot in more ways than one. The Germans began warming things up all along the line by throwing over more and more artillery and mortar fire. By mid-morning there had been several casualties in each company and the command post had been shaken up twice. The battalion commander issued orders that no man would leave his position unless absolutely necessary. Obeying his own order, he stayed in the hole.

The battalion's mortars and supporting artillery were returning more than they received, but there was no quieting the Germans that day. Martin was watching the situation with interest. One of his jobs was to receive and forward "shell-reps." A shell report, or "shell rep," was supposed to be sent in by any man who witnessed the fall of enemy artillery fire. The report included the exact location in which each shell hit, its caliber, and, as nearly as possible, the direction from which it had come. At the Fire Direction Center, the artillery S2 placed the location of each hit on the map and projected the estimated direction of flight back into enemy territory. The lines thus plotted always crossed somewhere. If enough of these rays intersected near the same point, it was a good bet a hostile battery was located somewhere in that vicinity. By studying the terrain, as indicated on the map, it was often possible to guess just about where that battery would be. Then, when the S2 was satisfied, from this information, that he had a good chance of drawing blood, he could take the matter to his own commander and ask for a counterbattery mission. If approved, the big 155's would reach out and search the selected area. Sometimes they were lucky. Sometimes they weren't, but every shell that burst in enemy territory was money in the bank to the infantrymen who heard it going over, so it was never a complete waste.

Martin was puzzled. He kept a rough record of the shell reps for his own information and by the middle of the afternoon he had enough data to make him want to talk to his boss. He called Lieutenant Colonel Cooper, the commander of the 110th Field Artillery Battalion.

"Sir," said Martin, "I believe the Germans have moved some more artillery in opposite us. The way these reports are coming in makes me think they are registering on us. What worries me is how they could be getting any observation on some of the targets they shoot at."

"We think the same thing," Cooper replied. "and I'm asking General Sands for some corps artillery to give us a hand with counterbattery today. Call me again if you get any definite ideas."

Some of the enemy fire falling that day was on targets that had never been hit before, and which couldn't possibly be observed from the enemy lines. The Germans had no equivalent of the American light observation plane that provided the artillery with a bird's-eye view of any front. Therefore there seemed to be only one answer to the accuracy of the fire—the Germans must have infiltrated artillery observers into the battalion lines for the express purpose of registering on vital new targets.

Major Johns ordered out several search parties. They beat through every wooded area and combed every hillock or bush-covered hedgerow. They examined every tall tree and even prodded into suspicious-looking ground that might have covered trapdoor-type holes. They found no observers. After two men were hurt by incoming shell fragments, the Major ordered them back to their holes, none the wiser.*

Martin was defeated. He said it was impossible for artillery to fire with such consistent accuracy from a map. If his first "only" answer had been wrong then all that was left to believe was that the German artillery had registered on all those targets while the area was still in their hands. Nobody could answer that question, but it didn't stop the accurate fire from coming in steadily.

The mortars were the worst, though. They were even more effective than the 88's there in that position at Dufayel, because the rolling terrain produced many dead spaces which the 88's with their flat trajectory could not reach. It was later that the men came to fear the 88's more than the silently falling mortar shells.

The German mortar gunners must have registered, too, because they had the exact range of every foot of hedgerow held by the battalion. On the 10th of July they covered almost every foot of every hedgerow. That sort of gunnery was rough on the men. They never knew when the first round would fall. But once it had splattered with its flat crash, they all knew that six or maybe a dozen more were coming, each one a little farther up or down the hedgerow. When you heard that first one you pulled the bottom of your foxhole right up into your

---

*Many times during the campaign in Europe did American units suspect that the Germans had observers concealed behind our lines. This probably did occur in some instances. However, the answer usually comes from a less mysterious source. The Germans told us after the war that our radio security was consistently poor, that by monitoring our transmissions they were generally able to keep themselves well informed as to our movements, and that by goniometric intersection on our transmitters they were able to locate most of our command posts as well as other installations. Our people never seemed to realize that in many German units were men who had lived in the States and understood American slang perfectly, and that the so-called double talk which we indulged in rarely fooled them. Even more interesting is the fact that our supposed short-range transmissions during the Louisiana and Tennessee maneuvers were picked up in Germany owing to a phenomenon involving reflection from the Heaviside Layer of ionized particles in the stratosphere. A study of these intercepts often told the enemy when our units were preparing for oversea movement. The German artillery was also skilled in sound- and flash-ranging, but this method did not, of course, locate for them anything except active artillery positions.—Editor.

belly and prayed. When you heard the second one you knew whether or not they were coming your way. If they were coming toward you it got right rough. Each round was a little closer, and they were so damned deliberate about it that the waiting was worse than the crash of the shell itself. You lay there and counted the seconds between the shells until you knew that the next one was YOURS.

The twenty seconds or so was the longest in the world because you'd never know if you were safe until the shell hit. It could hit anywhere outside your hole, even a matter of inches, yet you were okay. If it hit in the hole with you you'd never know it, of course. Actually, only a few shells ever made direct hits on foxholes, but some did and nearly every man had seen a foxhole that had been hit. There was always the little tail-fin section left on the surface, and after the litter bearers had come and gone there was only a pool of dark muck to show that somebody had been in the hole.

It happened twice that day.

A little after 1700 General Gerhardt came striding through the trees behind the command post hole. His manner was neither light nor gay. He came on serious business, that of giving orders for an attack. If he carried them himself they were important.

He wanted to brief all the company commanders but he didn't have time to wait for Able and Baker to worm their way out. Consequently he talked to Kenney; and to McCarthy, who had succeeded Captain Nabb in command of Dog Company; and to Mentzer, together with Major Johns and the staff. All crowded into The Hole.

"Gentlemen," he said, with an edge to his voice that was impressive, "the division attacks tomorrow morning at 0600. All along the line. This is the drive for St. Lo."

He stopped to consult a notebook. "Your objective will be the town of Belle Fontaine. Of course you will get details from Ordway. But I want to tell you that this is the beginning of a very big and very important operation. I can't tell you more now, but I expect every one of you to do your best tomorrow."

With that he was gone, Weddle and Grimsehl scurrying to get off the steps to make room for his passage, and his aide scrambling to get out of the phone hole and catch up.

Before he got well into the woods, the General stopped suddenly and called, "Oh, Johns."

Major Johns was on his heels. "Yes, sir?"

"Look, boy, you're the sole survivor of the three volunteers who wanted to come with me. Did you know that?" He didn't wait for an answer. "Whitehead caught an 88 the other day while you were back in those woods." He paused and looked sharply at the Major. "I don't know if it's lucky to ask to get into a war or not. But you stay in there and pitch. I'm counting on you."

He waved and was gone again before Johns could reply.

The staff ate their C-ration supper in thoughtful silence, waiting for the CO and Weddle to be called back to Regiment for particulars concerning the attack. They were called soon enough.

There were few details. The battalions would attack, as the General had said, at 0600. The 1st Battalion would advance in a southwesterly direction, with the village of Belle Fontaine as its initial objective. It was hardly a thousand yards, across country, but every man in the battalion knew it would be a long thousand. It was just as well that they didn't know just *how* tough that thousand yards was to be.

The 2d Battalion would move on La Forge and the 3d would be in reserve.

That was about all there was to it, except for the usual information concerning artillery support, supplies, location of the regimental command post, and that sort of thing.

Johns and Weddle got back just at dark. Though it was very quiet, the company commanders who were waiting in The Hole were uneasy. None of them wanted to attack from that position. It was too screwy a setup. But there was nothing they could do about it now. The Major had no choice in his order of

attack. From the direction of the objective he could do only one
thing, let Able and Baker take off from right where they were,
with Charlie, in reserve, protecting what would become the
exposed and dangerous left flank.

Johns expected trouble on that left flank because they
would be moving slantwise across the Charlie front, at least
at first. Even in that difficult terrain it was too much to expect that they could get clear without trouble. He told Kenney
to try to protect the flank with one platoon while holding two
platoons free for him to use to shove through a soft spot, if
one was found, or to bolster a weak place if they were hit
hard with a counterattack.

By the time the order got down to the platoon leaders their
part was pretty simple; all they, in turn, had to say was "All
right, gang, let's take that next hedgerow."

When the company commanders had gone, the staff dis-
cussed the plan of attack. The question bothering Johns most of
all was where to put the advance command post group. He
wanted to hold casualties to the barest minimum, yet he wanted
to be as far forward as possible. There were a number of good
reasons for this. In the first place, keeping the command
group close to the companies made a lot of difference in communications, particularly in this close, wooded country. A
clump of heavy trees or a high hedgerow could spell the margin
between having contact and not having it. That was of supreme
importance. Second, if he had to move to a bogged-down
company or to any trouble spot, he wanted to have the shortest
possible distance to go. Third, the group couldn't afford to
stay far behind, in any event, because they fully expected the
German paratroopers to close in around them as soon as they
started to advance. If the command post group were too far
from the rifle companies it would have a good chance of getting
cut off and destroyed or captured. Then there was always the
consideration that the men liked to know that the Old Man
was not far behind, and to see him once in a while when the
stuff was flying around. Major Johns was acutely aware of this,
but he'd already suffered losses in his command post group by

getting them up front and he didn't want that to happen again. There wasn't a good route of advance in the center so he decided to move along close behind Able. That would put the command post on the open flank, away from the known threat to the left but exposed to anything that might come from the right. If danger did materialize, the command post group could always help defend the flank then shift toward the center as soon as they could conveniently disengage.

At midnight the whole staff, less only the S4, was still in The Hole talking about the attack. The night was almost eerily still. Only a quiet voice or two and the occasional passage of heavy shells, high overhead, disturbed the silence.

There was no mortar fire, largely because mortar men don't like to fire at night. The flash of their guns, so comparatively close to the lines, looms bright and clear in the darkness and sometimes a little trail of fire follows a shell for several hundred feet up into the air, making it plain as a tracer and spelling out, "Here I am. Why don't you shell me back?"

There was a rare rifle shot or brief burst of machine gun fire as some gunner on one side or the other fancied he saw a target. But the stillness between was so heavy that these puny outbursts hardly made a ripple on the great pond of silence.

By 0100 the last patrol was in safely. Only two had been sent out, just to make sure the enemy was still in the same positions and to listen for signs of movement behind his lines. Nothing was stirring.

The radiomen turned on their sets and checked with each other as they did every half hour throughout the day and night, so they would never be completely out of touch for more than 30 minutes if the wires should go out.

The staff was uneasy. They didn't want to turn in. They couldn't say why; there had been other nights like this. They all sensed that everyone shared their own nameless fears.

Mentzer broke the spell. They had all come out of The Hole for a breath of air and were standing by the hedgerow, looking at the few stars that showed through a light overcast that had drifted in since dark. Mentzer was a light-hearted individual, not usually concerned with thinking deeply about abstract matters. He had been a cab driver back in Frederick, Maryland, home of his Headquarters Company. "Ah," he said, "them bastards are just tired after throwin' all that heavy stuff in here all day. They've shot their wad. I'm gonna hit the sack."

He turned and disappeared into the extreme darkness of the woods, headed for his nearby hole.

Down in The Hole the phone rang softly. Weddle went down to answer it, staying nearly two full minutes before he came back up, saying, "That was the Doc. He says one of his men saw a German out by the medics' latrine. I asked him how could he know it was a Kraut in this dark and he said because the guy crawled over a hedgerow not ten feet from him and he got a good look at his little paratrooper helmet silhouetted against some stars that happened to be in the clear just then. He said the guy grunted when he slid off the hedgerow and he didn't sound like any of our people. The Doc checked but couldn't find anybody else who had been out there. Nobody uses that latrine but the medics."

Major Johns snapped to full alert. "Doc's man was probably seeing things. Nevertheless get Mentzer to grab some of his people who are off duty right now and beat out the area. Get the whole A and P Platoon if you want to, but have a good look around. We can't take any chances."

He wouldn't have admitted that he was nervous. He just believed in playing it safe.

Weddle went after Mentzer while the Major turned to Grimsehl. "George, wake everybody up and check the CP close-in defense. Get the Commando Platoon on their toes. See that there is an alert, tight ring around here tonight—all night."

Grimsehl lost no time in moving out to look for Sergeant Turner, who had charge of the so-called Commando Platoon, which was a group of 10 or 12 men specially picked and trained for tough patrol work. They were kept around the command post for its defense when they were not out on a mission. In a quiet position a double guard at each entrance was usually enough, as all the others slept nearby in holes dug in a circle around the command post. Tonight the battalion commander wanted every man in every hole to be awake and ready for business. He proposed to take no chances on a quick rush by a few determined paratroopers overrunning the guard and tossing grenades into all the holes, including The Hole.

Suddenly a terrific firing broke out.

Every German cannon, mortar, rifle, and machine gun that had fired a round that day cut loose simultaneously. The sound of mortars coughing on the German side blended with the scream of incoming shells. Grimsehl and Hoffman slid down the steps of The Hole before the first round hit.

It was Ryan's war all over again on a broader front. The sharp roar of artillery shells overrode the flatter crunching of the mortars, while the vicious, snarling, still sharper crack of 88's stood out above both, and the ripping of German machine guns filled in the tiny intervals between explosions. Although the fire was concentrated chiefly on the edges of the gap between the two companies at the orchard, it was hitting all along the front. Some rounds tore into the field and hedgerow near the command post while others rushed overhead to burst in the trees as they searched for the mortar positions.

The phone rang. Major Johns grabbed it. "Red 6."

"Charlie 6, sir. We're catching hell down here with mortars and artillery. I think there is enemy infantry coming in under the fire."

Stoen broke in, the operator having wisely sensed a crisis and cut him into the circuit, "Same here, Major. Only I KNOW there's infantry coming in. They're already in the road with us."

His voice and manner were normally extremely quiet and easy-going. Now his tone was strident with urgency. Had it been anyone but Julian Stoen, the Major might have thought it showed near-panic. "Okay to both of you," he answered as calmly as he could. "Stuff's coming in up here too. Fight 'em and keep me informed."

He spun the crank and said to the operator, "Give me Regiment."

Nothing happened. You can tell when a field wire is dead because it is so very dead. The operator's voice was rising now, too. "Sir," he shouted, "that line is out. I'll get a crew on it right away."

Before Johns could lay the phone down it rang again. It was Stoen. "Sir, for God's sake put all the artillery we got down in front of the lines . . . you know my concentrations . . . call for all of 'em . . . . the bastards are all over us." The phone went dead.

Martin was frantically spinning the artillery phone crank but there was no answer and the crank spun easily. There was no resistance in the circuit, indicating that the line had been cut. Martin stuck his head out the entrance and called to the radio operator. "Call for concentrations 175 through 183 as fast as they can fire 'em. Tell 'em it's an attack. We need all they can give us."

The operator turned on his set and started calling. He called and called, but he got no answer. They all knew that the set at the Fire Direction Center was not on because they had checked in exactly 8 minutes before, and it would not come on again until 0200. That meant that for 22 minutes the batallion would be cut off from outside support of any kind. A lot could happen in 22 minutes.

The mortar observers, up with the companies, found their lines were out too; but they had radios, and the men at the mortar positions did not need orders to start firing anyway. They could hear what was going on. The mortars started pouring out shells before the first message came back. So, at least, the battalion had its own support working.

"That Kraut back by the aid station!" cried Weddle, suddenly. "He must have been part of a patrol that came through and cut all our wires! Hell, there haven't been enough shells falling to cut 'em ALL. The smart bastards! They even knew when we checked the radios, too."

Major Johns nodded. He was calling Able Company. No

answer. That wire was out. They were all out, front and rear. He took the 300 handset from Bein, his new radio operator, and tried to get Charlie Company. Kenney answered, reporting that his whole line was heavily engaged. There was no reply from Baker.

Johns cursed his impotence. His communications, with which he had been so satisfied, were shot to hell. For all the influence he was having on this battle he might as well be back at Division. It was up to the men on the front line now. He had no reserves and no way of getting any. He knew the radiomen were trying to get through to Regiment and the Fire Direction Center. There was absolutely nothing he could do but wait.

The enemy fire was still heavy. The German gunners pounded every company, then searched every position that might hold reserves. The command post was shaken up again and again. Bein's radio lost an aerial, which he replaced in seconds. One of the commando gang took a fragment in his leg. Tracers flew overhead in all directions, ricochets screamed and yowled, and the tearing crackle of German machine gun bullets never stopped.

Only minutes after the barrage hit, the hollow, clumping roar of grenades came from the direction of the Able Company command post. Major Johns rushed into the open to listen more carefully. The sound of the grenades kept coming, punctuated with the short high-pitched burrrrp, burrrrp, burrrrp of the MP 38*. The center of the noise was moving slowly but steadily toward the rear, right through the center of A Company. Johns' stomach crawled up in his chest again, so that nothing but a cold vacuum was left in his belly. His defensive line was broken! The paratroopers were running over Able Company! He took two running steps in that direction, then stopped. It would be pretty silly for him to go

---

*Maschinen Pistole Model 38 (Schmeisser), a "Tommy" gun issued to parachute troops. Americans called them burp guns, from the sound of their high cyclic rate.

tearing off into the dark in the middle of this melee, thus virtually surrendering control.

He turned to Grimsehl. "George! Send a runner to A Company to find out what's happened down there."

Grimsehl went to get the man, who in a few seconds trotted off down the hedgerow, his M1 ready in his hands.

Twenty age-long minutes crept by. The fury of the attack did not diminish. Johns stayed outside to listen, as he could learn more from the nature and location of the firing than he could from his useless radios and telephones. Twice he had to duck back inside, once when a battery volley struck along the other side of the hedgerow, and once when the enemy mortar fire started its orderly march down the near side. The German mortar gunners were, as usual, deadly accurate in their location of the hedgerow, but they were not so effective in the spacing of the rounds. One shell hit between the old phone hole and The Hole and the next struck harmlessly on the far side.

At last came the sound of still more artillery. But this was the good kind—the going-out kind. It was hard to distinguish it from the rest of the din. Nevertheless there are always lulls in any battle, no matter how fierce, and in these intervals the familiar outgoing whine came through clearly. But the volley went out much too far; the first few rounds would have no effect on the Germans, who were storming through the battalion defensive lines.

The artillery fire kept going out, way out, until both Martin and Johns were almost beside themselves with frustration. Suddenly the monotonous calling of Martin's artillery radio operator changed to sharp attention. He had got an answer!

"Fire mission. Concentrations 175 through 183 at once! Request all available fire. Enemy attacking strongly all along front!"

Thank God! breathed the Major. Then he yelled in Martin's ear, "Tell the FDC to tell Regiment what's going on and that if they have any reserves to rack 'em up behind us, we may need 'em."

The message went out quickly.

"On the wa-a-a-ay" came back as an answer.

This time the artillery hit much nearer. It had that authoritative crack to it which told that it was close in, almost as close as the German stuff. And it kept coming.

Somehow the wires to Charlie and Baker were re-spliced time and again. They always went out, but after that first 30 minutes or so they were in most of the time. When they were not, the 300's did the job. The companies had settled down a bit after the first shock and the operators did whatever was necessary to reestablish their communications. Kenny and Stoen both asked for reinforcements, both getting the same answer, "Sorry. There aren't any. Do the best you can."

There was no contact with Able. No runners came in to report, no fire missions were requested. Nothing! There was no longer any heavy firing in the direction of the line originally held by A Company, but there was plenty from an area to the rear of that line. Oddly enough, there was an occasional flurry of fire from well in front of the center. It looked very much as if the company lines had been completely overrun and were falling back.

Martin called for the A Company defensive concentration anyway.

Around 0300 the runner came back. His eyes were very big. "Sir," he reported, "there are Krauts in the A Company CP."

"Nuts," said the Major.

"Yes, sir, there really are."

"How do you know?"

"Well, I had a little trouble, running into people on the way. Some were Krauts, some our own men, so when I got close I crept up sort of easy-like. 'Fore I saw anybody in the road a Kraut challenged me and when I didn't answer he cut loose at me with a burp gun. Missed me, though."

"Nuts," repeated the Major. He didn't want to believe Able

had been overrun. He turned to look for Grimsehl but saw instead the man he really wanted. It was Private First Class Gay, Silver Star hero of a lone patrol back at the Bois de Bretel. Gay was sitting very calmly on a corner of The Hole, chewing gum. Johns snapped at him, "Gay! Get the hell down to Able and see for sure if there are Germans in the CP and what the situation is generally."

Gay looked at the Major. His jaw motion slowed to a halt. Then he remembered that he had a reputation to maintain. He rose, checked his carbine, gently detached a grenade from his belt, and started down the hedgerow fiddling with the pin on the grenade.

The German artillery and mortars began to let up some. They seemed more uncertain, as if they weren't too sure just where their own people were. They kept beating the flanks of the salient they had driven into the battalion line, but the rolling barrage under which the paratroopers had first come in had slackened materially. The savage ferocity of the small-arms battle was either increasing, or the lessening of the artillery and mortar fire let the sounds of the rifles, machine guns, submachine guns, and grenades come through more clearly. The indefinite center of the fire was coming from a point that moved farther and farther to the right rear of the command post. Major Johns could not be sure, but the sounds seemed to indicate that A Company was pulling back from in front of the enemy, fighting as it went.

Stoen had managed to report that his right was holding but he had had trouble on his left at the orchard. His whole line had been in action ever since the first shells fell. Germans had gone through his company, he said, on through the orchard in rear, but they had not driven him out of his position. There had even been two grenades thrown into his command post.

The center of the battle surged in close, no more than a hundred yards to the right of the battalion command post. Bullets cracked through the trees, chunked solidly into wood or earth, or snapped overhead in the clear. One long burst, flashing straight down the hedgerow, bored into the top of The Hole between the Major and radio operator Bein. It was beginning to look as if the command post were going to get into the fight. Johns ordered every man into a fox-hole. There would be no moving around and no shooting unless the enemy attacked in force. There was no use starting a fight with the little handful of people near the command post. If they had to shoot they would, but there was no point in asking for trouble.

Grimsehl loomed up out of nowhere, prodding a prisoner ahead of him with a bayonet. Some instinct led him to the Major who rose from his hole to see what the S2 had got from the prisoner. "Sir!" Grimsehl said excitedly, "I got this bird from a couple of A Company men. He says they are hitting us with four companies, three infantry companies in the assault and one engineer outfit fighting as infantry in reserve—all paratroopers and about 110 men per company."

"Four companies! And on a narrow front! Wait till Regiment hears this. Maybe we'll get some help now!"

The paratrooper, his hands locked behind his head, must have understood a little. He smiled as if confident that he would not be a prisoner for long.

Grimsehl faded into the dark returning a moment later without the prisoner, whom he had given to a commando for safekeeping.

"He says they had committed the reserve just before he was grabbed, which was about 0215 or 0230. They were already through the A Company center and right flank by then and they shoved the reserves on through to keep going. But I don't know where they could have got to, because the fighting still isn't much past our line here."

While he was speaking, the center of the battle surged toward the rear, as if it had just gotten free of snag. There was a beating of feet up the hedgerow a few yards toward A Company and the sounds that men make scrambling over a hedgerow. Johns and Grimsehl sank to the ground. The safety on Hoffman's M1 clicked loudly as he pushed it forward into the "Off" position.

But the rushing sounds went straight to the rear, punctuated by brrrrps from German guns. They did not pause at Mentzer's domain or at the aid station. They were headed for the mortar positions.

Major Johns whispered to Bein, "Call Dog and tell them some Krauts are coming toward them from the direction of Battalion."

Bein called, but the only answer he got was the sound of firing from the direction of the nearest mortar position.

The telephone operator, taking the Major by the arm, whispered in his ear, "Phone, sir. It's Regiment. Colonel Ordway."

"Johns? What's going on up there?" The Colonel was excited too.

"Full-scale counterattack, sir. Prisoner says four companies, 440 men, hitting us. Didn't you get my message through the artillery?"

"Yes, but they just said an attack."

"I asked for help. Able was overrun and maybe part of Baker. I think you better . . . ." Realizing that he was talking into a dead line, Johns rang for the operator. "Send the wire crew out again, and ring Message Center for me."

Sergeant Wilson answered the Message Center phone himself, "Yes sir?"

"Sergeant, haven't you got that radio working yet?"

"Yes sir, it's working, but we can't get an answer from Regiment." The sergeant sounded completely unperturbed about the whole business.

"If you ever get through, tell 'em they're going to have Krauts back there very shortly if they don't send me some help to restore these lines."

"Yes, sir. I'll write a message and bring it to you later for signature."

"Oh for Pete's sake! All right." Johns dropped the phone to look for Martin. He found him at a post on the hedgerow, watching the dark field beyond.

"Martin! Get your people to tell Regiment that we have been hit by an enemy force of 440 men, that our line has been broken, and that we are requesting reinforcement."

"Okay, Major, but I'll have to encode that, which will take a while."

"Encode hell. The Jerries know about it. Send it in the clear." The Major was having "security" trouble again.

"If you say so . . . ." The artilleryman repeated the message to his radio operator who reluctantly put it on the air.

The Artillery Fire Direction Center was horrified at the breach of security. They lectured the operator briefly but thoroughly. He replied with a rude sound that was not in the Signal Operating Instructions, adding. "The Major said send it. We need help and the Krauts know it. Now get it for us!"

Kenney called for artillery fire at a new point. Instantly Martin, his operator, and the Fire Direction Center became coldly precise again. They had been firing concentrations on every spot where the paratroopers could possibly form up or through which they would have to move to reinforce the attacking force. Most of the Division artillery and some from Corps must have been supporting, because the whine, scream, crash, roar, crack, and rumble of the shells going overhead and thundering down into enemy territory was almost constant. The sound was extremely comforting, even though the small-arms fight was still raging behind the command post.

A man staggered up to the command post and nearly fell into Martin's arms. Only some instinct had prevented the CP guards from shooting him, as he had made no attempt to answer their low challenge or to halt. It was an officer, a forward observer who had been with Able Company.

He was panting, incoherent. Martin and Johns half carried him down the steps into the command post, where they sat

him on an ammunition box that served as a chair. In the light
of the single candle he made a horrible sight. Blood was
smeared over his face, his hands, and his shirt. But Martin
could find no wound. The man was dazed, dumb. He sat with
his head down, still panting, paying no attention to questions.
He stared at the blade of a hunting knife in his right hand.
It was still sticky with blood, as he raised and lowered it.
He seemed almost to be weighing the knife. He opened and
clenched his fingers around the handle, never taking his eyes
from the red-stained blade.

Martin heated some coffee over a K-ration box and forced
it gently on the forward observer, who was a close friend. The
young officer took the coffee and began to settle down. The
wild look went out of his eyes. His trembling lessened until
it nearly ceased. Finally he began to talk, the words falling
out in chunks, sometimes incoherent, "We were out on Able
OP 2 . . . . I was asleep . . . . the stuff started falling all
around us . . . . Before I knew what was going on . . . . the
Krauts were in there with us . . . . They killed two Able boys—
right in front of me . . . . I held up my hands and my radioman did too. . . . They took my pistol belt . . . . then the
others went on and one Kraut pushed us toward the rear, his
rear. . . . We walked a long time . . . . I don't know how far
. . . . or where we were . . . . then some of our own mortars
came in close. We stopped and the Kraut looked around for
cover. There wasn't any so we ran a ways . . . . then the
artillery started . . . . it was hitting in front of us. We stopped
again . . . . and found some old German fox holes. They had
tops on. The guard turned his back on me. He was kicking at
a hole to see if he could get in it . . . . and my radioman
jumped him. My man jerked off his helmet, hit the Kraut in
the back of the neck with it. . . . Then I remembered I still
had my knife." He pushed the bloody blade forward and looked
at it for a long time, his fingers still closing and opening around
the hilt.

"I jerked it out." He stopped talking and put his head down

almost to his knees, still holding the knife at an awkward angle in front of him. He didn't move for a full minute—then, with an effort, he sat up again and went on. "I jumped him just as he turned around . . . I hit him with the knife and it went into him . . . then I hit him again and again and again. I couldn't stop hitting him even after . . . after I knew he was dead. My radioman pulled me off him, finally . . . We started back."

Major Johns was bouncing with impatience to ask questions but something held him in restraint until the man stopped. "Where were you? How did you come back? Did you see any more Krauts?"

The lieutenant looked at him dully, as if he didn't understand. But he answered. "I don't know. We didn't see anybody until we got here. I don't know where we were, or how we came back. I didn't know where we were until . . . until I recognized the battalion hedgerow."

It was obvious they were going to get no useful information out of this man. He was another combat exhaustion case, shocked more by the awful experience of killing a man with his own hands than by the fire he had been under and the fact that he had been captured. The Major motioned to Martin, who led the still-dazed man away, and sent him to the aid station.

Gay came back from A Company. He answered the challenge flippantly and slouched into The Hole. There were no grenades hanging from his belt. He reported.

"That runner was right, Major. There WAS some Jerries in the CP."

"What do you mean, 'was'?"

"Just that. There ain't so many now as there was before I got there, least not so many live ones."

"What happened?" The Major was impatient. It was obvious that Gay was enjoying the spotlight again and wanted to draw it out.

"I crawled up to the edge of the sunken road right over the

CP, coming in from around on one side. I couldn't make out who was there, so I made a noise and some bastard challenges me in Dutch. I answers him in Dutch, too, but it don't sound right to him and he asks for the password. I gives it to him with grenades, and hightails it out of there. The stupid bastard never even got a shot at me."

Johns couldn't help smiling. "What about the rest of the line? Could you tell anything about it?"

"Naw, Major, it was too dark to see anything, but there was some shootin' out on the left front and a helluva lot in the right rear. None at all along the road where most of the line used to be."

"All right, Gay, thank you very much. Stick around close, I may need you again."

Gay went out and took his place on the corner of The Hole. He treated himself to a fresh stick of gum.

Counterattack Countered / *11*

NO BATTLE goes on for hours without lulls. This one, fierce as it was, was no exception. After the flurry of fire back at the mortar positions there was a long pause in the small-arms firing although the artillery was still going over, mostly outward bound now. As Gay went up the steps of The Hole the firing started again, back by the mortars. It grew until it was a first class row, with grenades, burp guns, and rifles all mixed together.

It lacked the size of the earlier fighting, but not ferocity. Nor did it rise and fall in volume quite so much. It gave the impression of determined, plugging fire, kept up by a comparatively few men on both sides, men who weren't going to quit. From the mortar positions it began to move slowly back toward the front again.

As soon as the direction of the sound was definite, the Major began to exult although he could not be sure that the battle had turned. He was puzzled because the sound of German burp guns stood out clearly and dominated the other firing.

The sounds came closer and closer, then died out completely for a few seconds. In the near silence the sound of running feet came not far from the aid station. Then an M1 rifle cracked sharply 8 times from a point no more than a hundred yards back of the command post hedgerow. A burp gun answered. More M1's fired. Two or three other burp guns opened up. Then a light machine gun joined in, its tracers flying toward the enemy lines, a few ricocheting off the hedgerow.

The running feet pounded nearer. In another momentary lull there came again the sound of men scrambling over a hedgerow. Then a burp gun and several rifles fired from the far side of the hedgerow. The machine gun and other burp guns answered them. A rifle grenade burst on the hedgerow itself. More running feet, then grenades and scuffling noises, more grenades. Then came the clear cry, "Goddammit, somebody kill that sonuvabitch before he gets away again."

Every man in the command post group laughed aloud at that. They knew the show was about over. The battalion's lines would be restored before morning.

The firing, with more bloodthirsty yelling, receded toward the A Company line.

Kenney called from C Company to report that the attacks on his line had let up and they were now free from any flanking threat. Stoen, his line out and the radio not working at the moment, sent a messenger to say that they were holding. He had picked up about a squad of A Company men who had been wandering around in the rear. They were using the squad to bolster their own right flank.

There was still no word from Able Company.

It was after 0400. The dawn would soon help clear things up one way or another. If it showed most of four companies of paratroopers in the lines formerly held by Able there might be some trouble. On the other hand if the Krauts were scattered and had not been able to consolidate a position during the darkness, it might be possible to pull some men away from Charlie and Baker, to clean up such enemy as were left.

It occurred to Johns that if the enemy were still around, the command post group might find itself with a fight on its hands as soon as people could see. He again ordered everyone to stay out of sight until he could tell what the score was. There had never been a thought in anyone's mind of withdrawing, even though the attack had carried well to their rear.

The line to Regiment was in again and Colonel Ordway was on the phone. Major Johns gave him a brief report. "Sir, things are getting quiet up here again, but I can't tell yet who owns the area. I don't have the faintest idea where any part of Able is. Baker may have lost some of its left platoon by the orchard, although Stoen tells me they are still in most of their original positions. The Germans got clean through our middle and went as far back as the mortar positions but I think we've got everything in hand now." He waited while a long burst of machine-gun fire snapped overhead, then added, "But you never know."

Colonel Ordway was impatient. "Some sergeant from A Company rushed in here about 3 o'clock with a wild disaster story. Said the whole battalion was destroyed and he was the sole survivor."

"One of MY men said that?"

"Yes, one of YOUR heroes. That was bad enough but he put the wind up for a battalion of 4.2 mortars that are digging in behind you. That whole gang took off." The Colonel paused a moment, then went on, "He picked up about half of my Cannon Company as he went through the woods, too."

Johns was nearly speechless—a man from the Red Battalion —a sergeant too—running away from the enemy! He sputtered into the phone, "Why .... why that dirty ....! I'll court-martial him for cowardice if it's the last thing I do!"

The Regimental Commander ignored him. "Can you attack at 0600?"

That stopped Johns cold. It was the first time he had even thought of the attack and, if he had, he would of course have assumed that another outfit would be put in their place. People don't attack too well after fighting for their lives half the night.

"Colonel," he answered, "we couldn't attack a hot breakfast at 0600. I've got most of one company, at least half of another, all of my headquarters, and Lord knows how much of my Weapons outfit. I don't know anything about Able Company yet, nor do I know that we aren't going to be fighting Krauts out of the CP in the next ten minutes. What about the reinforcements I asked for?"

"Nothing doing. Division wouldn't let me send you anything. They still won't believe you had anything but a combat patrol up there. They know about your prisoner's report and I told them about the runaway sergeant. But they still wouldn't let me turn loose anything. They wouldn't even believe what I told them about the 4.2 battalion running off. Had to send their own man down to check, but he'll be until noon getting back with a report."

"Very well, sir, I think we can handle the situation alone now anyway, but I repeat that I can't guarantee ANYthing. You may have a good part of our hostile paratroopers in your lap by the time it gets light, because I believe a lot of them just kept right on going after they got through us. I don't have any idea where they could have got to, but it's quiet now. Stoen and Kenney have even stopped calling for artillery for the first time in more than 3 hours."

That ended the conversation. Johns swung around on Weddle and Hoffman, cursing fervently. "That goddam Division! The ornery SOB's wouldn't believe what we told 'em! I hope that bunch of Krauts gets clean through to where they are, if they can walk that far! Maybe they'll believe us then!"

Stoen called in. The wires had been restored again. He reported that his position was secure and that he was sending a patrol out to the left to see what he could find in the Able Company line. He also said that his 60-mm mortar people, whom he had directed to pull back one hedgerow in order to keep them out of the fight, had found all three of Able's 60's, abandoned. They had picked them up, together with their ammo, and had fired all 6 guns all night long until they were now down to only a few rounds per gun.

Johns looked toward the spot in the darkness that he thought was occupied by Weddle. He did not often call the S3 by his first name, but this was a special occasion. "Leroy," he said, "I want you to take about six of the commando boys and go down to Able to see if you can tell what happened and what the situation is. I figure it's better to do it in the dark, taking it easy, than it is to wait till it gets light and maybe run into something and get into a fight. Don't get involved in anything unless you have to. If you find it advisable, stay down there and get things straightened out, but send me a message so I'll know what you're doing. Watch out for that Baker patrol, although I don't think you're apt to run into it."

Captain Weddle groped for his helmet and M1, said "Okay," and was gone up the steps.

Once more there was nothing for Johns to do but wait.

It wasn't long until the sky began to lighten. There was no word, of course, from either Weddle or Stoen. It was too soon to expect anything. But the Germans started to throw 88's into the area, which was encouraging. They wouldn't be doing that if they had any reason to believe their own troops were occupying the lines. Johns went outside to look around. As he did so an 88 smashed viciously into a tree just behind The Hole. He grinned as he sniffed the acrid smoke. Dallas and his German paratroopers, hunh!

It was a little past 0500, light enough to see clearly, when the first runner came from Weddle. He was grinning broadly as he trotted up, rifle in hand. "Sir," he said, "Captain Weddle says tell you he has found what is left of two whole platoons of A Company and that Sergeant Shaff has the old CP back again."

He saluted and turned to go back to Weddle. The Major returned his salute, calling after him, "Tell the Captain that makes me very happy."

A little later Stoen called in to say that he was occupying every foot of his old line and that his patrol had returned to tell him about the two Able platoons that were still in position. He had lost a lot of people but didn't know how many more were being found all the time. He had also lost the two .50 caliber machine guns that Regiment had ordered them to use in the attack that morning. Neither Stoen nor Major Johns was concerned about the guns as they had thought all along that it was silly to try to use such heavy guns in an attack in that kind of country.

Weddle got back about 0630 with a strange story. He came

into The Hole, demanded a breakfast ration, and sat down on the shelf before he would tell it. Finally he got started.

"Here's what happened to A Company, as near as I can tell now: The mortars and artillery hit them sudden and hard. They hit the outposts at the same time they did the main line. Every SOB in the company put his head down. The Krauts come in under that fire like they loved it. Shaff said they weren't thirty yards back of it. They run plumb over the outposts before the sentries knew there's a Kraut within a hundred yards, so the main line got no warning. One sergeant looked up and saw the shine of a shell burst on a box of machine gun ammunition a Kraut is carrying and he hollers, 'Krauts,' but by then it's too late in most places. The Germans poured right over the edge of the road and run up and down it throwing grenades into the holes where the guys were still hiding from the artillery, shooting anything that moved.

"That bird you got running the company says he was stunned by a grenade in the first assault. He wasn't able to get out of his hole, or to give an order. He seems to be okay now, except a little shaky. He's trying to get things together. He's damn lucky he isn't dead.

"Anyway, the Germans ran through the company CP in nothing flat. Everybody that isn't killed takes off for the rear. That's where our sergeant hero that went back to Regiment come from, I think. But the two platoons in the middle are cut off. You know they aren't all in the road. They can't run if they want to, 'cause they know by now that there're Krauts behind 'em, probably more than in front. So they stayed right there, fighting like good little boys all night long. That was the shooting we heard out front from time to time and couldn't figure. Kee-rist! There's dead Krauts and our dead people all over the place.

"Those of Able that take off, about a platoon plus, altogether, I reckon, hit for the battalion mortar positions. They join up with a few guys from Baker and beat the Krauts back there by quite some time. Then the noncoms and a couple of officers who are around—I still don't know who—rally the whole gang, put them in some sort of position along with the mortar crews. By the time the Krauts get back there they're ready for 'em and kick hell out of 'em. I heard about one bird who waited for a Kraut to come right alongside of him, then raises up, grabs the Kraut's burp pistol, kicks the guy in the crotch, and shoots him with his own gun. That was why we heard so many burp guns. Our guys were taking 'em away from the Krauts and using them against 'em. Our boys like the Schmeissers better'n anything we got, for this kind of fighting.

"This took most of the night. It didn't go quick, mostly because the Heinies were taking it pretty easy after they get through the line, like they don't want to lose contact with one another. Then they had that scrap down by the mortars. Some of the Germans pulled back, just as slow." The S3 stopped, took his helmet off, and scratched his head seriously.

"You know," he went on, "I just can't figure out what happened to all those paratroopers. The boys from Able said there must a been at least two hundred went through the orchard. But I don't believe there was more'n about 40 or 50, maybe 60 at the outside, ever got as far as the mortars."

Johns interrupted, "Could be a lot of 'em got separated in the dark and decided it was no good so they filtered out around the flanks, or went back the way they came."

"Yeah, could be. Then we got to remember that Kenney and Stoen and the two Able platoons had a quota apiece. From the way the Krauts chewed Baker there must'a been quite a few in that crew.

"And I nearly forgot—the artillery knocked hell out of a lot of Germans before they ever got going. That was probably what saved our tails, really. The Able boys said that first concentration, the one that hit so far out, went right into the middle of something, because they heard all kinds of yelling and screaming and carrying on out there. Could of been their reserves, I guess.

"Well, however it happened, it all boils down to the same old story: they hit us, pushed through, took casualties, and got disorganized. We counterattacked and shoved 'em out again—just like the book says."

Grimsehl came in with more details obtained from his prize prisoner. The man, who was from the headquarters company of the German battalion they were facing, seemed to know all about everything. He claimed that the whole attack was a direct result of the visit of the medical officer two days before, when the truce had been requested and granted. The Major stared hard at Grimsehl when he reported that, and the S2 flushed. If this were true the battalion had paid a terrible price to save the life of that one American they had got out of the orchard alive.

Grimsehl went on, "He said that medic came back and told their commander that he had been in our lines and they were lightly held. Of course, he never was in our main line, only in an outpost. If he thought that was the main line I can see how he would believe it to be pretty thin. But I guess they got a surprise when they hit Baker and Charlie, who wouldn't give. Anyway, the German battalion commander decides to have a try at us, because we are sticking out a little and they wanted to straighten their lines and maybe get back the main road behind us, there. He got some more artillery to come in for the show. They were registering and covering it up by firing so much yesterday. Then he got that company of engineers to fight as infantry and act as a reserve.

"This prisoner says what Weddle guessed about our artillery is about right, because the Germans took one hell of a beating in that first concentration. It knocked the engineers cockeyed while they were forming up and delayed their push through the orchard quite a bit.

"I think they had a couple of platoons worrying Charlie and maybe a couple more trying to get around Baker's right, while the rest hit right in the middle. But by the time they got through they were so shot up that the engineers didn't have what it took to roll us up. So they chickened out when they hit the mortars, and decided to quit."

Major Johns accepted the story without comment. It was

probably correct. But at that moment he was more concerned with what was going to happen than with what had already happened. He wanted to know how many casualties he had suffered, to get the companies untangled, bring up more ammunition, and see that the men got a little rest. They hadn't had much sleep lately. It still did not occur to him that the attack order would not be cancelled. As far as he was concerned, the 1st Battalion had had enough fighting for the day.

He called the companies for a strength report, and told them to hurry up the reorganizing process. All companies reported some dead, but none had an accurate count as yet. The Doc reported that the aid stations had treated 42 casualties, with more coming in all the time.*

---

*The facts concerning the German attack were all verified in a German after-action report which the 29th Division captured later at Brest. Major Johns' estimate of the number of troops involved, the casualties suffered, and the progress of the action were all confirmed exactly, showing that the Battalion's information was accurate. Division, which had exhibited such skepticism, was mildly embarrassed, and the Battalion was ultimately awarded the French Croix de Guerre for the action.

Rough Day / 12

THE ASSISTANT DIVISION COMMANDER, Brigadier General Norman D. Cota, came down at about 0730 to see what was holding up the attack. He was unimpressed by Major Johns' account of what had happened during the night, but could see that the battalion was not in condition to jump off. He said something about the urgency of the situation, then went back up the path toward the rear, leaving an irate battalion commander behind him.

Johns could understand the need to attack and to attack as quickly as possible, so that the enemy troops in front of him would be held in position and not be shifted to face other American units that were attacking. But he knew that if he were forced to push his own men into an attack before they were ready they would be defeated before they had fairly started. The Germans could then move at will to resist the attack elsewhere. Furthermore, no matter how much guts and firm will to fight that men may possess, they cannot do much good without ammunition, and at the moment there was mighty little of that on the 1st Battalion lines. Except, he thought to himself, what is lodged in dead Krauts.

He called all the company commanders on the telephone and explained just what had occurred, emphasizing the need for them to get going as soon as possible. He would, he said, give them enough time to get ammunition and food to all the men. Also he prodded Mentzer to keep after the Ammunition and

Pioneer Platoon, who were responsible for getting fresh ammunition to the companies.

The company commanders were not happy at the prospect, but they had all attacked on previous occasions when they didn't want to, so they went about getting ready as efficiently as possible.

Regiment called periodically all morning. If it was the Colonel, he got a polite report on progress. If it was a member of the 3 section he was told exactly what he could do with his foul-named attack, then invited to come up and lead it himself if he didn't like the way the battalion was doing it. Most of this sort of thing was usually banter, but today a thread of earnestness ran through the retorts. The nerves of the battalion officers were drawn pretty fine, and they did not enjoy being harassed from above.

By 1100 the battalion was almost ready to go. Able and Baker had been unscrambled, ammunition and chow had been brought up, the men had eaten a C- or K-ration, and some had even had a chance to catch a little rest.

The casualty reports, still incomplete, were appalling. Able and Baker had lost between 40 and 50 men apiece. Charlie had lost only a few, but the Weapons Company had taken a beating on machine gunners. They also had lost their company commander. Little Lieutenant McCarthy was dead.

Grimsehl went out to bring McCarthy's body in as soon as his death was reported. He said the youngster apparently had been coming back from checking a mortar observation post when the barrage hit. Caught in the first enemy rush, he had died fighting heroically. The bodies of two dead Germans lay near him, and his carbine had been fired a number of times. He was facing the enemy, his body riddled with a dozen or more burp gun slugs. Death had been instantaneous.

Command of Dog Company then passed to Lieutenant Leutz, a promising newcomer. He was full of fire and energy, and he knew his stuff. But he had not as yet acquired the seasoned judgment of Nabb and the cool, calm efficiency of McCarthy.

Major Johns, however, was satisfied that Leutz would make a splendid commander once he had the burden of responsibility long enough to give him steadiness. Since he was a ball of fire in combat, the Major was satisfied that he would shine in his first day of command.

At 1110 the battalion commander and a carefully selected advance command post group moved down the hedgerow to a point just in rear of the right flank of Baker Company's most advanced platoon. Hoffman and Mentzer were left at The Hole, which would be the rear command post. The aid station and mortars would stay in position, the mortar crews providing protection for both command post and aid station if necessary.

The men of Baker Company, a little surprised to see the Old Man and the staff almost in line with them, were still nervous and jumpy. They resented having to launch this precipitate attack with no time to rest after the big fight during the night. But they would do it, whether they liked it or not. They always did.

Johns was amused to hear a sergeant on his left quelling a complaint about the demands of war. "What the hell did you expect, a 40-hour week?"

At exactly 1130, five and a half hours late, the Major gave the command to attack. He did not stand out in front and drop his arm as he had done the first time. If he'd tried that this time he'd have hit the ground dead before he could move an arm. No more than one squad could have seen him anyway, so thick was the country.

Nor did all the men move out together, in parade-ground formation. The squads and platoons of the assault echelon slipped quietly, sometimes timidly it seemed, over a hedgerow and started at a run for the one on the far side. One platoon, with more aggressive leadership, and shouting "29 LET'S GO," leaped the hedgerow in a headlong charge.

They all met the same reception—rifles, machine guns, and burp guns. But the German mortars and artillery had lost their punch. Or at least so it seemed at first, whereas Martin's people and the dead McCarthy's men were out for blood. Concentrated fire on small parts of the German line was too much even for the paratroopers. Their line broke in one place, the defenders knocked out by tree bursts.

Baker Company swarmed into the breach; in a few minutes the whole enemy line gave. Every company made exactly one hedgerow, but there they stuck. Johns later suspected that the enemy withdrawal was planned. It left the attackers, without holes, against new hedgerows on which the Germans had undoubtedly registered earlier. The Germans themselves could pull back a hedgerow to a new position yet lose nothing.

Nor did it take the paratroopers long to locate the advancing right flank and launch a counterattack on it. Machine gun and rifle fire clipped the leaves from trees and bushes close over the heads of the battalion command post group. They were in shallow holes dug by B Company men earlier, but the fire was uncomfortably close. Then the enemy mortars began to step down the front as accurately as if the gunners could see every GI behind the hedgerow.

This was not going exactly as Major Johns had planned. He had expected the attack to move forward, leaving his command post about one hedgerow behind so they would be out of most of the observed fire and yet close enough to the companies to get protection. Instead, the right flank was held back by Lieutenant Stoen, with the Major's approval, to meet the already threatening encircling movement. Half the men in the command post group became part of the front line. Some of them were doing the first battle firing they had ever done.

If this kept up, somebody was going to get hurt. And there was no point in needlessly exposing men who could do no good where they were. The Major and Weddle, Grimsehl, and Martin could do their jobs as well from a little farther back. He hated to move from his advanced position, but had just about decided it was essential, when bullet clipped bark from a tree a few inches from his ear. There was something personal about that. It clinched the argument.

"Move back 100 yards," he ordered the command post group.

The new position wasn't much better. They weren't getting

as much small-arms fire, but the enemy mortar fire was getting worse. There was no protection from it.

The battalion, making no progress, was taking heavy casualties as a result of that first short advance. One episode was truly tragic. Able Company reported the loss of an entire platoon that had fought its way into a short length of sunken road which had turned into a trap. The Germans had let them get into it but the moment the last German clambered out the far side, there was a cascade of mortar shells, every one squarely in the middle of the road. Not a man in the understrength platoon escaped unhurt.

Mortar bursts marched across the command post group once. There were no casualties, but Johns could see no point in remaining there either. They pulled back another hundred yards or so to the corner of two low hedgerows. The new position was no more than 400 yards from the old hole, and they could as well have gone back there, but the Major would not do that. His battalion being in the open, the least he could do was stay out with his men, if not in the very front line.

A feeling of apathy began to descend on the whole outfit. The officers and men were not at first conscious of it, but defeat hung in the air like a palpable thing. Johns felt that the companies were not trying as they might. He suspected that they were digging in and had no intention of pushing. But he, too, was apathetic. He made little effort to inject life into the attack.

His new command post was at the junction of two paths that led to the front. Just on the other side of the hedgerow corner one path branched off to the left toward Able Company. Another ran straight ahead to Baker. Both lanes were already marked with blood. Wounded were stumbling back in a steady stream, their arms, legs, and heads wrapped in red-stained bandages. Some stared wildly, in the first stages of shock. Others leaned heavily on more fortunate buddies. Still others smiled widely, oblivious of the fire. These last were the ones with the "million-dollar wound," a clean hole in arm or leg that would put them out for a long time but would leave them sound when healed.

Calls came constantly for litters. Five for Able. Three for Baker. Two for Charlie. Two more for Baker. Three more for Able. Of course there weren't that many litters, or litter bearers, but it gave a fairly accurate count of the badly wounded although it did not include the walking wounded who always outnumbered the litter cases. Neither did it include the dead. For every four men wounded there was nearly always one man dead.

As the afternoon wore on the battalion commander watched the wounded, called for more artillery fire, and prayed for darkness. He was not doing a very good job of "leading" a battalion in the attack. He crawled up to each company once, finding that their reasons for not advancing seemed sound. "If only," he thought, "we could get enough artillery in one place, we could blast a hole and get going." But there wasn't that much artillery. The whole division was attacking, and the other units needed support too.

By late afternoon the CO would have admitted that he had shot his wad. He was all out of drive and his morale was low. A dead man lay on one side of him, shot through the belly early in the battle, and a man with a great hole in his thigh lay on the other side. The man with the wounded leg had managed to climb over the hedgerow before he collapsed, so Johns had dragged him into his hole and given him a shot of morphine while waiting for an empty litter.

While the Major wondered dully what he might do next, he saw a hand come over the nearby hedgerow. It was groping uncertainly, searching for a hold. It found the root of a bush and was followed by a ghastly caricature of a face. The man had been struck by a fragment that had slashed across his nose and both eyes in a great jagged cut from which the blood still flowed. Johns watched in dumb horror as the man pulled himself up on the hedgerow and then fell over on the near side. He rolled several feet beyond the base before he could pull himself together and resume his painful crawling on hands and knees. Only then did Johns find his voice. "For God's sake, GET that man," he shouted, leaping to his feet.

A runner and a commando got to the soldier first. They laid him gently down next to the hedgerow. The commando tore open a first-aid pouch and gently bandaged the awful wound. It was impossible to tell if the man had lost his eyes. The runner put a handful of sulfa pills into the man's mouth and gave him a canteen of water. The man gagged, swallowed, then lay back limply. In a moment he started to struggle to his feet. The CO put his hand on the man's shoulder, saying, "Take it easy, son, we'll have a litter squad here for you in a little bit."

The man calmly threw off the restraining hand and struggled to his feet as he said, "That's okay, sir, I can make it and there's a lot of others need the litters more'n I do."

Major Johns nodded to the commando and the runner. They put an arm under each of the man's shoulders and walked him slowly toward the aid station.

The commander went back to his shallow hole. In a little while the aid men came and took away the man with the bad leg. He looked down at the blood where the man had lain and where it had gotten on his own pants. He shuddered slightly. He couldn't help it. This was a very rough game they were playing.

The German artillery was perhaps not so intense as it had been the night before, but it was methodical and thorough. The enemy had to use some of their guns on other fronts also, but those they used on the 1st Battalion they used in concentrations, pounding first one target then another. But they didn't have observation, thank God. Consequently a lot of the fire was falling harmlessly in the open fields. At that moment it was walking methodically down a hedgerow to the rear. There were no men there, but the majestic trees that topped the 'row were rapidly being reduced to blackened stumps and heaps of green rubbish.

Johns watched the destruction absent-mindedly. The trees were a good hundred yards from his position, hence there was no danger. He started when a big man literally slid into the hole with him.

It was Lieutenant Colonel Smith, the Regimental Executive.

Smith was panting from running down the hedgerow.

"What's the matter, Johns? Why aren't you getting any-where?" Smith gasped.

The Major pointed to the bloody trail, to the dead man, to the shells that were still savaging the trees, and finally in the direction of the nearby front from which came the plodding sound of mortar fire. His eyes were lacking their usual snap, as he answered dully, "They're too tough."

Smith blinked several times. He was obviously trying to think of something to say, something that would inspire this listless battalion commander to new effort. "Well," he finally brought out, "you gotta get going right away; Regiment has got to move—you just gotta get going."

Johns shook his head. He wasn't having any. "Not today," was all he would say.

Then, for some reason, both men looked up the hedgerow toward the rear. Colonel McDaniel, the new Division Chief of Staff, was striding toward them, oblivious of the fire. Just as he reached the command post a volley of four rounds screamed into the field just beyond the hedgerow. The concussion tumbled him into the hole with the Major and Smith. But McDaniel did not lose his natural dignity and he was smiling as he said, "Hello Johns—Smith—how are we doing?"

Johns made an effort to perk up a bit, but his voice lacked conviction or force as he told McDaniel all about the situation.

The Chief of Staff surveyed the scene, weighing it all very carefully before he answered. When he did, his tone was serious and he was not smiling.

"Johns, when you were on maneuvers in Louisiana, or at VMI, and while you were studying at Leavenworth, you saw situations where units had to be sacrificed knowingly in order to get a job done, didn't you?"

The battalion commander nodded.

"When you saw those things you probably never thought very much about them, just accepted them as a matter of course in war, didn't you?"

The Major nodded again.

"You never stopped to think, probably, that there might come a time when you and your unit would be the one that had to be sacrificed to enable the parent unit to accomplish its mission?"

The Major's eyes were opening wider as he shook his head.

"Well, I don't know for sure, but maybe this is that time. I DO know that this is the highest ground on the corps front— the key to the entire defense of St. Lo. Corps expects us to break it, and we think you are the man to do the job. At whatever the cost. Now don't let us down!"

Without another word he got to his feet and walked back the way he had come. The Regimental Exec tagged after him.

Johns watched them go. Suddenly he remembered that the General had said the day before, "I'm counting on you." He turned to Weddle, who had watched the little drama with detached interest.

"Leroy," the Major said as he squared his shoulders and pointed to the sinking sun, "take a damned good look at that sun, old boy, because it's probably the last time any of us will ever see it. Let's go."

Johns never knew, later, just what he did the rest of that afternoon and early evening. He remembered moving the command post forward again and he knew that he had needled the company commanders unmercifully, threatening them with relief from their commands, begging, pleading—anything he could think of that would work best with the individual at the moment.

He found that there was a comparatively weak spot in the German lines opposite Baker again. He badgered Martin into persuading the artillery to give him all the fire that could hit that spot at one time. That meant a lot of guns. When they all fired three rounds as fast as the gunners could load them, a hundred yards of German-held hedgerow went up in flame and smoke and dust. Again most of Baker Company streamed across the field and into the gap blasted by the artillery.

That took the heart out of the paratroopers, who began to fall back all along the line. It was no rout. The Germans retired from the flanking threat Baker posed, having gained

a place in their main line. But they fell back slowly, fighting
every foot of the way.

Major Johns wanted a reserve very badly just then—to throw
into the gap and have it fan out behind the enemy, trapping
those who faced the rest of Baker and all of Able. But since
Charlie was as heavily engaged on the left flank as the others
were in front, he did not dare pull out any part of it. So the
chance was lost.

The tenacious paratroopers slowed the weakened battalion
again. But they could not stop it entirely. The company commanders and the platoon leaders, together with the battalion
CO, had thrown off their apathy, taken a second wind, and
were not to be denied.

At dark, thanks to the inspired leadership that had been
provided in a few short minutes by Colonel McDaniel, the
German line was broken beyond repair. The battered American
battalion had made 500 bloody yards. The command post
group found a short stretch of muddy sunken road on the edge
of the yard around the little farmhouse that showed on the map
as the "village" of Dufayel and which gave its name to the
grim battle of 11 July. There they established their command
post for the night.

As dusk faded into darkness the firing began to diminish,
only to flare briefly again on the left. Then it died away into
silence. Kenney called in to say there had been a light counterattack on his left flank. He had easily kicked it off.

The Major did not ask for permission to halt the advance.
He gave orders to dig in for the night after he was sure the
companies had close contact on their flanks. He ordered
Kenney and Stoen, on the flanks, to pull their lines to the rear
as best they could so that the battalion position was in the
form of a rough open U.

He had been out of contact with his rear command post and
with Regiment ever since the attack had again begun to move
late in the afternoon. He had no idea where the other units
of the regiment were, nor did he care particularly at that time.

His battalion had been fighting alone with no support on the flanks for so long that they felt as if the war were a private affair between only themselves and the paratroopers they faced.

He told Grimsehl to make the usual arrangements for contact patrols as soon as they had established communications with Regiment and found out whom they were to contact and where. But he cared little whether or not the enemy might try to strike past him at something in his rear. The battalion had about had all it could handle, merely looking after itself.

He sent no patrols to the front. Outposts were sufficient security for the battalion. The idea of maintaining contact with the enemy never even occurred to him. If he had thought of this strict, inviolable rule of war he would have broken it as unhesitatingly as he did without thinking of it. If the enemy wanted to withdraw that night they could damn well do so without hindrance from his outfit.

The men dug in. Half of them slept while the other half kept watch. Officers and noncoms kept themselves awake by sheer willpower, checking constantly on the outposts and the men on watch. There must be no chance for another debacle like Colonel Warfield's 2d Battalion had experienced, or even like the near debacle of the night before.

Around 2300 the wiremen got the telephone circuits to the rear command post and to Regiment working again. They had laid wire as they advanced, but it had been knocked out as fast as they had laid it, so that not once had the command group been able to use the phone. Major Johns talked first to Hoffman, who reported all clear and quiet. The aid station was working frantically to get the flood of wounded evacuated. The A and P boys would be up with ammunition any minute. Food and water would follow as soon as they could get to it.

Regiment received Johns' report with surprise. Colonel Ordway was glad to hear they had made some progress. He remarked that no one had made any significant advances that day. The attack would be resumed at 0800 the following morning.

Weddle found a comparatively large dugout with overhead cover near the end of the sunken road. It was big enough for three men if they were willing to cooperate very closely. He, Martin, and the Major crawled in and dragged the phones after them.

Weddle, whose spirits seemed to be more elastic than the commander's, remarked sleepily, "Looks like we might see that sun again after all, Major." The latter muttered, "You haven't seen it yet, bud, so don't get so cocky."

But they did see it. In fact, the sun was well above the horizon when the companies moved forward again. The scouts darted forward cautiously, slipping from cover to cover, expecting to draw fire at any moment. They made the first hedgerow, where the Germans had been the night before. No fire. They peeped over the hedgerow, still expecting a trap.

No trap. No Germans.

The enemy obviously had pulled out right after the counterattack on Kenney's flank the night before. Johns remembered that there had been no firing after that and he smiled to himself at all his caution of the evening and earlier that morning, especially that morning.

It was just light enough to see, when the three officers unscrambled themselves from one another and crawled out of the hole to stretch and to rub circulation back into cramped legs and arms. Weddle claimed the Major had scraped all the skin off both his shins with boot heels. Martin accused Weddle of deliberately poking him in the eye with his elbow so he would pull his head down and give Weddle more room. As soon as they were out, Johns borrowed an entrenching shovel from Bein and looked around for a good place to dig a cat hole.

The road itself was far too confined for such purposes, from a practical if not esthetic point of view. Also it was still too early to be wandering around in the open fields on either side of the road or in the open courtyard of the hamlet of Dufayel. There was still a chance of a wandering German patrol and Johns had no desire to be shot with his pants down, at least not for so prosaic a reason. He settled for a cow shed near the house.

He started for it, then turned back. They had searched all the buildings the night before but had not occupied them because they were such inviting targets for a raiding party. There was no guarantee that there were no Germans in them now. He remembered Vierville and Colombieres where the snipers had come back for days. Though there was no one in sight he knew Able Company was well on the far side of the house, screened from view by a heavy hedge of young poplars. He decided definitely that the shed was no place to be visiting alone.

The ubiquitous Gay was on guard at the end of the road. Johns motioned to him to follow, saying, "Come on, Gay, you can guard me and the road both from the inside edge of that shed."

Gay laughed, hitched up his rifle, and moved over to take his new post in the shed.

The balance of the simple operation took place uneventfully. The Major, amused at his own caution, was reminded of one of the first lectures he had ever received on the subject of "security." "You don't even go out to take a crap," some instructor had said, "until you are absolutely certain of your security." He wondered if the instructor had meant this literally.

The companies continued to advance, but they weren't rushing into anything. They took it easy, moving across wooded fields and orchards until they came out on the slope of a long hill that led down to Belle Fontaine, less than a thousand yards in front of them. As they cleared the last of the heavy country and started down the slope, they heard some firing on the far right. With glasses they could make out the 2d Battalion, working down another slope still closer to the town.

As soon as the men came out of the cover of the heavy country the German artillery, silent until now, opened up. The first volley hit just in rear of Baker Company's leading elements. It was only minutes before a runner panted up, looking for the Major.

"Sir," he reported, "Lieutenant Stoen is hit. Lieutenant Kordiyak sent me to tell you we are getting Lieutenant Stoen back to the aid station and that he is taking command of the company."

"How bad is Lieutenant Stoen?"

"Not too bad, sir. Fragments in his back and right arm, but the aid man says he'll be all right."

"Okay. Tell Lieutenant Kordiyak to carry on and try to do as good a job as Lieutenant Stoen has been doing."

Stoen out! That was a bitter blow. He'd made a fine company commander. Well—he was beginning to get used to that sort of thing. Kordiyak had a good reputation too. He remembered all the good things he had heard about Lieutenant Chadwick and wished him back for a spare—but . . .

The scouts finally ran into what they had been looking for, and dreading, machine gun fire. The leading platoons halted, while the leaders studied the situation to decide just what they were up against. From their reports it was easy to see that the battalion was opposed by only a few small groups, acting as delaying forces. But their fire, as deadly as any other, demanded respect. The company commanders were inclined to hold their men under cover and use their mortars, both 60-mm and 81-mm, to blast out the Germans before trying to continue the advance. This method took longer, but it saved a lot of men, and the battalion was woefully short of men just then. The Major did not attempt to push any faster. If their progress was slow, it was steady.

However, it also became apparent that it was going to be a toss-up whether men saved by not assaulting machine gun positions would be sacrificed later to the enemy artillery fire. While the mortars worked on the enemy, the enemy artillery worked on all men who were halted, above ground, and waiting. Then the German mortars started firing again, too.

Johns selected a hedgerow corner where he could lie flat on his back to rest while Kordiyak rooted out two German machine guns that were holding them up. He was awakened by

Lieutenant Fink, the forward observer from the Regimental Cannon Company, who wanted to know if it would be all right for him to shoot into the town. For answer the Major snapped, "Don't ever ask me if you can shoot at ANYthing that's in front of us. You knock it flat and then TELL me about it, but don't you ever ASK me again if you can shoot!"

The observer was a little startled, but he liked the idea.

Johns sat up and put his back against the hedgerow, comfortable in the warm sun and not very worried about anything at the moment.

A mortar shell burst squarely on top of the hedgerow, a foot above and back of his helmet.

For an instant he did not move. Then he clapped his hands to his ears and rolled sideways to the ground, waiting for the next round. It didn't come. After thirty seconds Grimsehl and Weddle ran to the Major and took his arms. Grimsehl said something, but Johns only shook his head, gently, pointing to his ears. Weddle looked him over carefully. There was no blood anywhere. Then Martin looked at the shell crater with practiced eye and announced, "Didn't touch him. Not a single fragment got below the edge of the hedgerow."

Johns was a little dazed, but not for long. When he thought he had himself collected a bit he said. "I'm okay, except I don't think I can hear anything very much."

Grimsehl came close and shouted, "Are you sure?"

He could hear. The shout hurt his ears.

Grimsehl, in a lesser tone, suggested they move back a little way to a sunken road they had passed. They started the move, shortly encountering a very interesting sight. No man in the group was a stranger to sudden death, so they were able to examine this bit with cool professional interest.

It was a German paratrooper, his little helmet still fast on his head as he lay with his back against the side of the road, his hands clenched tightly at his sides, his eyes staring up at the sky, and his teeth showing as he still bit down hard on his lower lip. Both his legs were cut cleanly off just below the hips. He was quite dead.

Johns looked at him for a moment, then stepped up on the side of the road to look at the field on the other side. He spotted one of the missing legs a good thirty yards out in the field. He couldn't find the other.

Martin wanted to know more about what had produced the effect. He crawled out into the field and came back in a moment to report. "4.2 mortar. Field's covered with craters. They tell me the shells often split up in long slivers that would cut ten men in two, just like that." He nodded at the corpse.

"Wish I had a camera. I'd like to show this to the 4.2 people after they had that big panic the other night on account of these paratroop boys."

They stayed in the sunken road until nearly noon. Then leaving Hoffman and Mentzer to make it a rear command post, they moved out again. Just before they moved into a little draw that promised a good location for another advance command post they came across two mortar tubes, a big pool of blood, and two dead mortar men. Both the tubes had holes in them. One was the exact size of a quarter and as smooth as if drilled. Leutz came up as they looked down at the two dead men. He said glumly, "One round of artillery. Hit right there." He motioned to a crater a few feet from the dead gunners.

The draw made a good spot, so they settled down again, the phones were hooked on, and the CP was in business. Major Johns noted that Martin seemed restless, and that none of his men were with him. "Where're all your boys?" he asked.

"They stayed back near where we were before—where you caught the mortar round—said they'd send runners to us." He looked back. It wasn't far to where they had been. "I think I'll go back for 'em."

He came back in a few minutes, his face grey and his voice trembling as he fell on his knees before Major Johns and grabbed his arm. "Major! Come back and look with me. They're dead. All dead."

They all jumped up and walked back. There against the hedgerow, sitting knee to knee and looking quite comfortable, were the five men of the artillery liaison party. Martin was right.

Every man was dead. Only Sergeant Fischhaber, who was not with the group, had escaped.

A mortar fin lay on the edge of a fresh crater made by a German 80-mm mortar, not ten feet in front of the silent group.

"And after all the times I've told 'em and told 'em not to bunch up like that." Johns shook his head sadly and headed back for the draw.

Not long afterward, the Germans suddenly quit and took to their heels. The companies started in pursuit but they had not got far when Regiment ordered that the 1st Battalion would break off all action and march to La Forge where it would become Regimental reserve.

Just Forget About Your Flanks / 13

BY DUSK they had moved into La Forge, the village that had been their original objective in the attack launched nearly a month ago. Since they were well behind the new front lines, the men, except for one out of each squad, could clean up and catch up on their rest.

That night 53 new men reported to the battalion. The Major had a chance to check up on his outfit. He found that the official report of casualties of the day before, the 11th of July, totaled 187. However, neither he nor Weddle was convinced the report was accurate, because the foxhole strength reports from the companies didn't tally with the official numbers. There was always the chance that more official casualties from the preceding day would be reported. In any event they figured they had lost at least 225 men, not counting artillerymen.

The Quartermaster graves registration and salvage units, which had already moved in behind the advance and had cleared the battlefield of dead and equipment, reported picking up 87 dead German paratroopers. If they had found that many there were bound to have been others who were carried off by the enemy; the usual ratio of approximately 1 dead to each 4 wounded would indicate that the Germans had taken around 350 to 400 casualties during their night attack and the next day's fighting. So the battalion had inflicted a 2 to 1 loss on the enemy. This was strictly jack-leg figuring, but it was encouraging, especially when it was remembered that all the enemy killed in earlier skirmishes had been removed only two days before.

Despite the receipt of the 53 replacements, the battalion was still woefully short of men. Of all the casualties about 180 were in the rifle companies. This was an average of about 60 per company, around a third of the strength with which they had come into the position. Even now, with the replacements, they couldn't count more than 110-115 men per rifle company, which was a little less than two-thirds full Table of Organization strength. The appalling part was that nearly all these men had been lost between 0135 and 2130 of the same day.

The battalion, then, numbered about 650 men, half of the total being in the 3 rifle companies. Headquarters and Dog were nearly at full strength, although Dog was still short a few machine-gunners.

Three days later a rejuvenated 1st Battalion moved through the lines of the 3d Battalion at La Luzerne, another little village about a thousand yards beyond La Forge. Blue (3d Battalion) had been trying for four days to fight their way off the Line of Departure but couldn't get going. The men were so exhausted that they hardly bothered to answer when Red swaggered through with remarks like, "Stand back, boys, and let men show you how to do a job."

That black but victorious 11th of July was forgotten. The number of German casualties was on every man's lips, but not a soul outside of the staff could tell you how many the battalion itself had lost. Morale and esprit, carefully fostered from above, had gone sky-high again. The men had beaten the much vaunted paratroopers twice on their own grounds and they were damned well proud of themselves. Meanwhile Blue, having had its dark days too, was glad to take time out.

By 0330 on the morning of 15 July Red Battalion was in its jump-off position. And a very peculiar position it was, too. Kenney and his Charlie Company were on the right, Kordiyak with Baker were on the left, and Able was in the center—but in reserve. This peculiar lineup was the only way they could figure to fit the troops to the ground.

The battalion front extended from a paved road (the Isigny-St. Lo Road), which was the right boundary, exclusive, some 1300 yards to the left. The road led to St. Lo, less than two miles ahead; and the 1300 yards included two clumps of woods, one on either flank, together with about 600 yards of wide-open field in the center. To attempt to move out into the open was obviously impossible as both clumps of woods were strongly held by the enemy, and Blue had found that the field was absolutely untenable. There were no hedgerows or other cover; every inch of ground was covered by hostile flanking fire from the woods, including fire from some multibarreled 20-mm guns that could reach from one end of the front to the other.

The 1300-yard front was a long stretch for the 300-odd men of the three rifle companies. The peculiar terrain made it necessary for the battalion commander to split his force into two attacking groups, holding a reserve company to shove through any weak spot in the enemy's lines which they might find or make. Johns had let out a yowl, back at Regiment, when he had seen the operations map and been shown the front over which his men were to attack. But it had been a vain cry. He asked that Blue be given the somewhat smaller left flank, just to hold, if not to attack. The Colonel had said no, Blue was too beat up to do any more fighting. Bitterly, Major Johns thought about how "beat up" his own unit had been the morning of the 11th, yet still ordered to attack. He had already forgotten how impotent they had been most of that day.

So he studied the maps, wondering how he was going to cope with four open flanks instead of the usual two. For four they had, as orders were to attack both woods. There were no friendly units on the immediate right or left. The 35th Division, which had the zone to the right of the road, including the road itself, had not been able to come up abreast of La Luzerne, leaving a 400-yard gap extending to the rear of his right. Every opposing yard had a German in it. There didn't seem to be any enemy on the wide-open extreme left, but it was so open that it could not be used for maneuver. That left the interior open flanks. Fire from one woods could cover the other. The Germans, with their machine guns and 20-mm cannon, were certain to make sure of this. Any GI who showed himself on either side of that open field was inevitably bound to be seen and fired on from the other side.

As Johns considered these problems, Warfield, the regimental S3, had had to go and make that classic remark, "Just forget about your flanks!"

As if the flank troubles weren't enough, it seemed as though the Germans had a perfect defense along their fronts as well.

When the Major went up for a reconnaissance he understood why Blue hadn't been able to get going. Charlie Company faced a little open stretch of marshy ground, beyond which were hedgerows and woods. Baker Company would have to cross or skirt a deep gully with steep, open sides, bare of cover. Neither company could do anything but attack straight ahead.

And so, at 0330, the battalion was lined up for that straight-ahead assault. A platoon of tanks, having been attached for the attack, was formed up just behind the advance command post, which Major Johns had placed just to the rear of Charlie Company's left flank. The 3d Battalion would support the 1st Battalion with their mortars and heavy machine guns. In addition, all the fire of the Regimental Cannon Company was theirs for the asking because Red was carrying the ball all alone that day. Not even White was attacking. Thus Johns' men had lots of support, and it looked as though they would need all of it.

At 0345, while the men of the leading companies were fingering their rifles and fidgeting nervously, toughing out those last long minutes before the jumpoff, the enemy beat them to the punch again.

The Germans opened up with everything they had. But Red Battalion, pretty used to that sort of thing by then, was unimpressed. The hostile artillery and mortars were not nearly up to the standard set in Ryan's war and the Dufayel counterattack, while nobody minded small-arms fire when they were safely behind a hedgerow, even when 20-mm stuff was flying around pretty thick.

Nevertheless it made a very nice show, to say the least. The Major said, "Here we go again," leaned back in his shallow foxhole, crossed his arms back of his head, and looked up at the tracers that flew 6 to 10 feet overhead. The German fire came from straight ahead and from the left front. The tanks opened up right over their heads, with their .50's. Blue cut loose with their prepared supporting fires from the left rear, and the 35th Division, not to be left out of the fun, joined in from the right rear. That accounted for every part of the compass except the right front, which the Germans over there obligingly filled in. The result was a crisscross of screaming ricochets, snapping machine gun bullets, crashing mortars, and roaring artillery. The whole effect was deafening. The damn tanks, Johns decided, were worst of all because the muzzle blast of the .50's was right in his ears.

Oddly enough, almost all the enemy counterfire was high. Not a single man in the leading companies was hit by that steady, heavy maelstrom of flying steel. Although the enemy fire didn't last long, Regiment, fearful that it heralded an attack by the Germans and preferring to meet it from behind hedgerows rather than to run head on into it in the open as they launched their own, postponed the battalion assault until 0600.

Then Baker and Charlie moved out. Charlie was lucky. They made it across the marshy ground before the Germans woke up to what was going on. The first hedgerow on the far side, for some reason best known to the enemy, was only outposted. Kenney's men drove in the outposts and seized the hedgerow in a matter of minutes. This was more than Blue had accomplished in three days. But there they stuck.

Kordiyak tried to get around the deep draw and into the woods from the right. It looked as if this was the only way in. Unfortunately the Germans knew it as well as Kordiyak did. The smoke he put on them didn't bother them much because, with their guns sited on the narrow approach the enemy didn't have to be able to see clearly to cover it adequately. Kordiyak's first rush was repulsed with losses.

The tanks might as well have been back at Ordnance for all

the good they did. On account of the marshy ground they couldn't get up close enough to support either company. Their platoon leader tried hard but after he stuck one tank so thoroughly that he had to abandon it, at least temporarily, he gave up trying to move the heavy vehicles. Then he wisely started an inch-by-inch reconnaissance of the front on foot, looking for the few feet of firm ground he needed for getting his tanks rolling.

The battalion commander watched Kenney for a while, then went over for a look at B Company. He found them lined up behind a low hedgerow facing the Germans across 150 yards of a deep ravine. They were methodically pounding the opposite hedgerow with 60- and 81-mm mortars while the artillery and more mortars smoked the right flank. A determined little group of men crawled around in the shallow folds of the field that gave them their only cover and only chance of getting into the German-held woods.

As he walked down the hedgerow, bent nearly double, Johns came to a man lying on the ground, his leg in a bloody bandage. It must have been a million-dollar wound because the man was quite cheerful and alert as he waited for the litter bearers. He waved to the commander and warned him, "Watch that gap up there, Major; there's a sonuvabitch across the way has it zero'd, and he shoots every time anybody comes across."

The Major looked at the gap, about 8 feet wide, and at another man on the far side, in almost the same condition as the man he was talking to. The other man, just as cheerful as the first, gave more advice, "Take it fast, sir, and he can't shoot quick enough."

So Johns, going along with the game, got down into an exaggerated "starting" position, dug his toes into the ground, waved his tail around in the air, then suddenly took off as hard as he could go in the bent-over position. A shot cracked through the space, but he was well past the gap as both men cheered.

He found Kordiyak, talked with him awhile, and watched the 60-mm mortars firing from just behind the hedgerow. He wondered at their accuracy as he saw the projectiles rush straight

into the air then fall close behind the German-held hedgerow
less than 200 yards away. It was close range, even for a 60.

He stayed long enough to satisfy himself that Kordiyak was
trying hard and skillfully. Then he ducked successfully back
across the gap in the hedgerow, thumbed his nose in the direction of the German rifleman, and sauntered thoughtfully back
to the command post. There he found that Regiment was sending the 2d Battalion in a wide sweep calculated to take the Germans in the left woods from the rear. It was an obvious move
that would probably succeed, provided there weren't a lot more
Germans in the way.

As he talked with Weddle and Hoffman something rapped
him sharply on the shin. He drew his leg up to rub the bruised
spot, puzzled by what could have caused the sudden blow. Then,
seeing what it was, he leaned down to pick up the still warm
but quite spent German machine gun bullet that had struck
him. He put it in his pocket for a souvenir.

Kenney and C Company were doing a magnificent job.
Stopped cold after their first success, Kenney had "developed
the situation" as carefully as he could. In this case that meant
that he had observed every part of the enemy's line while both
sides kept up a constant interchange of fire. Kenney had decided that the Germans' left flank, next to the road, was their
weakest spot, probably because they were not numerous in any
event and did not expect an attack on a flank that could be
dominated by fire from the other side of the road, which was
still German held because of the lagging 35th Division.

There was a ditch along the road that Kenney found to be
deeper than it looked. He knew it could develop into a trap,
but it offered the only hope for an advance. He chose his best
squad leader, gave him a full squad, and sent him to crawl
across the 200 yards that separated the two lines. Kenney
realized that if the men were discovered it would mean almost
certain death in spite of the heavy covering fire set up to blast
the far hedgerow if need be.

While the squad inched its way up the ditch the rest of the
company made a feint that was almost an all-out charge. They

smoked the German hedgerow with white phosphorus from the 81's and blasted it with artillery and all the Cannon Company fire. The men yelled and fired as fast as they could with all their weapons.

The ruse would probably never have worked against the cooler, tougher paratroopers they had been fighting before. But the Germans now opposing them were not paratroopers. They were part of a Volksgrenadier division who, although they did a good job of fighting, lacked the skill and fanaticism of the picked parachute regiment. Anyway, it worked. Kenney's squad poured over the hedgerow under the supporting hail of fire the rest of the company was pouring out. The German flank gave way completely. Kenney shoved the rest of the platoon up the ditch, then sent the other two straight across the field while the Germans were still confused.

That action netted one hedgerow and 28 prisoners besides a dozen dead and wounded. Kenney didn't lose a man.

But the defeat of that one enemy group did not cause a rout. The attack bogged down again. The terrain beyond the new hedgerow was exceptionally rough. It was only lightly wooded but there was some underbrush, an unusual thing in France. The Germans had honeycombed the whole area with foxholes and gun emplacements that covered each inch of open space without ever letting the attacking forces see where the fire was coming from. Kenney tried another push on the right, making some progress. But he could not roll up the flank because of the rough country. The men who had moved up were exposed to their rear. Furthermore, long-range fire from the 35th Division, now 600 yards to the rear, was worrying them. They were inclined to be contemptuous of the 35th's ability to hit anything at that range, but Kenney, fearful that that friendly but too-distant unit would bring up a tank at any minute, pulled his men back. Major Johns got on the circuit to Regiment to request for the third time that somebody please tell the 35th damn Division that the people on the left of the road were—or at least had been—friendly.

Kenney thought they could risk the 35th's fire if they could get the left flank up at the same time. But one well-placed, stubborn hostile machine gun stopped that flank attack cold. The German gunner got half of the small squad that tried to rush him through smoke; and the attackers had to withdraw, dragging their wounded with them. Mortars and artillery left the German undamaged. Rifle grenades couldn't quite hit the narrow slit through which he was firing. Two grenadiers, trying to take extra careful aim, had also been hit by concealed German snipers. When the Major arrived it looked as though progress had stopped.

Martin, for once, was not at his side so, using the battalion radio to the rear command post and the artillery phone from there, he adjusted 18 successive rounds from one gun of the 110th Field Artillery Battalion in a vain attempt to sharpshoot the machine gun out of existence. But he couldn't hit it, and after each round burst on or near the hedgerow the enemy gun would reply with a derisive burst.

There was only one answer—a tank.

And, miraculously, a tank appeared! The tank platoon leader had kept trying to find a way to cross the marshy area, and when C Company made their new gain it enabled him to explore new ground. Finding a narrow hard spot he waved his remaining four tanks across.

One steel monster lumbered up behind Johns, who yelled instructions to the tank commander. The gunner watched carefully while an infantry squad leader fired a clip of tracer bullets at the slit that hid the machine gun, then swung his short-barreled little 75 into line. It crashed once and almost simultaneously with the muzzle blast came the crack of a white phosphorus shell as it hit the slit. The smoke blossomed up from behind the hedgerow, indicating a direct hit. With that, a single paratrooper came running toward them.

A few moments later everything on the company front cut loose, the company charged, and another 100 yards of French real estate changed hands.

The lucky, or very skillful shot had flushed out the first paratrooper seen that day. He wasn't the last one they saw, but he was undoubtedly the maddest. Two riflemen gathered him in before he had time to recover from his shock, and brought him straight to the battalion commander. The man was typical of the elite of Hitler's Army. He was a big, fine-looking youngster in his early twenties, blond and sturdy. And he was completely furious at the fate that had made him surrender. He sneered at Major Johns and the grinning riflemen who held their bayonets at his side, but he answered no questions. They never found out what had impelled him to run the wrong way. It was very obvious, however, that he had not intended to surrender. They assumed that he was dazed or blinded by the explosion of the tank shell and did not know which way he was running.

Johns went forward to examine the machine gun emplacement that had held up a company for an hour. He found the answer to its near invulnerability. The gun itself was fastened firmly in position, with a string leading from the trigger around a corner of the dugout position into another hole from which the gunners could observe. Thus they did not have to man the gun itself except to change belts and barrels. Johns found one gun that had been knocked out by rifle fire, and the one still in position bore marks where it had been hit before the tank shot had knocked it over. One of the crew had also been killed by rifle fire, while the third man had been wounded by the tank shell. The Major wished every machine gunner in his outfit could have seen that position as an illustration of what skill, tenacity, and guts could do to build and defend one machine gun position.

Those were but two examples of what went on all day. By dusk Kenney had advanced perhaps 500 yards while Kordiyak still had not crossed the ravine in his front. The tanks were of little help after their first dramatic appearance because the terrain was so uneven they could seldom find a target. One was knocked out by one of the big German bazookas and the rest were pulled out by Regiment as soon as it was dark.

The fighting had had its lulls but it had been as sustained as bitter fighting ever is. C Company had taken losses comparable to those suffered on the 11th. Charlie Company was now so depleted in strength that it could no longer handle the 300 yards of woods on its front. As dusk settled the battalion commander sent A Company in on the left so as to take no chances of losing their gains during the night, and to have a fresh force to take up the fight in the morning.

But darkness did not stop the attack. Kenney was a whirlwind of leadership. He was up and down his front from one end to the other, not once stopping to rest or eat. He encouraged his men, estimated each situation as it arose, and came up with some sort of answer. Some plans worked, some didn't. When one was unsuccessful he'd try another—and another. Just before dusk, a mortar round hit so near him that the concussion slammed him into the side of a hedgerow, knocking him cold. The round had exploded in a small hole or Kenney would have been killed.

His radio operator reported him seriously wounded, but Kenney himself corrected the report, said he was all right, and wanted to keep right on fighting. The Major was of the same mind, so the fighting went on into the darkness.

Thirty minutes after complete darkness, the Germans launched one of their typical flank attacks. It had been cleverly planned. Slipping across the open field they tried to come in behind Able's left. But it was against just such an attack that Able Company had been put into the line, with their flank drawn well back. In attacking Able, the Germans ran headlong into a fresh force. Not many of them got away from the machine gun and rifle fire and grenades that Able dealt out to them.

Nevertheless, the enemy scored. Able 6 was struck out with a bad wound just when the Major had decided that perhaps the man was proving himself. What was worse, Kenney caught another mortar shell in almost exactly the same way as the first. Only the hole wasn't quite so deep this time, so the brave young fighter stopped a handful of small splinters of steel with his legs and back.

Kenney regained consciousness before the litter bearers could get him out. He tried to get up to go back to his company, but Johns ordered him out and would listen to no argument. Kenney was too good a man to risk any further and he had done his job for the time being. His company would roll of its own momentum now.

Two brand-new replacement officers took the two companies. Lieutenant William R. Todd, another Texan—hence, prima facie, a good man—inherited Able; and Lieutenant Leonard E. Dettman took over from Kenney.

The German counterattack succeeded in halting the advance on the right, largely through the commotion caused by the almost simultaneous loss of the two company commanders. The battalion commander ordered the men to dig in for the night, moved the command post up to the first hedgerow Kenney had taken, and retired to it to take stock of the day's action.

He found the casualty report discouraging. Not a company counted over a hundred men in the line. To balance that somewhat, Grimsehl reported that nearly a hundred prisoners had been taken, almost all by C Company. Kordiyak was still along his ravine but he came in to the command post long enough to give a brief report and to vow that he would get into the woods that night or die trying.

The Major decided to let him try that night, and if he did not succeed to pull him away from the left and "forget" that flank entirely. They could continue to smoke it, as they had been doing periodically all day when men on the right side of the field had had to expose themselves on their open left flank. Every time that had happened they had drawn fire from the rear of the left woods, but smoke had cut down the accuracy until the enemy fire was completely impotent.

The 35th Division kept firing into their open right flank, wounding at least two of Johns' men during the afternoon. Oddly enough, the Germans on the other side of the road ignored them completely. Either they were too busy with the 35th Division to notice the 1st Battalion, or the road was their boundary and they didn't care what happened on the other side of it. That was helpful, in spite of the action of the 35th

Division. Of course, the fire from across the road could have been accidental, but the Charlie Company men blamed trigger-happy new troops who shot at anything they could see, in spite of orders not to shoot across the road. Major Johns, in his report to Colonel Ordway, complained bitterly whereupon the good Colonel promised to take strong remedial action.

The night was not quiet. Patrols from both sides kept running into trouble, little bursts of firing marking each encounter. The artillery and even the mortars blasted away periodically, the latter firing whenever a patrol needed covering fire to help it out of a tight spot.

Kordiyak, as good as his word, got into the woods. But he couldn't stay. He sent a large patrol well out into the field, much as the Germans had done earlier on Able's flank. The men, crawling slowly every inch of the way, were able to come in from behind the German flank and for a few minutes it looked as though they could roll it up. Kordiyak pushed a platoon across the open at a run, but before he could bring up the rest of the company the woods erupted Germans from every direction, with the result that the attack was repulsed with heavy losses on both sides.

Just before dawn, when everyone was keyed up to continue the attack despite the fact that no orders to that effect had come down, Regiment called to say, "Hold up. Do not attack until further orders."

For once, an order not to attack was a disappointment. The battalion had had a rough day and a hard night, but they were making ground and they wanted to go. Reluctantly the men subsided, dug their holes a little deeper, and waited.

It wasn't hard to figure why they were being held back. The 35th Division was a full 800 yards to the right rear and nobody knew where the 2nd Battalion was. There had been no contact patrols during the night and no firing had been heard on the left. That left Red Battalion 'way out front and all alone. As usual, they were clay pigeons. It did not take a great deal of perception to see that someone, having had a look at that "big picture" back at Division, had decided to hold them up lest they get further out front where they could be cut off and gobbled up by a superior force.

When he thought about that the Major was glad the 3d Battalion was still in La Luzerne, barely a thousand yards behind.

The morning passed uneasily. For one little group it must have been the most nerve-racking period of their lives. Just before dawn a messenger came into Kordiyak's command post. The man came from the patrol that had gotten into the woods earlier in the night, and which Kordiyak had thought was lost. The messenger reported that most of the patrol was intact and that they were holed up near the corner of the woods, unknown to the Germans. They would stay there until Kordiyak launched an attack next morning. Could he please do it at dawn?

Kordiyak was wild. He pleaded to be allowed to attack and the Major carried his request to Regiment where it was gently but firmly refused. A company attack could start the whole front boiling again and they did not want that yet. The patrol would have to wait.

So wait they did, until 1415. Then the word came down, without explanation, "Continue the attack at once."

As soon as the companies began to move, putting into effect the plans they had made during the night, it was apparent that the enemy had not wasted their time. They had dug in and probably received reinforcements. In a very few minutes the battle became a bitter struggle at close quarters.

The ground was so rough and so heavy with brush that the front lines were not clear to either side. In places they were so close together and so confused that neither side could risk using mortars or artillery for fear of hitting their own people. Calls for more grenades came in constantly. The brrrp of German machine pistols blended with the crack-crack-crack of M1's as the antagonists fought it out with small arms. Casualties mounted by the minute.

Major Johns dissolved the improvised Commando Platoon and sent the men back to their companies. Orders had come from Regiment to put every available man into the line. Close behind these orders arrived a group of frightened drivers, clerks, and other rear-echelon people who had never fired a shot in anger. Johns was loath to put such men into the fight because he knew they would be at least as much of a liability as an asset. It is not necessarily the fault of the individual, but a man who serves in the rear almost always develops a "rear-echelon" complex of fear for the unknown terrors of combat. To feed such inexperienced soldiers into a hot fight was to make great demands on the leadership ability of hard-pressed squad and platoon leaders who would have to spend more time shepherding the new men than they would in fighting the enemy.

But the regimental orders were adamant. Everybody went in.

The Major eyed Barbeaux speculatively. Weddle caught the look and cried, "Ye gods, Major, not THAT. He'd get his whole squad killed."

Barbeaux was reprieved.

The fighting went on. It was not a constant hack-and-slash thing, as those who have never experienced battle might think from what they read or hear. War is made up of countless individual actions which do not necessarily take place simultaneously. True, there are concerted charges by large groups but these are rare; a hard-fought battle inches along after the opposing forces have come to close grips.

Riflemen take cover when they are fired on, and seek a target. Artillery and mortar observers choose places from which they can get the best observation of enemy lines. They pick likely places on which to drop their fire, although they may never see an enemy. Squad and platoon leaders move about, sizing up the situation before they make an attempt to destroy or drive away an enemy machine gun or take a strong point that is holding up their advance. Company commanders do the same, gathering reports by radio, by runner, or by crawling up to their platoon leaders and talking with them.

All these actions take time. A "bitter" battle may "rage" for hours, but there will be long minutes when not a shot is fired by either side, simply because neither knows where the other is, exactly, and is reluctant to expose his own position by firing blindly. During these pauses the planning is going on as information is gathered. Finally, a decision having been reached, the plan for the next little move is passed down to the men who will execute it—from company to platoon to squad to the men themselves. That takes still more time, since a squad leader may have to crawl tortuously to each of eight or ten men in order to tell each one what to do.

When such a plan has been made and orders given to carry it out, this still does not mean that every man will leap to his feet and charge forward. As a matter of fact, that seldom happens. The plan may provide that a single mortar will fire two or three rounds of smoke on a suspected machine gun position while a half dozen men crawl a few yards and attempt to get close enough to shoot accurately or throw grenades into the enemy position. If this is successful a number of men may worm further forward or, sometimes, actually jump up and run a few yards. If they fail, someone usually gets hurt. A new plan must be made, starting all over again.

An attack may well go on that way for a long time—as it had, indeed, gone on the day before—with a machine gun being knocked out here, a man or two being killed or wounded there. Eventually the leader of the stronger force, usually the attackers, may decide that he has weakened his opponents enough to warrant a large concerted assault, preceded by a concentration of all the artillery and mortar support he can get. Or the leader of the weaker force may see that he will be overwhelmed by such an attack and may decide to pull back to another position in his rear.

Thus goes the battle—a rush, a pause, some creeping, a few isolated shots here and there, some artillery fire, some mortars, some smoke, more creeping, another pause, dead silence, more firing, a great concentration of fire followed by a concerted rush. Then the whole process starts all over again.

The defender will almost always hold out some reserve, even though his front line is being torn to bits. At least he should. He may inflict all the damage on the attacker that he can, while giving ground slowly; then, when he thinks the attacker is weakening, or when the defense has reached a certain piece of ground that the defender has chosen for the purpose, he launches a counterattack with his reserves. The attacker has used much of his strength, his men are tired, probably short of ammunition, and are almost inevitably somewhat disorganized. The defender throws fresh troops into a counterattack over ground his men know. Unless the attackers are very strong they must inevitably suffer. Often they are defeated and thrown back or destroyed, as happened to the enemy in their night attack at Dufayel.

Such counterattack tactics have been standard almost as long as there have been organized armies. The Germans employed them so regularly that they were never a surprise. But the enemy could never seem to muster the strength necessary to make their counterattacks stick. Their efforts often halted an advance, as they had the night before, but they rarely gained back any ground and were almost always costly to the counterattackers. Even the best and most proven tactics still require judgment, and the force to do the job. The Germans rarely had enough of either.

Such was the course of that battle on the 16th day of July between Red Battalion and the Germans just northeast of St. Lo.

In the middle of the afternoon the CO moved up close behind A Company to watch their contingent of former battalion commandos go into the line. Sergeant Turner, who had been in charge of the platoon, was with them. Seeing the Major he fell behind long enough to say, "Sir, we're going in there and help our buddies from old A Company lick hell out of those bastards, but when we get through I'd sure like to come back and get me another bunch of commandos for battalion." His cool voice ended on a rising note.

"All right, sergeant, you get us into St. Lo, and I promise you I'll get you another platoon of your hell raisers just as soon as we can spare them from the companies." Johns returned the sergeant's salute and watched the man as he ran to catch up with the others.

An hour later a Weasel, a small all-purpose tracked vehicle, flying a Red Cross flag, clattered out of the woods, carrying a load of wounded on litters. The battalion commander, who was passing the spot, stopped when he saw the wounded. The little commando sergeant lay on the litter on the near side. Seeing the Major he yelled to the driver to stop.

Johns went over to him and the boy, both his legs wrapped in dirty, bloody bandages, grabbed his commander's shirt and pulled himself up on the litter. He was crying openly and unashamedly as he burst out with a flood of invective, "They got all my boys, Major . . . We didn't even get off the LD. I let you down, Major, I let you down."

He stopped and sobbed bitterly before he could go on. Major Johns could feel his own throat constricting as he held the tightly gripping hands that shook him again and again as the sergeant poured out his grief and rage and disappointment, "We had to get that gun . . . damn the dirty bastards, goddam, goddam, goddam . . . I let 'em get me with a f - - - machine gun and they got all my boys, too . . . goddam, goddam." He sobbed again, uncontrollably, while the Weasel driver began to let his clutch take hold. "But I'll be back, Major sir, I'll be back—I'll be back . . ."

"Sure, boy, and I'll have your old job for you any time. You just take it easy and get those legs fixed." The Major was walking slowly by the side of the litter, trying gently to disengage the grip on his shirt. The sergeant let go and fell back on the litter, exhausted. Johns looked up at the aid man, who slowly shook his head. The sergeant would not be back.

Heavy Going / 14

ALL THREE COMPANIES were committed and were doing the best they could. The Major, going to see all three of them, had discovered that there was nothing he could do or suggest that would be of any great help. He felt that the continued presence of a senior officer often bothered a company commander who was doing a good job, unless there was some specific help that the commander could render. So he found a centrally located, fairly well-covered spot where he sat down. One by one all the staff officers found him, the phones were brought up, and a regular forward command post was formed, without an order ever being given except when he warned them all to stay well spread out.

He reached into his jacket pocket for his pipe. His hand fumbled momentarily in the pocket and he scowled. Then he brought the hand out of the pocket, holding the pipe in two pieces. He said a very bad word!

That one pipe was his only means of smoking. An inveterate cigar smoker, he found no solace in pallid cigarettes. His supply of cigars having been long since exhausted he depended heavily on the little pipe. In fact, the pipe and the French bayonet he had wheedled out of Morris and which he carried constantly, were his prize possessions. Now the pipe was broken.

He examined the damage carefully. The stem had been snapped off cleanly at the shank of the bowl. He decided it could possibly be repaired with the tools at hand, one sharp pocket knife. He fished about in his pockets until he found the knife and began to dig at the broken piece in the shank.

While he whittled at the pipe the fighting went inexorably on, and the sun sank toward the trees. He was still thinking of pulling Baker away from their woods on the left where, so far as he knew, they had made no progress. True, he hadn't heard from Kordiyak in more than two hours, but a runner was out looking for that officer at the moment. The Major did not expect anything very surprising from that flank.

He was more concerned about what might occur in the immediate future on the right flank. Able and Charlie were making progress, a few yards an hour. It was only a matter of time until they got through a little group of houses that were just ahead now. The map showed that the woods were considerably wider on the other side of the little settlement. It also showed some open fields on the right flank, which meant that the right-flank unit wouldn't be able to watch the road with anything but patrols or an outpost—and probably neither in daylight—because the Germans would be able to see and fire on anyone who moved out into the fields. If they couldn't watch the road there was always a chance that some eager-beaver German, discovering that fact, might send something down it to catch them in the rear. The 35th Division was maintaining the 800-yard interval quite accurately, although they had stopped shooting into his rear. Major Johns hadn't heard from the 2d Battalion all day. Even Regiment was very reluctant to say anything about that unit. Johns had been counting heavily on them to come in and help Kordiyak with his woods, which was in fact the only reason he had not already pulled Kordiyak away from his profitless job.

He made up his mind that if the 2d Battalion had not put in an appearance by early dusk he would move Baker over to the right, hang on to what he had there, and to hell with the left woods. Regiment would just have to agree, or risk losing all that had been gained.

He was also concerned about finding some means of digging a reasonably large 6-hole that night because they had had none the night before and Regiment had got stuffy again about the lack of overlays. Weddle had told them frankly that he couldn't give them an overlay, nor could he be absolutely sure of the exact position of the companies. There were no hedgerows in the woods and no unit knew exactly where it was on the map. No one was able to work up a great deal of concern about it as long as the artillery stayed zero'd just in front of them the way it had been all along. Warfield bitched about it but refused an invitation to come down in the dark to make a survey with some suitable instrument, such as a 6-inch rule.

The whittling and the thinking and the fighting continued. Just as the sun was sinking into the trees the Major made the last adjustment to the stem of the pipe and had the satisfaction of seeing it fit with acceptable smoothness. Looking up to see if anyone had a piece of tape to hold it together, he was astonished to see a wireman holding a short length of rubber tape, waiting to hand it to him.

He thanked the wireman, wound the tape carefully around the crude joint, searched his pockets again until he found a battered packet of Granger, stuffed the bowl, lit it carefully and puffed experimentally until he was sure it was going to work. It did. He leaned back against the side of the shallow hole in which he was sitting and puffed away, still speculating about how to move Baker Company.

He was startled to hear a sigh of relief from Mentzer, who had been sitting next to him without saying a word for at least a half hour. He looked questioningly at the still dapper S1.

"Sir," said Mentzer, "you'll never know how glad I am you got that thing fixed."

"Why? What do you mean?"

"Because, Major, that's the only way most of us have of knowing how we're doing. You get all the messages, or you go and see, or you talk on the radio, and then you never say a damn thing to anybody except Weddle, and he never says anything either, so we don't know what's happening except by watching that pipe."

Johns took the pipe out of his mouth and looked at it care-

fully. It was a very plain little pipe. Not nearly what he would
have chosen, had he had a choice. He could see nothing unusual about it. "What do you mean?"

"Well sir, if it just puffs along, slow and easy—like now—
we know we're doing okay. If it starts going fast, we know
things aren't so good; and when the fire and sparks start coming
out of it we look for a hole."

Weddle laughed and the Major flushed. He had no idea his
reactions were so important to the men around him, or that he
didn't pass on the news. He looked up at the wireman, who had
been with him every day since the night attack, and at Bein,
who rarely left his side. They both nodded, grinning.

"That's right, Major," they said in chorus.

"Hummph!" Johns looked at Mentzer, "You should have
been with us the other day, after that night attack. I don't think
I ever even lit it."

"Yes, and look what happened, too. If I'd been up with you,
or if I ever am up with you when you forget all about that pipe,
I'm gonna find me a hole and pull it in after me." The adjutant,
laughing, got up to go back to see about digging a hole so
Regiment could have its overlay that night. Bein and the wireman nodded again in solemn agreement.

There was still no word from Kordiyak, so another runner
was sent out with a message ordering him to break off on the
left, move through the village behind shelter, and come up prepared to go into position on line in the right woods.

In a surprisingly short time the Baker company commander
stormed furiously up the path that led to the command post.
Without saluting he launched an attack on the Major, "Sir,
why the hell did you have to pull us out just when we were
going good, after all this time?"

The battalion commander was slightly nettled. "What do you
mean, 'going good'? You hadn't done a damn thing but get
shot at all day for two days that I know of. Not that I blame
you. I don't think *anybody* could crack that job."

"That's what I mean. Dammit, we DID crack it!"

"Just what do you mean?" snapped the battalion CO, rising. "You didn't get into the woods, did you?"

"You're damn well right we got into the woods. We'd been in 'em for two hours and were doing fine when I got your order to pull out."

"Well for God's sake why didn't you tell me? You ought to know I'd never have pulled you out if I'd known it."

"Major, I sent you three messages in an hour, telling you we were inside and going good."

Johns swore. "Three messages, yet I never got a one. I never even bothered to go over and check up. Never in the world thought you'd do it."

Kordiyak was beginning to simmer down. "Well, we sure did. I had one hell of a time getting the boys to turn loose and come out, or start out. They're some still covering the rear. I couldn't figure your order, but guessed you knew what you were doing after I sent all those messages. So out we came."

"Okay, boy, I'm sorry. But I really need you over here more now anyway. As a matter of fact I think it was a mistake to leave you over there as long as I did, except I wanted you to keep the Heinies amused so they wouldn't come over and help their buddies on this side, and I kept hoping White would come up and grab 'em by the tail."

He drew on his pipe. "Now, here's what I want you to do: Take the Able runner, here, and go up to have a look at Able's left flank. They're on the left of the woods up ahead about 300 to 400 yards. I want you to go in along that flank with plenty of depth to the rear, to guard against another counterattack like they had last night. Also take a little of Todd's front. Todd knows you're coming. You knew he had A company now, didn't you?"

Kordiyak shook his head. "All I knew was I had a woods to get into."

"Well, he has. The Able CO was wounded last night and so was Kenney. Dettman has Charlie. They both know you're coming because Todd is going to take over a little of Dettman's front so he can pull a platoon loose and bend it back around the right flank. In that way we'll have most of a full perimeter tonight and can kick off practically anything they shove at us."

Kordiyak nodded, found the runner, and set off for A Company's left.

By dark, in spite of the rough country, or possibly because its configuration helped conceal the movement, the switch was made. All three companies were now in another rough U-shaped position. The fighting, which had been slowing gradually for some time, had about come to a stop before the change began. The Major worried for the last thirty minutes or so, for fear the nightly counterattack would hit ahead of schedule.

He needn't have been concerned. It hit right on time, a half hour after full dark, and in the same relative position as the one the night before. Kordiyak had just gotten well into position when the mortars started falling heavily again, telling that the Germans were coming. But the attack was held off with little trouble, as both sides seemed pretty half-hearted about their fighting by then.

Johns used the counterattack as an excuse to tell Regiment he was halting the advance if it was all right with the Colonel. It was, and Regiment got its overlay that night in record time.

Orders for the next day came in by liaison officer before midnight. It all boiled down to one sentence, "Continue the attack at 0630." But with the message came another big overlay of the type that is used in giving orders. On the tracing were a number of large, irregular circles marked "Objective A," "Objective B," and so on. These circles were commonly called "goose eggs," and when the tracing was laid on a map and properly oriented each would fall on some tactically important piece of terrain that was easily recognizable both on the map and on the ground. The goose eggs were the source of a lot of kidding for S3's and G3's. The men on the ground were fond of saying, "Give a G3 a pencil and a map and he can win a war in nothing flat."

The overlays with their goose eggs were very useful, though, as they assigned definite objectives for each unit, defined boundaries, showed enemy positions sometimes, and gave other pertinent information. They also saved a lot of talking, which improved radio security. If a battalion wanted to report its location the S3 only had to look at the overlay, figure their position relative to the nearest objective, and report, for example, "We are so many yards short of Objective Q." But a goose egg had one big disadvantage. It was easy to draw on a map with a pencil but damned difficult, sometimes, to secure on the ground, with men.

The fact that the battalion was five minutes late getting started the next morning, 17 July, didn't really matter because though they didn't know it, they weren't going anywhere that morning. The Germans had apparently decided on that during the night. They had dug in deeper and possibly gotten a few reinforcements from the other side of the field between the two woods because the 2d Battalion still hadn't shown up and no one was worrying the other woods at all, except for periodic artillery fire and smoke.

Hence by noon the 1st Battalion hadn't gained an inch although they had suffered a lot more casualties. The men were tired. Morale was sinking slowly in spite of the new company commanders' determination to make a good showing. The men went through the motions, but the zip was mostly gone as exhaustion and frustration took their toll.

Major Johns looked over his little front carefully. He decided that something new would have to be done. He had been leaving it pretty much up to the companies to do what they wanted, cooperating carefully, of course. But now that wasn't getting anywhere. He and Weddle evolved a tactic they called "shouldering," which they decided to give a try. It wasn't new, probably, but it fit the ground and the problem and they thought it would be successful.

The operation took time, but it did work. The idea was to concentrate as much mass as possible against a narrow front instead of continually probing all along the line as they had been doing. To do this Johns carefully withdrew part of Able Company, filling in the gaps by spreading Charlie still thinner. He ordered

Dettman to mass his men behind a short stretch of front well to the right flank and pull his leading squads back about 30 yards. Both maneuvers were done slowly and cautiously, so as not to tip off the Germans. Then Martin and Lieutenant Fink concentrated all the fire they could command, together with the battalion mortars, on about 50 yards of the enemy line. They put smoke on the line not hit by the high explosives, so as to blind and confuse the enemy and keep him from supporting that part of the line about to be assaulted. Then Dettman shoved his pitiful little "mass" of about 60 men close in under the heavy artillery fire against the small part of the front prepared by the fire.

The maneuver worked. It couldn't help but work, really, because the Germans were as thinly spread and as tired as Red Battalion was, and they couldn't stand up to a concerted attack which closely followed a really heavy barrage of artillery and mortars.

Dettman made about 50 yards, more than they had gained all day. But the terrain was so uneven that this local success did not result in the Germans giving up all their line; and flanking fire was not effective owing to the short ranges and poor visibility caused by brush, trees, and cut-up ground. So they tried the tactic again on the left. Here, Kordiyak was able to make a similar gain. That was too much for the enemy in the middle of the short front. They pulled back to straighten their line.

The idea was good enough to try again and again. It worked almost every time. But on one occasion the Germans caught on. They moved forward when they were tipped off through the withdrawal of men in a short sector. Thus they knocked the attack back, only to be caught themselves when Todd saw what was happening. Guessing that the Germans who had come forward would be vulnerable on their flanks, Todd quickly sent flanking attacks against them under cover of smoke. This gained another 25 or 30 prisoners and almost cracked the German line. In any event it discouraged the enemy from trying to come forward any more. By dusk the battalion had gained 200 more tough yards.

Just before dark the last rush carried the battalion line to the far edge of the woods. The Germans now knew they couldn't hang on any longer. As soon as the artillery hit for the battalion's last push they took off across the short stretch of open fields that separated the woods in which they had been fighting from another smaller wooded area. Baker Company rushed into the gap and stepped on the top step that wasn't there. A whole platoon, seeing the Germans running away, spread to the left, forgetting the other enemy-held woods to their flank and rear, across the open field in the center of the battalion zone. They fetched up against a small hedgerow that marked a lane. There, with their backs to the woods for which they had fought so hard, they lined up to shoot at the fleeing enemy.

But while they did that, the German machine guns and the automatic 20-mm cannon in the woods behind them took careful aim and cut loose. When the enemy stopped shooting, only three Americans were left out of the 18 that had been in the platoon. Most of the others were dead, struck by the little HE shells fired by the 20's.

At the same time, but further inside the woods, Kordiyak was hit and carried out. By the time the reports got back to Major Johns it was clear that Baker Company as a fighting force had about had it. There was only one officer left in the company, and only a few noncoms. The surviving officer was probably the least experienced in the battalion, but there were none to put over him.

Moments after the destruction of Baker's platoon, violent mortar fire shook Able Company. Johns decided that as long as they had their objective, or part of it, they would stop for the night and set up a complete, all-round defense. He knew Baker was in bad shape, and Able and Charlie had been that way all day and weren't getting any better.

He looked at Weddle, "Leroy, run up and see how your old gang is making out. I'm sort of worried about 'em. Maybe you can buck 'em up a little."

Weddle picked up his M1, checked the safety, stuck a couple of grenades in his jacket pockets, and took off up the trail to B Company. While the rest waited to see what information the S3 would send back, the Major saw that Grimsehl and Hoffman prepared the inevitable overlays for Regiment. Meanwhile he wondered just how long they could go on fighting as they had been for three days.

He was also concerned because the command post was at least 600 yards to the rear of the nearest company. He did not like to be so far back during an attack but decided that it would be difficult to operate a command post from inside the tiny perimeter of the scrawny rifle companies; and anywhere else in the woods would be dangerous. Here they were somewhat out of the way besides being far enough back to be out of most danger from roving enemy patrols. He decided to leave the command post where it was for the night.

The Germans knew the terrain perfectly, of course, so it was not difficult for them to register their mortars on the one good path that led through the center of the rough ground. They knew that the Americans would use it, just as they themselves had, to bring up supplies, to evacuate wounded, run messages, and to perform all the other tasks that fall to a battalion every night. So, naturally, they kept their mortars pounding it intermittently. Weddle, who chose the wrong time to make the trip, dodged shells all the way.

About 30 minutes after Weddle left the CP the 300 radio stopped its frying noises and the S3's voice rasped out, "Red 6 this is Red 3." Then, without waiting for an acknowledgment Weddle gasped out a message, "Sir, Baker is in one helluva shape. They couldn't hold a half squad with broomsticks. Able isn't any better. The German mortars damn near got me three times on the way up. If you come up, watch that damn' path. It's hot as a pistol."

He cut off as suddenly as he had come on the air.

The Major went numb as the import of the fact that Weddle had put that information on the air struck him. It was all right to disregard tight radio security when you were in a fast-moving situation, but here was terribly damaging information that would be good all night. Grabbing the handset he yelled, "Watch your security! Over."

Weddle came back, "My God, I thought I had the telephone!"

The wires were in and it was not unusual for radio and telephone handsets to lie side by side, but Weddle would know the difference in an instant under normal conditions, even though the handsets themselves were much alike. Hoffman said, "Those mortars must have been right close, to rattle ol' Weddle like that. That boy's in a regular funk."

The CO was too angry to be amused. He swung around to the staff. "Now listen, you birds. This is an order. Every man in the command post group will provide himself with an M1 rifle, ammunition, and grenades. Major Hoffman will set up a small perimeter defense in this area where you will all dig and occupy foxholes tonight. At no time will this group retreat one inch without orders from me or, in my absence, from Regiment.

"Able and Baker Companies are in one helluva shape. You heard what Weddle said. If the Krauts hit us tonight, like they always do, they may come right on through. I'm going up to spend the night with Able Company.

"Hoff, give me your M1. You can get another from the salvage pile. I'll also take that bandoleer of ammunition and some of these grenades." He directed the last to Gay and another man from the "I" section.

Silently Hoffman, Gay, and the other man handed over the items named. Hoff hated giving up his pet M1 but he realized that the Old Man thought the outfit was about to be overrun and was going up to the point where he expected the attack to strike. There are times when every leader must lead in person. It looked as though this was one of those times. If a good M1 would be of any help, Hoff was glad to let the Major have one.

"A Company runner!" Johns snapped as he checked the rifle and hung the grenades on his belt.

"Yes, sir."

"Take me up the quickest route to A Company."

"How about the mortars?"

"F . . . the goddam mortars. Get going."

Not a shell fell the whole way, but it gave Johns an eerie feeling to walk slowly through the dusk over that broken ground, with cover all 'round. It reminded him of other long-ago times when he had walked stealthily with Mr. Richard Kleberg through a woods on the King Ranch, hunting deer. A bush rustled nearby, banishing the reveries. Deer don't shoot back, nor throw grenades.

The Able Company command post consisted of two fairly deep foxholes about 20 yards back of the hedgerow that bounded the far side of the woods. The holes were occupied by two of the most redoubtable characters in the company, First Sergeant Alton Shaff and Private "Red" Higley, the radio operator. Shaff, at 42, was probably the oldest man in the battalion by a wide margin. He was undoubtedly the most respected. Furthermore, he was a fighter. Word had gone round that he had killed a paratrooper, the night of the German counter-attack at Dufayel, by choking him to death with his bare hands. Shaff modestly denied this. What really happened, he said, was that when he had crawled back up to his command post in the early dawn he found one lone German desecrating his old foxhole. The sight of this had so enraged him that he had carefully rolled a grenade to a point where it would do the most good, thereby removing the last enemy and avenging the disgrace to the First Sergeant's foxhole.

Higley was completely out of sight in a hole dug under a rough mound of hard earth that stuck up from the surrounding flat ground. He had rigged an extension on the wire that led from radio to handset, enabling him to do his job in relative comfort and safety.

The First Sergeant was glad to see the Major. Lieutenant Todd was down the line a ways seeing that his flank was tied in properly with Baker; he would be back in a minute. Yes, they had had a pretty rough time the last few days, but he reckoned they'd make it.

The doughty old noncom always reckoned they'd make it. He was an incurable and obstinate optimist on whom the entire company leaned heavily. Company commanders came and company commanders went, but First Sergeant Shaff remained, apparently indestructible.

Todd did return in a minute or so. There was no trace of excitement or concern in his voice. He greeted the battalion commander as casually as if he had been host at a dinner at the Officers' Club. "Good evening, sir. How are you tonight?"

"I'm fine, but how are you and Able Company doing this evening?" Major Johns was just as casual. If both officers knew that a counter-attack could hit any moment—one that would almost surely break their line—no one would have ever guessed it by listening to the tone of their voices.

"Oh, we're okay, Major. Had a little trouble late this afternoon, but I hear that wasn't anything compared to what Baker got."

"Yeah. That was a little tough, losing that platoon, and Kordiyak getting hurt. 'Bout how many men've you got now?"

"I don't really know yet, Major, not exactly. Seventy-five or eighty. Maybe a few more or less."

"How do they feel?"

"They're tired, of course, but they're still going." Then he added, "They're a good bunch of men, Major."

"Of course. Now where are your lines?" He knew, approximately, where they had been reported on the map, but he hadn't tried to fit the map to the ground just yet.

"Oh, we tie in with Baker 'bout 75 yards down this hedgerow to the left. And it's not much over that, maybe a hundred or a hundred and twenty-five yards, over to Charlie on the right." He pointed down the hedgerow toward the Isigny-St. Lo highway.

"Where is your front?"

"Right here." It was completely dark by then. Todd turned

a little to one side and jerked his head at the hedgerow that loomed close in the faintly starlit night.

Although the Major was surprised to find the company command post within grenade distance of the most advanced riflemen, he made no comment. He asked, "Any reserves?"

"Yes, a few. I've managed to hold out a small squad. Five men in it. And there's always me and Shaff and Higley." His teeth showed clearly as he grinned in the darkness.

"Good. Keep 'em handy. You may need 'em before this night's over."

"Yeah, Major, I know. And it's about that time, too."

"Have you got a hole somewhere near that you can give me? Thought I might stick around, just so as not to miss any fun if we have callers."

"Well, let's see. Shaff, where can we put the Major for the night? Got a hole already dug around here somewhere?"

Johns broke in, "I can always dig one if you haven't, of course."

"Sure, Lieutenant," answered Shaff, moving nearer. "He can have Berkovitch's. Berk won't be needing it any more and it's a good, deep one." Walking the few steps to the hedgerow he pointed down at an open hole perhaps two feet back of the base. It was a typical front-line foxhole. A man could sleep in it, yet step out of it and be ready to fire over the hedgerow.

Johns and the company commander followed Shaff to the hole, where the Major carefully laid out on its parapet his bandoleer of ammunition and four or five grenades. He stood the M1 rifle against the hedgerow, then thought better of it and slung it over one shoulder. Todd and Shaff both carried theirs that way.

Shaff smiled to himself as he watched the Major handling the stock in trade of the rifleman. The commander handled the rifle as if he knew what he was doing, thought Shaff, but he lacked the easy familiarity with the grenades that comes naturally to the man who carries them constantly for days. The Major carried them only on special occasions.

Todd went on down the hedgerow to visit Charlie Company, leaving Shaff and the battalion commander to peer over the hedgerow into enemy territory. Johns could make out what he took to be the shape of another hedgerow not more than 75 yards to the front. It puzzled him because it did not seem to have any business being out there. It was a lonely chunk of ordinary hedgerow, topped with trees, and about a hundred yards long. But it didn't seem to connect with another hedgerow at either end. He wasn't even sure it was a hedgerow at all, because although the stars were reasonably bright it was impossible to see details at 75 yards. The hedgerow was discernible chiefly by the characteristic pattern of the trees against the sky. He stared at it a long time, then asked, cautiously, "Is that a hedgerow out there, Shaff?"

"Yes, sir."

"Who owns it, us or them?"

Shaff smiled again. "We do, sir. We've got a three-man outpost at the far end and a three-man strongpoint with a BAR* in our line opposite the near end. It comes up to about thirty feet of the line a little further down."

The Major failed to see the near end, where it blended in with trees nearer his hole. He looked at it carefully again. It was an ideal spot for a patrol to work in very close to the line before being discovered. He would have suggested strengthening it with another outpost or two, but he knew Todd was employing his men as best he could, and he did not like to interfere with the manner in which a company commander ran his outfit, unless it was very clear that interference was called for.

Shaff sensed his thoughts. "There's a wide-open field on the other side, sir. The outpost can see or hear anything that comes across it."

"Unh-hunh—good." Johns was somewhat relieved.

They went back to the company command post where they talked quietly for a few minutes.

---

*Automatic rifle.

Interrupted by the characteristic "pop" of a grenade fuse they looked up in time to see two little streams of fire from the fuses of two grenades which arced out over the hedgerow. They had been hurled by the men on either side of the battalion commander's home for the evening. The grenades roared, followed by a half dozen more from all along the hedgerow. Shaff and the Major lay flat and watched.

Johns' stomach did its usual acrobatics, while that cold, empty feeling took over in his midsection. The back of his neck prickled and his hands began to sweat.

Here comes the counterattack, he thought.

Several more grenades blasted flashes into the night, but nothing seemed to be coming back across the hedgerow.

The CO, getting over his initial fright, scuttled to his hole. He had come up to get into this fight and had already sat out the first of it. He grabbed a grenade. With shaking fingers he worked the pin loose. Then he eased up until he could see over the hedgerow, looking for a target. There was no movement on the far side. He waited a full minute, then edged cautiously over to the nearest rifleman. The man was holding a grenade with his right arm half-cocked back, the fingers of his left hand on the pin, ready to pull and throw. His rifle was at his elbow as he stood straight up, looking intently into the darkness.

Johns looked too. He could see a few bushes, but nothing that moved. "What was it?" he asked softly.

"Don't know. Just a noise, like something moving."

The counterattack seemed to be over. It was well past time for it. As the Major bent the pin slightly in the grenade to return it to "safe," he thought that was certainly the puniest effort the Germans had made yet—no mortars and not even a shot fired. Then he wondered if the enemy would try something different this time. Laying the grenade down by his hole he went back to Shaff, who had not moved except to unsling his rifle.

The sergeant said, "The boys are a little jumpy tonight. We haven't had much sleep lately."

Johns decided that was undoubtedly a masterpiece of understatement, especially the part about sleep. His stomach slid slowly back into place as he wiped the palms of his hands on his pants. He was trying to remember when he had slept last. It seemed as if maybe it was the last night they had been in reserve. But that was three nights ago. He knew he must have slept some since then. He couldn't remember, but it served to remind him that he was awfully sleepy at that very moment.

He whispered to Shaff, "If you don't mind, I think I'll try to catch a little nap. Let me know right away if anything happens.

He walked to his hole. Shaff smiled as he answered softly, "Have a good night."

Johns lay down full length on his back and wondered briefly what had happened to the man who had dug the hole that fitted him so nicely. Then he looked up at a constellation of stars he could not recall having seen before. It puzzled him for a while, but he never had been very good at astronomy and he decided seriously that it had probably been there all the time.

The next thing he knew Sergeant Shaff was shaking him. "Better wake up, sir. We're going to hop off in a few minutes."

He grunted and opened his eyes. It was seconds before he remembered where he was, "Unnh—oh, hunh. What's that?"

"Major Hoffman called and said it was to be at 0630 for this morning again. Our first objective is a road junction about 800 yards ahead."

He sat up and looked at his watch. It was exactly 0600. He put his helmet on and stood up straight. Shaff pulled him down quickly. "I wouldn't do that, sir. Its been awful quiet, but you never can tell. This hedgerow ain't very high."

"Oh. Yeah. Thanks." Johns sat down on the side of the foxhole and shook his head sharply. He was having trouble coming awake.

Shaff handed him a K-ration. It was a dinner unit, the one with the cheese. "Sorry, Major, but this is all we have left."

"Never mind. I'll have to go back and see what the score is anyway, and I'll get one back there. You keep it."

He got up again, more cautiously this time. As he started to move toward the rear in the typical hedgerow stoop Shaff said quickly. "Oh, by the way. The enemy that counterattacked us last night is still out there if you want to have a quick look."

The Major, curious at the gleam in the sergeant's eye, took a peek over the hedgerow. Just on the other side lay the biggest hog he had seen since he left Texas.

Foothold in St. Lo / 15

BACK AT HIS OWN command post Major Johns looked at the latest overlay from Regiment. It showed the 2d Battalion to be at least a thousand yards to their left and well to the rear. The 35th Division was still holding its own, exactly 800 yards behind them on the right. We're still all alone out front like clay pigeons, he thought grimly.

While he looked at the overlay and the map, word came back that the companies had hopped off on time. Weddle called Regiment to report that interesting item. They waited, a little tensely, to see what would happen next.

They waited a long time, but there was no sound of combat. It was like that other morning, just after Dufayel. The scouts had moved out cautiously, followed by the companies, equally cautiously. But there was no firing. Within an hour they had walked, slowly, the 800 yards to that first objective.

Weddle called Regiment to report, "Mission accomplished." Major Johns did not let him say there was "no resistance," lest Regiment might gain false hopes that might be very short-lived.

Now Regiment didn't want to believe the report!

"Are you SURE?" yelled Warfield over the telephone.

"Yes, dammit, I'm sure," retorted Weddle. "I'm standing up straight right in the big middle of Objective A. We haven't fired a shot. It's just a hike, so far. But that doesn't mean it'll stay that way."

There was a lot of silence over the phone before the word

came back, "Okay. Go on to Objective B."

They went on to Objective B, a small farm and orchard another 600 or 800 yards ahead. They went very slowly, still looking for a trap and careful not to bypass anything. But the advance was lightning-like compared to the three days it had taken them to make that first thousand yards out of La Luzerne.

Regiment was more ready to believe them this time, probably having received reports from other units by then. There was no doubt that the Germans had withdrawn, possibly all the way into St. Lo.

During the next two hours Regiment gave them five different missions, countermanding three of them. At each order the battalion would start off in a new direction, only to be pulled up short or change direction by a new order. Any other time they would have been thoroughly exasperated over such indecision at higher levels, but today—with nobody shooting at them—they couldn't have cared less. Warfield and Whittington got rather more than the usual amount of ribbing, being assured that they could come down and visit the battalion in perfect safety. But they themselves were too harassed from above to take advantage of the opportunity, or even to get very sore over the irony.

Just before noon a fairly reasonable-sounding order came down. "Seize and hold the main road at RJ at 51.0-64.3." Looking at the map Major Johns found the road junction described by those coordinates to be almost at their elbow and less than a mile from St. Lo. In ten minutes they were sitting on the RJ, with Weddle happily commenting that he had already been able to report "Mission accomplished" more times that day than he had during the whole previous time he had been S3. This was no exaggeration.

Next orders came down by liaison officer. Whenever a regimental "bird dog" of this kind came down to a battalion it meant either one of two things: something really hot or the Colonel wanted some first-hand information about how the outfit was doing. This time, it was the former. The dope was that a special task force was being formed back at Division to go in and take St. Lo. It was being made up of part of the Division Reconnaissance Troop, some tanks, and some tank destroyers. At the time nobody in the battalion thought to wonder where the supporting infantry was coming from. In fact, nothing at all was said about infantry. The force was to be called Task Force Cota.

There were more orders for the battalion, too. They were to cross the highway and go into St. Lo by a trail that was shown on the map as a thin dotted line. The 29th Division boundary had been changed just to let them do that, as the 35th Division was still too far behind. That gave the entire town to the 29th Division. Major Johns' 1st Battalion of the 115th Infantry was the nearest unit to the objective.

It took them an hour to search out the several large buildings of a big farm that was perched on the side of a low hill just where the road and the highway met. That done, A Company started down into the narrow, sunken trail. It was just after 1300.

Todd had his scouts out and flankers extended far enough on both sides of the road to pick up any possible ambush. But the battalion CO hoped to sort of sneak in the back door. He didn't want to cut too wide a swath, so he kept their front as narrow as possible. The scouts, having penetrated 500 yards from the main road, were a scant thousand yards from the edge of the town before the Germans showed their hand again.

A half dozen machine guns opened up simultaneously on the scouts and both flank patrols. In minutes all of Able was engaged. Since the ground to the left looked best, the Major lost no time in sending Baker around that way with orders to drive hard and punch through without fooling around. But Baker didn't get far. The Krauts had plenty of machine guns— at least enough to stretch as far as Baker had tried to go. So the Major kept Charlie in reserve while Todd and the one officer left in Baker Company fed their little squads into the line, each one looking for a hole a little farther to a flank.

It was no go. Every thrust met another German machine gun. The enemy had no mortar or artillery support, and very few rifles, but their machine guns alone were so numerous and so well placed that they covered every inch of the front and were not to be knocked out easily. The two companies silenced a few and took some prisoners, but they couldn't make a hole.

The commander had hardly found a spot for a temporary march command post when the first batch of wounded were carried out. Todd and Dettman led the pack! Both were on litters, Dettman out cold. Todd, who was quite conscious, stopped his bearers long enough to give the Major a clear account of just what had happened. Dettman, as CO of the reserve company, had been with Johns what seemed like only two minutes ago, but had slipped off to go up and have a look at the situation so he'd know what the score was when Charlie was sent in. He had just found Todd and they had climbed a hedgerow together, getting caught in the same burst of fire. The front, so Todd said, was a solid mass of machine gun bullets. Nobody was going anywhere until they could get enough artillery to knock out a few of the guns. Rifle grenades and bazookas were not enough. There was too much open space in the fields to let a patrol get close enough to blast a single one of the closely ranked automatic weapons. Todd was weakening fast, so Major Johns waved the aid men on. As they went the lieutenant raised himself on an elbow and called, "I'll be back, Major, I'll be back."

That really fixed the command situation in the companies! Todd had been the last officer in A Company, all the others having fallen in the last three bitter days. Sergeant Shaff was in command. Dettman had also been the last officer in Charlie. except for one young, inexperienced replacement, Lieutenant Liquori.

Johns looked at his S3. "Leroy, how would you like to have your old command back?"

The big captain grinned broadly. "Well, now, Major this is one hell of a time to be taking over an outfit, but I'll take ol' Baker any time, anywhere. What's more, we'll go!"

He ran off down the sunken road toward the tearing sound

of the German guns.

Orders came from Regiment to send some men to grab another crossroad. The map showed it to be an important point. Johns sent Liquori with a platoon of about eighteen men.

Grimsehl brought in some prisoners whom he took farther to the rear to see if he could pry any useful information out of them.

Mentzer was somewhere in the rear. With him were two new officers, Lieutenants Barnes and Ellis, whom the Major wished were up at the front. Although both were without command experience, they had joined at Bois de Bretel and should have learned something by now. He had been keeping them with the staff, but this would be as good a time as any to make platoon leaders out of them.

Thus only Johns and Hoffman remained in the command post, along with the usual gang of runners and radio operators and wiremen. Lieutenant Leutz and Sergeant Wiskamp trotted up to report that the mortars were ready to shoot. The forward observers were already with the companies. The mortars began coughing from the rear while Leutz was reporting.

The situation stayed that way for about fifteen minutes. Then a runner trotted in, all out of breath. "Sir," he panted, "you are to report to Colonel McDaniel back on the main highway. I'll show you where he is."

"Right." Major Johns turned to Hoffman. "Take over, Hoff. I'll be back as soon as I can but don't commit Charlie unless you're absolutely sure you can break through or somebody else does get through and Charlie can run with the ball."

He trotted after the runner.

In the courtyard of the farmhouse by the main road he found Grimsehl with Gay, questioning a single German soldier. He stopped to see if they had learned anything.

Grimsehl reported. "This man says he's not a German, sir."

"I don't give a damn if he's a Chinaman. Does he know anything?" Johns broke in.

"Claims he doesn't. He was part of a machine gun crew that Able knocked out with a rifle grenade right off the bat, but he says his sergeant just put them there and told them to shoot the Americans."

"Doesn't he know anything about how many others there are?"

Gay growled, disgustedly, "This man's a Russian who volunteered to fight with the Germans. The Russkies are so damned dumb they don't know nothin! But they can kill you just as dead as an SS man can."

Colonel McDaniel was in a neat little summerhouse on the sheltered side of the main road, not far forward of the farmhouse. He was brief.

"Johns," he said, "The task force has already gone up the road and is starting into town. I want you to pull out of whatever you've got hold of and follow them in on the main road. General Cota and your new regimental commander are already up there."

"Yes, sir. We're tangled up with a couple dozen machine guns right now but I can get loose okay. Did you say 'new' regimental commander?"

"Yes. Colonel ————." The Major lost the name in the rumble of a passing tank.

"What happened to Colonel Ordway?" The Major's voice held deep concern.

Colonel McDaniel answered softly, knowing that Johns had a very high regard for Ordway, "He's all right. He's being moved up to corps."

Major Johns did not pause for long. "Right, sir," he answered, "I'll be out of here and into St. Lo in nothing flat."

He ran all the way back to the command post, hoping he had enough men left to cope with whatever Germans were in the town.

Mentzer, who was coming down the trail looking for him, got in the first word, "Sir, I just brought up 29 replacements. The companies need 'em so bad I put 'em right into the line."

For a brief moment the Major was aghast. To slap fresh replacements into the middle of a firefight wasn't exactly the way the book said it ought to be done. They'd probably lose half of them before they could get loose from the machine guns. But there was nothing he could or would do about it just then. The companies *did* need men.

He acknowledged the information with a nod, then snapped, "We're pulling out of here and going into St. Lo down the main road. See that the Doc is informed. If you've moved any ammo up here get it out, because I'm not going to leave many men here to protect you."

At the command post he grabbed the radio and called for Weddle and Shaff to come back. He wouldn't put the new order on the air, and they were so close it would be quicker for them to come back than to send a message.

When they got there he directed each to leave a squad, together with one mortar forward observer and the Cannon Company forward observer, to keep the German machine gunners amused, pull the rest out, and start them down the road. He would meet them at the farmhouse.

He directed Liquori to start Charlie Company moving at once. By the time he reached the farmhouse the men were beginning to file past him, turning right on the main road and heading for the town that had been the XIX Corps objective ever since D-day.

He hadn't long to wait for the others. He told them to follow Liquori, then remembered he had sent Hoffman after the platoon that had gone to the crossroad. But Hoff wasn't long in getting back either. He was annoyed with what had happened to the platoon, but the Major had no time to listen. The platoon was back with the company, and that was all that mattered at the moment.

"Come on, Hoff," he exulted, "let's go to St. Lo."

They swung off down the road with the last of C Company, passing the more slowly moving men on either side of the road. Before they had gone far, the sound of incoming artillery fire came from not far ahead. The crashing roar of the shells told them it was pretty big stuff, at least 150-mm. They were behind a hill at that point, but the map had already shown them that the last 800 yards or so of the road would be wide open to observation and fire from the high ground on the far side of the town.

In a few minutes they reached the open part of the highway. They could see some of the ruins of St. Lo ahead, but after a quick look Johns was more interested in what was going to happen to his men on that road. On the right side was a steep bank, almost vertical. The left side fell abruptly into a stream. There was no place to go except straight ahead.

As the next shell screamed in the men hit the ditches on either side. It burst in the middle of the road. Long seconds later one or two noncoms began to get to their feet and call to the men to get up and get going. Presently the next shell yowled in. The action of the men was repeated. Nobody was hit, but the fire was retarding the advance, and men were beginning to pile up behind. In a minute they would be bunched up so that a shell would wipe out one or more squads.

Johns noted that the German fire was coming in slowly. There couldn't have been more than two or three guns firing and as they were all big ones they didn't fire rapidly. That was a break. But just one of those big shells in the wrong place! As the next one began to howl, the men began to look for deeper spots in the ditches.

Johns yelled, "Keep going, dammit, it's not here yet."

The men kept going for several more seconds, running hard now.

The shell was nearly on the ground before the Major yelled again, "DOWN!"

Although the men hit the ditches, Johns was too excited to remember he was in the middle of the road. He went down on one knee. The shell burst a hundred yards ahead. Again, nobody was hit. The instant it burst, the Major was up, yelling, "LET'S GO!"—running as he yelled.

His men got up and ran too.

Hoffman and Grimsehl, catching the idea, moved farther back down the line of men, to relay commands and call the signals on the shells. When the next one hit, all three officers did the same thing. None got off the road.

Here and there, noncoms, without orders, began to fill in the gaps, staying in the road themselves. By the time the third shell hit, the whole column was working as smoothly as if it had been a parade-ground drill, and they were losing no time.

They kept going. A few men were hit, but not many. Oddly enough not an officer or noncom was knocked out of the middle of the road though each leader only went down on one knee.

One shell burst not 25 yards ahead of the Major, but it hit just around a small bend in the road and he was sheltered by the bank. He ran forward into the smoke and dust, nearly falling over a man who was rolling crazily, half in and half out of the ditch. Johns grabbed him by the arm to help him to his feet, crying, "Come on, boy, let's go."

The man tried to get up but stumbled awkwardly forward. Only then did Johns look down and see that the soldier had no feet. He was trying valiantly to stand on the stumps of his two legs, where his feet had been sliced cleanly off just at the ankles. Johns laid him gently back into the ditch and changed his tone. "Maybe you better take it easy a while, son. You stay here until one of your buddies gets here. There'll be one along in a minute."

The man himself was an aid man, and not another was in sight, but the battalion commander had no time for one man, so after a quick look to see that the stumps were not bleeding profusely, he patted the man on the back, saying, "See you later, bud." Then he ran to catch up to his place in the column.

A little farther down the road, after another burst, he saw another man lying in the ditch, not making any move to get up and go on although he didn't seem to be hurt. Johns stopped, grabbed him by the arm, and yelled again, "Come on, man. Let's get going!"

Looking blankly up at him the soldier pushed a camera forward, saying plaintively, "I'm a cameraman."

This rocked the Major for a moment. "Well, you can't take pictures in that ditch. Get going!"

He had just reached the foot of the hill where the road crossed a little stream before winding up the far hill into the town itself, when a cry came down the line, "Battalion Commander to the head of the column."

With the cry came a jeep. The driver recognized Major Johns and swung his little vehicle in a tight turn, scarcely slowing down long enough for the officer to jump in. They gunned through the column, while the Major stood up waving his souvenir bayonet and yelling "Come on gang! let's go!"

Some of the men cheered and waved and yelled back. Morale was going up with every step.

Just on the edge of the ruined houses the commander caught a brief glimpse of a sight that stayed with him for a long time. Death was nothing very new or unusual, but dead civilians were a novelty. By the side of the road lay a headless, legless torso, clad in a light blue blouse and a darker blue garment that covered the lower portion. It looked as though it had been there for a long time. Johns took time out to wonder if it had been a man or a woman. Not that it made much difference.

They passed another jeep stalled in the middle of the road, the driver slumped forward over the steering wheel. "Machine gun got him," said the Major's driver laconically.

At the top of the hill, on the edge of the main part of town, just past a large cemetery on the left, the driver ducked into an archway that provided good cover. He stopped the jeep and pointed up the street. "The Colonel is up there a little ways. He's looking for you."

Johns jumped down and ran up the street. Standing in the middle was a strange colonel who must be the new regimental commander. Johns trotted up, saluted, gave a parade-ground report, and waited orders. The new colonel shook hands, whereupon they got down to business.

"There are tanks or tank destroyers at nearly every crossroad in the town," he said. "But they haven't got any infantry to cover them and they need men on the ground. I want you to grab four or five men and send them to each one before they get knocked off by enemy infantry."

While the Colonel talked they were moving up the road toward a corner occupied by a tank. Major Johns looked back to see how Charlie Company was coming. As he looked, he saw a little Mexican-American soldier stop at the foot of the hill, kneel down, make a quick sign of the cross, and run ahead. Nearly every man following did the same thing until a little break in the column of men prevented the next man from seeing it, so the inspiration was lost. If he had had time, Johns would have pondered further over this demonstration of the power of suggestion and the solace of faith and prayer.

The Colonel was still talking about protecting the tanks when the first Charlie Company men caught up with them. Without waiting for the battalion commander to do anything, or asking for the company commander, the Colonel grabbed the first four men he saw, saying quickly, "You men. See that tank down there?" He pointed to a tank just visible down a side street. "You go down there and guard it and don't leave it until you are relieved."

The men obediently ran down the side street. The Colonel grabbed each little group of four or five as they came along, repeating the process, sending them in all directions from the crossroads they had reached, without regard for the number of noncoms he might get in one bunch, or if there were any at all. Liquori came up as the second group was sent off, whereupon the Major tried to introduce him to the Colonel, with the idea of giving Liquori the job of sending his own men out. The Colonel paid no heed, but continued enthusiastically with his self-appointed chore of company commander, scattering Charlie Company to the four winds and completely destroying its value as a fighting unit. Meanwhile he made no provision for liaison between groups, central command, or communications.

He also tried to send the 60-mm mortar men out. But they had already had orders where they were to set up; they simply stared at the Colonel in wonder, paying no attention to his orders. He grabbed a sergeant by the arm, telling him to get those men back to take orders. But Sergeant Payton looked the

Colonel straight in the eye and said, "Dammit all, SIR, those men are armed with mortars. What do you want them to do? Shoot from the hip?"

The Colonel, letting Payton go, snared more susceptible men while Johns took Liquori off to one side and said, "Looks as if you won't have any company in about a minute. Now you watch where those men are going, as best you can. When things simmer down a bit, you unscramble the squads and establish a more organized defense."

Liquori nodded. He was so mad he was almost crying because of the cavalier treatment he was getting from a strange colonel who was ruining his company at the start of what promised to be a big action. Major Johns didn't blame him. He wasn't very happy about it either.

Fortunately, the Colonel got enough protection for his tanks just before the last of Charlie Company came by. If there had been one more platoon of tanks to guard, there wouldn't have been any riflemen left to clear the town.

Johns sent word to Weddle and Shaff to hole up their companies along the sides of the road, under cover, then to report to him themselves. Grimsehl came up, waited for an opening, and asked eagerly, "Sir, may I have A Company?"

The idea had not occurred to the Major. Shaff was as capable a company commander as any man in the battalion, but here was an officer who wanted the job. He himself could get along without an S2 if he had to. "All right, George, you can have it. Now stick around."

Artillery fire was still falling along the road below, but none was striking in the town itself. There was a little small-arms fire here and there, but on the whole the situation was remarkably quiet.

The Colonel had moved out into the middle of the crossroads and was looking up a long, straight road that led due east out of town. It sloped gently upward for at least two miles before disappearing from view over a ridge. Men were streaming across the road about a thousand yards from their corner. The tank opened fire on them with its .50-caliber machine gun.

The Colonel screamed, "Stop that firing. That could be the 2d Battalion."

Major Johns watched the men crossing the road. They looked like Germans to him and the 2d Battalion had been so far away the last he'd heard about it that he doubted that they could have got that far so quickly. He ventured an opinion to that effect. The Colonel snapped back, "Maybe they are Germans but we can't take a chance on shooting our own men."

Not having heard the yells to stop firing, the gunner was doing his methodical best to hit fleeting targets at long range. He wasn't doing much good. Not one fell down. The Major watched him for a second then, reluctantly, crawled up on the tank and yelled into the turret, "The Colonel says cease fire."

As he jumped to the ground he heard the familiar snap and crackle of machine gun bullets a few feet overhead. It blended with the last burst from the tank's .50, but there was no mistaking it. Taking the Colonel's elbow he said, "Sir, I don't think you ought to stand out here. We're being fired on."

The Colonel shook his hand off. "Nonsense. That's our fire."

Again came the deadly snapping, nearer this time. Johns thought the next burst would probably be on target. He started to move behind the nearest house, leaving the Colonel where he was, but thought better of it and firmly pulled him around, pointing to the side of a house behind them. Brick dust was still floating in the air. A number of fresh scars showed where the last burst had hit.

The Colonel squinted through his glasses and said, "I see what you mean."

They moved quickly to cover behind a building. The next string of bullets snapped past them, one of them screaming off the side of the tank.

Another shot—a rifle shot this time—slammed loudly against the side of another house behind them. Johns thought he had caught sight of movement in the upper story of an old hotel across the wide corner. He raised the M8 submachine gun he had picked up the night after he had stayed with Shaff, and let off a whole clip of .45 slugs in the general direction of the window. He didn't know if he had really seen anyone or not, but he had an urge to shoot at something, which was as good an excuse as any he was apt to get. Though he never found out if he hit anything, there were no more shots from that direction for a while.

This had taken no more than two minutes. The Colonel was giving orders again. "I want you to clear the town as quickly as you can. There aren't many Germans in it, but there are a few and I want it all clear. Your battalion is the only infantry we have with the task force. As you are the ranking officer you will be in command of all troops in the town."

He looked closely at the Major, who nodded, trying to conceal the elation he felt at knowing that he would have command, on the ground, of what would undoubtedly be an historical action. The Colonel thrust a map at him.

"Here's a large-scale map of the town itself. Now get going."

Major Johns turned to look for Weddle and Grimsehl, his two staff officers turned company commanders. Both were almost at his elbow. He drew them to one side and divided the town between them.

The City is Ours!

IF THEY HAD realized how large the city of St. Lo really was they would probably have been appalled at the idea of clearing it with the handful of men they had, because the two companies together couldn't count a hundred riflemen and the Colonel had already scattered what might have been a reserve. But they didn't know how big the town was and they didn't stop to think about it.

Major Johns drew the boundary down the main road that ran through the town. He gave Weddle half and told Grimsehl to clear the other half all the way down to the river. "I'll stay right here until we find out what the score is," he added.

The command post thus established was far from being centrally located, but the layout would make communications from the rear easier, and the Major didn't realize at the moment that he was located so far from the middle of things. Anyway, it was merely a starting point. Looking at his watch, he checked time with the two officers before sending them off. It was a little before 1600 hours.

Weddle and Grimsehl ran back to their companies. Major Johns returned to where the Colonel stood talking with General Cota. He saluted the General, who said nothing. The Colonel turned to Johns. "I want you to set up an antitank defense for the entire city. Coordinate it carefully and mark it all on the map. We may get an armored counterattack in here any minute. I'm going back to my command post, which will be in

/ 209

that distillery at the foot of the hill. You passed it on the way in here—the big building west of the road."

Johns nodded. He remembered smelling it. As the Colonel and the General left, he took a deep breath of freedom. He was alone in command of what was, to him at least, the biggest and most important city yet seized by the Americans in France. The fact that they hadn't really seized it yet did not occur to him.

Able and Baker began to move out. Grimsehl took a long time to brief his noncoms. But he did a good job, so that when he got through they knew exactly what they were going to do and how. Weddle hadn't needed so long; he was at home with Baker Company.

As the men began to move out, bayonets fixed, rifles ready, and grenades handy, the few Germans left in the town began to come to life. Gunfire and grenades marked the progress of the troops as they set about clearing St. Lo.

The battalion commander was left almost alone. He had dispatched all his staff officers to other jobs, except Hoffman, concerning whose whereabouts he was ignorant. That left Bein, the runners and wiremen, and Barbeaux—a group a lot different from the one which stepped out into the field at the Bois de Bretel, 20-odd strong, that morning a month ago.

Looking around he began to size up the immediate situation. The first thing that struck his eye was a little alley that led into unexplored territory. He had noted, subconsciously, that neither company had sent men down it. What was worse, it was so close to the boundary that there was every chance that no one would be sent down it. It was too close to leave uninvestigated.

A few men from Charlie Company were still around, but Liquori was not in sight. The nearest thing to a noncom was a private first class with the look of a new soldier. Johns wondered if he was one of Mentzer's 29 replacements. However, there was no time to worry about that. He motioned to the PFC and three other men, standing nearby. They came forward, rifles ready.

"See that alley there?" said Johns, pointing. "I want you to take these three men and go down to the end of it, looks like about a hundred yards, where you will set up an outpost. Lieutenant Liquori will come around later to see how you're doing."

The PFC squinted down the alley, nodded a trifle uncertainly, and started toward it. The others followed, but the Major was too preoccupied to note that there had been no briefing, and no assignment of positions or duties. They just trooped off down the alley together, like a bunch of men going to the post exchange.

Two minutes after they left, the sound of German machine gun fire came from the direction of the narrow passageway. Johns turned to look. Out of the alley pelted the four men, straight toward him. The private first class panted, "Sir, there's a machine gun down there!"

The battalion commander didn't know whether to be amused or angry. There was no telling what new men were apt to do if they didn't have the leadership of an experienced or well-trained noncom or officer. He decided to be gentle. "Yes, I heard it. Now, tell you what you do. You take these three men again, assign one to a place where he can shoot at the gun, or where you think it is, then take the other two and see if you can't come around behind it and get it for me."

The PFC took that in, nodded somewhat less uncertainly, motioned to the men to follow him, and started purposefully back down the alley. In not more than five minutes there came in rapid succession the sounds of the machine gun, a few rifle shots, two grenades, and running feet. Johns had moved across the street, looking for the best place for a temporary command post. He turned toward the mouth of the alley wondering what would come out this time.

Two Germans showed first, running toward him at full speed. Before the Major could bring his submachine gun up he saw the PFC and one other man prodding the Germans from behind with bayonets. They spotted him and poked the prisoners in his direction. They stopped in front of him before he noticed the MG-34 the PFC was dragging behind him.

The man dropped the machine gun in front of him saying, "Here's the gun you wanted, Major, but this is all that's left of the crew." He was a bit hesitant as he added, "We had to kill two of 'em, sir."

Major Johns gulped, nodded, and motioned to Gay to come get the prisoners. The private first class and his helpers jogged back toward their new outpost. The Major looked after them wondering just what sort of training or indoctrination they must have had, first to run away from an enemy without trying to fight back and then to apologize for having killed two! He looked down at the battered German machine gun, kicked it idly, and reminded himself to be more careful in issuing orders to new men. They were apt to take things a bit on the literal side. He was sure that the PFC had actually thought that the CO himself had a personal desire for the machine gun they had knocked out, and that he would have gone to any ends to retrieve the gun itself in order to bring it back, just because the Major had added that "for me" when he had ordered them to "get" the gun.

These were the first of a great many prisoners taken that day. The German defense, in no way coordinated inside the city, consisted of isolated little groups here and there. Some fought a little before giving up, while many didn't even go through the motions, coming out willingly, hands overhead, at the first shot or grenade into a house.

Lieutenant Leutz ran by the CO's corner looking for an observation post for his mortar observers. It was only seconds before he was back, herding four prisoners with his .45. He grinned and waved as he handed the prisoners to an "I" section man, then ran off again. In ten more minutes he was back with four more. This time he called, "Kee-rist, Major they're everywhere. I find 'em in every good OP I go into."

The German artillery was still pounding the road to the rear. Not a round had fallen inside the city. It was apparent that the German command did not yet know that they had lost St. Lo.

A stranger would have thought the battalion was on a picnic.

Everything was going their way, and it's easy to have fun when you're winning. The men laughed and shouted at one another, fear and fatigue forgotten in the thrill of taking the Corps objective. There were only a few real fights in the mop-up. After the easy going, when some enemy group did elect to hold out, the men, indignant at such surly lack of cooperation, usually went in and finished things quickly.

Major Johns himself had never felt better. He was elated past any experience in his life. Everything was lovely and everybody was doing fine. It was like being ringmaster for all six rings at once in the biggest show on earth.

While he was directing the private first class to take the machine gun and watching Leutz bring in his prisoners, a thousand other events were going on. The commander of the tank that guarded what was still the command post corner asked for permission to shoot down what looked like an observation tower near the crest of the hill on the road to the east. It must have offered a wonderful view, which made the tanker think maybe it was the place from which the fire on the road to the rear was being adjusted. Johns told him to blast away.

After fiddling with his controls briefly the tank gunner cut loose with the 75-mm cannon. Nothing happened to the tower. He fired again. No result. He tried again and again, but he couldn't hit it. After all, at 1800 yards a spidery tower with a little box on top makes a small target.

A tank destroyer captain, appearing from nowhere, watched the firing. He waited as long as he could stand it, then asked Major Johns, "Let me have a crack at it, please sir."

"Sure, go ahead."

The tanker was miffed, but he'd had his chance. He pulled back, after which the tank destroyer waddled into place. The tank destroyer gunner was cranking his longer gun around to bear on the tower when Johns remembered he had an antitank defense plan to get together for the new Colonel.

He walked into the house on the right corner. The front room was a shambles of broken plaster and wrecked furniture. On a scarred table he saw a little metal figure. He picked it up and

found it to be a toy mouse, made of some dull grey metal with
a plain bolt and nut on the bottom, as if it were intended to
be mounted on something, such as a radiator cap. The mouse's
tail was broken and there were two small holes in his body.
Examining it carefully he decided it was about as beat up as
the battalion. He tossed it to Barbeaux. "Put that in my musette
bag. We'll keep it as a souvenir of the first American command
post set up in St. Lo."

Barbeaux glanced indifferently at the battered rodent, managed a weak smile, and stuffed the toy into the musette bag.
His normally sorrowful mien thus far had successfully with-
stood the enthusiasm and elation that had seized the rest of the
outfit. His attitude was that of one who was by no means convinced that St. Lo was such a wonderful place in which to be.
As a health resort it seemed to be lacking in certain particulars.

Major Johns moved through a narrow doorway into a small
room on the right, a few steps away from the corner room itself. This room was not quite so messy; besides, it contained a
larger table. He looked around briefly, then called to Barbeaux,
"We'll make this the CP for awhile. See what you can do about
straightening it up a little."

He examined a chair for booby traps, swept the table more
or less clean with his arm, spread the map, and sat down to
study the town plan. He was hardly settled when a terrific concussion shook the room. Plaster rained from the ceiling. Dust
jumped into the air from floor, sills, and furniture. Barbeaux
slid under the table in one quick motion while the Major leaped
up and started for the door. He thought the house had been hit,
but when he reached the opening he could see the muzzle of
the TD just outside, smoke curling up from it. The gunner
had just had his first try at the tower. The muzzle blast, so
close, was as powerful as a shell burst.

He went back to the table, shook the plaster from the map,
and resumed his study. When the gun blasted again he found
himself halfway to his feet before he realized that he knew perfectly well what it was. Plaster again showered him and the map.
Barbeaux still seemed to like it under the table.

Patiently the Major shook the map free of plaster and bent over it. Later he couldn't understand why he hadn't simply taken the map to another house, but at that moment he was too engrossed in the antitank plan to have any other ideas. People do funny things sometimes.

The tank destroyer fired again, this time getting a reaction from the enemy. The plaster had hardly stopped bouncing on the map when a shattering sound blasted chunks of brick through the door to the corner room. At the same instant, the motor of the tank destroyer roared and its tracks scraped on the stone pavement as it pulled back from the corner.

The tank destroyer captain stuck his head in the window at Major Johns' elbow and yelled, "88 at the foot of the tower. He's shooting at us."

Johns got up, moved to the doorway, and looked up at the front of the house. There was a new hole in the left wall, toward the street, perhaps a foot and a half in diameter and ten or twelve feet from the ground. The sound he had just heard was an 88 armor-piercing round going through the walls of the next room.

He went back and sat down again. After all, there was another brick building across the street between his room and the 88.

The tank destroyer moved forward, the gunner snapped off another shot at the base of the tower, and the motor roared as the gun pulled back. Another solid shot smashed by the front of the tank destroyer, ricocheting off the far wall of the building.

Johns was beginning to lose interest in the antitank plan. He had never seen a duel between a tank destroyer and an 88, so he stood in the window to watch as the gun moved up to have another shot. It wasn't quick enough that time. The blast of its gun and the metallic, wrenching, squealing impact of an 88 round hitting the armored vehicle came almost simultaneously.

The tank destroyer was able to pull back from the corner, but that was the end of the duel. Oil flowed from the engine, making a pool in the street just outside the Major's window. The hit was mortal to the vehicle but neither the gun nor any of the crew had been hurt. Unfortunately, there were no targets it could shoot at from where it crouched now, unless the situation changed and it was needed for very close-in support.

That marked the end of the picnic. Some smart character with the 88 undoubtedly began to pass the word around, so that the local enemy high command finally heard about it— the Germans didn't own St. Lo any more. They began to take action accordingly. Their artillery was reinforced by a number of new guns, together with any number of mortars. Their fire moved up the road, passed the cemetery on the edge of town, and centered on the new command post area at the crossroad.

The artillery shells screamed in and burst while the mortar shells flew silently through the air. But their hollow, flat explosions were sharpened by the confining walls of the buildings. It was lucky that the artillery projectiles arrived a few seconds ahead of the mortars, for they thus warned the men who were in the open. Even so there were several men hit in the first concentration that worked over the corner. From then on it was a very dangerous place.

After hitting the corner, the fire moved back to the trees along the cemetery. The Germans, who knew all about the effectiveness of tree bursts, used them deliberately every chance they got.

This left the command post corner at least temporarily free, so the battalion commander went out to look for the tank destroyer captain he had seen earlier. The antitank plan was getting to be a nuisance and it had just occurred to him that he was in command of all the troops in the town. So why shouldn't he give the job of making the plan to a man whose regular work was to kill tanks?

He started across the street as another volley of artillery burst in the trees a hundred yards down the road. Looking in that direction he saw Weddle running out of the smoke and dust, holding his left arm just below the shoulder, his eyes wide and wild.

When he saw the Major, Weddle yelled, still running, "Major, Major! The bastards done blowed my arm plumb off!"

He ducked into the command post with Sergeant Brooks, his Operations Sergeant, hard on his heels. Johns followed. He had seen Weddle's right arm quite clearly, still firmly attached to his body. So far as he could see there hadn't even been any blood on it. Although this was twice in two days that Weddle had been shaken up, he didn't think there was anything very much wrong with him that a few minutes' rest couldn't cure. But he changed his mind as soon as he got into the little command post room where the S3 was sitting, gasping for breath.

Brooks, sobbing, was carefully cutting away the officer's field jacket and shirt, exposing a wide, deep gash just below the shoulder. Johns' stomach turned over quickly when he saw the wound. It was no longer funny. The bone was shattered, with sharp, splintered ends sticking through the bloody, pulpy mass of torn flesh. Weddle was damned near right, they had almost "blowed his arm plumb off."

The S3 moaned, his eyes closed, as he leaned back to let Brooks do what he could with the nasty wound. But he pulled himself together in a moment or two and opened his eyes to look at the CO.

"I was just coming back to tell you," he ground out between clenched teeth, "that we have our side of town all clear, with men out on the edge, when the artillery caught me in the middle of the street." He flinched, and his face twisted in pain when the aid man who had taken over from Brooks inadvertently twisted his arm as he sprinkled sulfa powder into the wound.

Then he went on, "Chadwick is back. Didn't know it until I saw him. Came just before we pulled out of the little road back up the hill. You can put him in command. He's good." He was gasping the words out now, "Major, can you get me out of here? I don't want to lose this arm . . ."

"Sure, boy, we'll get you out. Just try to relax now. Don't worry about it. Take it easy and we'll have you back where they can fix it up in no time."

Colonel McDaniel, coming into the room just then, sized up the situation at a glance and said to Weddle, "My jeep is outside. You can go back with me in a minute."

The aid man gave Weddle a shot of morphine from a syrette and stuck the needle of the little tube into his collar so they would know in the rear that he had had a "shot."

McDaniel turned to Major Johns, "How's everything else?"

"Weddle finished clearing his half of the town just before he got hit. I expect Grimsehl to report that A Company has cleaned up the rest of it any minute now."

"Good. I brought up a Division flag. Your Sergeant Davis and PFC Bein just hung it on the corner. We got movies of it."

He turned to Weddle, "Come on, Captain, I'll take you back now."

Weddle leaned heavily on Brooks, who was still sobbing from the shock of seeing his captain so badly wounded. Weddle and Brooks had been together a long time and the Major knew the sergeant would be no good around the command post for a while, so he motioned to him to go along and look after the wounded S3.

Colonel Mac's jeep was crowded with wounded men as he started the dash back down the hill and through the artillery fire again. That first mile of road to the rear provided an exciting trip for anyone who traveled it that day.

Johns turned back to the antitank plan. He still hadn't found the tank destroyer captain. He had just brought the map into focus again when a voice called in the window at his elbow, "Major?"

He looked up to see a strange artilleryman, a first lieutenant. "Yes?"

"I've just come down to relieve Lieutenant Martin. He's going back to be Battalion S3."

"All right. Have you got all your observers set up okay?"

"Yes, sir. I've been around to all the OP's and I can tell you we've really got some good ones. Even if they did shoot one of the cathedral spires down while I was off looking for somebody to put in it."

The lieutenant was very cheerful about the whole thing as he sat down in the window and leaned back comfortably against the bricks.

"Fine." The Major had missed Martin earlier, but hadn't had time to worry about him. He knew that Martin would do his job. He wondered what this new man's name was, but didn't bother to ask. He wanted to get that AT plan out of the way.

He managed to get a start this time. He had made several little diamond-shaped marks, indicating the positions of tanks, before he was interrupted again. This time a bullet cracked like a bull whip against the side of the building a couple of feet over the new liaison officer's head. The lieutenant leaned forward and looked diagonally across the street in the direction from which the bullet had come.

"You know," he said casually, "I think somebody is shooting at me."

"Hmmph," said the Major, making another diamond. He decided that he would have to dig up a bazooka team to put at another corner.

He heard footsteps outside and the lieutenant's voice as he said, "I wouldn't stand there if I were you, soldier. I believe a sniper has this place spotted."

The footsteps retreated and the lieutenant leaned back against the window jamb again, apparently enjoying the warm sunlight.

The Major made another diamond and wondered where he was going to get all the bazooka teams it was beginning to look as if he'd need.

There was a sharp "chunk" at the window sill. The lieutenant grunted, hopped off and started back down the street, holding his left leg at the thigh and limping. Major Johns, completely amazed, leaned out of the window, to hear the lieutenant say, to no one in particular, "Dammit, I KNEW that sniper had me zero'd."

Johns looked across the street, realized suddenly what he was looking for and pulled his head back hastily. Some people, he decided, were just plain nuts. He never could figure out why that lieutenant had stayed there and let himself be shot, or why he himself had not dragged the man under cover after the first bullet smacked into the bricks. That damned antitank plan must have been responsible.

He found his place on the map, but hadn't made another mark when the sound of incoming artillery, big stuff, made him raise his head. It was coming close. In a few seconds his little world jumped and rocked as the shells crashed into the street at the corner, not 20 yards from where he sat. One hit the corner of the house where Sergeant Davis had put up the flag. Bricks flew. The flag crumpled into the street. Another hit just short of the outside wall of the command post house, blowing in the window and a few bricks from the sill. Plaster and dust rained down on him. A few brick chunks rattled around his room—at least he supposed they were brick chunks.

He said a four-letter word again as he shook the plaster off the map and looked under the table for his pencil. Barbeaux handed it to him.

Hoffman's voice called in at the window, "Hey, Major, you better get the hell out of here. They're gonna knock this whole corner down. We've got you another place all fixed up across the street anyway. I've been looking all over for you."

"Good. This place has too much plaster on the ceiling anyway." He folded the map, walked out the door and diagonally across the street to what had been a small cafe. Hoff snared Barbeaux and put him to work cleaning up the back room. There were still a number of good tables and chairs in the place, so in a few minutes it became a very presentable command post.

Grimsehl came in shortly, his face beaming with the success of his first mission as a company commander. "Gee, sir. We had one rip-snortin' good time—grenades, bayonets, 'n everything. Got lots of prisoners. But we're spread awful thin along the edge of town. No real line at all, just a series of mutually supporting strongpoints with all the gaps covered by fire. This place is too big to cover right and there's a lot of it across the river that's crawling with Germans. We see 'em all the time, moving around out in the open. The men are having a wonderful time, sniping at 'em."

The CO looked at his watch. It was only 1730. He could hardly believe that they had gotten into town and cleared it in a little over an hour and a half. He watched the second hand to see if it was running, then checked with Hoffman to be sure. He reflected briefly that if the Krauts had wanted to defend the place the way the Russians had hung onto some of their cities, it would have taken a division or two to get it, not one tired, half-strength, beat-up battalion.

He went over to where Bein had the 300, which he used to call the rear command post, still back at the farmhouse, instructing Captain Mentzer to report to regiment that the city of St. Lo had been cleared and was now secure as of 1730 hours, 18 July 1944.

Lively Graveyard /17

MAJOR JOHNS had not found the tank destroyer captain. He knew now that he would never get the antitank plan done by himself. What Grimsehl had said meant that he would have to move part of Baker Company from the north and east sides of the town over to the south side. The 2d Battalion was supposed to move into the race track on the extreme east edge of town but the 1st Battalion was still responsible for all the rest of it. He started out the door again, but, changing his mind, turned back to tell Grimsehl something.

He had just opened his mouth to speak, when the window and door exploded inward. The room reverberated and shook from magnified repeated explosions of terrible power. Plaster and dust mingled with smoke that billowed through the open door, filling the room with the sharp, acrid smell of high explosive. Three mortar shells had hit in the middle of the street just outside the command post.

The Major staggered against Grimsehl, who caught him by the arm. He shook his head and brushed bits of plaster and glass from his shoulder. Luckily, the window had already been broken, so there remained only a few small fragments of glass in the corners of the mullions. Parts of the frame fell to the floor.

Hoffman had been standing in the rear of the room, his back to the door, when the shells hit. As the dust and smoke cleared enough for the Major to see him, Hoffman was in the act of turning and sinking into the nearest chair. His face was already grey and his legs were trembling visibly. He gasped, "Oh God, they got me!"

"Where're you hit, Hoff?" Grimsehl and Johns called together, rushing toward him.

"In my leg. Here!" Hoffman put his hand on the back of his left thigh.

They looked, but could see no sign of a wound. Then they found two small tears in the olive drab trousers. The Major took out his knife to rip them down so they could get at the injury. As he did so, he suppressed a smile as he thought of Hoff's melodramatic, "Oh God, they got me" over the two little bluish holes they found and bandaged.

Hoffman, fainting from shock, rolled forward out of the chair. They caught and laid him on the floor on the Major's field coat which Barbeaux, with remarkable presence of mind, had brought from the back room.

In a few minutes the Exec came to, had a drink of water to wash down the handful of sulfa pills which all wounded got immediately, and was waiting patiently to be taken to the rear so some medic could dig out the shell fragments. He was a little sheepish about having passed out with such a small wound, but these episodes are beyond the control of the individual. In fairness to the well-liked Hoff the reader should know that the medics later cut some 16 pieces of steel out of his legs and back.

The CO went to the door and looked out into the street. His eyes widened in consternation. The place was a shambles. Dead and wounded were scattered from the side of the knocked-out tank destroyer clear back past the entrance to the cafe. An aid man was tending one of the wounded. Another injured soldier was already sitting up against the wall of the first command post smoking a cigarette, his legs in fresh bandages. The Major didn't stop for a count just then, but learned later that the three mortar rounds had killed three and wounded seven men. They had been bunched around his headquarters in spite of innumerable orders to stay away from a command post anywhere. Every man had been hit.

He went out to help. He worked his way past the tank destroyer, giving a hand here and there. Then he remembered that he was still looking for the tank destroyer captain. He hoped maybe there would be someone in the vehicle who could tell him where he might be found. There was no one in it, but as he walked around the hull, there was the captain. He was lying peacefully on his back, dead.

With a gasp Johns knelt down to look for signs of life. He took the limp hand to feel for a pulse. There was none. As he laid the arm down, very gently, he noted a massive gold ring which he examined carefully. He could read "Virginia Military Institute, 1940." Another gallant schoolmate whose name would be added to the long roll of honor. Captain Sydney A. Vincent, Tank Destroyers, would not have to worry about the antitank plan for St. Lo.

The Major went back to the cafe as soon as the wounded had been cleared out. For the moment, the dead were left where they had fallen.

Bein was waiting for him to give him a message, but pointed instead to his throat. "You're hit, Major! Are you hurt?"

Johns looked blank. "Hell no, I'm not hurt. I'm not even hit. What's the matter with you anyway?"

"But you are, sir. There's blood running down your neck." Bein came close and looked at his commander's throat, while the Major gingerly put his hand to his Adam's apple then looked at the fresh blood on his fingers.

He could feel that it was only a scratch, but the cut bled profusely. The top of his shirt front was already stiff and sticky with blood. An aid man stuck his head in the door about that time and Bein yelled at him to come in and fix up the Major. The man laughed when he saw the tiny nick. He cleaned it up, dusted sulfa powder on it, slapped a band-aid over it, made an entry in a notebook, and went out again saying, "Okay, Major, you've as good as got the Purple Heart."

"Nuts," said Johns as Lieutenant Barnes came in with a message he had got somehow from Chadwick. It read, "Have 37 men left on line. Lieutenant Blank* useless. Can you give

---

*A pseudonym.—Editor.

me a hand?"

The Major read the message and said to Bein, "Call him and tell him I'll do the best I can, but am making no promises."

Barnes broke in. "Liquori was also hit a while ago. Let me take what's left of C Company and go up there."

The Major had intended keeping Barnes and Ellis to replace his defunct staff, but if Liquori was out and Chadwick's company was in such bad shape, Barnes could do more good there. "All right," he answered, "you go out and round up all of Charlie that isn't guarding tanks, and any strays you can find. Let me know how many you get. Then move them up to a position as near in between Chadwick and Grimsehl as you can find. The threat is all going to come from that high ground to the south and southwest. If you get a good spot in the middle you can move to either flank and help both. Don't forget, you're the only reserve I have, so don't go jumping all over the place without orders from me—you're still directly under my command. I want you to support by fire any time you get a chance, but don't move unless I tell you to. Savvy?"

Barnes did. Beaming, he galloped out of the command post on a manhunt.

As soon as he left, another man stepped up to the battalion commander. It was the photographer who had been in the ditch on the way into town. He asked quietly, "Sir, may I talk with you for a moment?"

"Sure, what's on your mind?"

The man looked all around, then drew as close as he could, practically whispering in the commander's ear. "Sir, I took pictures of Sergeant Davis and PFC Bein when they put up the Division flag, but I just discovered that I didn't have any film in the camera." He paused and looked down, embarrassed. "I guess I was a little excited at the time. Do you suppose you could get one of your men to come out and put it up again so I can get some more pictures? It got shot down a little while ago anyway, you know."

Major Johns laughed, but was sympathetic. "Sure," he said, "just a minute."

He looked around. Bein was the first man he saw. "Come on, Bein, you're going to hang the flag again."

"Sir?"

For answer, the Major went out the door, the photographer following.

The house on the left corner had been shot up pretty badly. It had several more holes in it and the 88 on the hill was still firing into it occasionally, apparently in the blind hope of getting to something on the other side. Johns chose the old command post as a more appropriate and less dangerous spot. The photographer gave the flag to Bein then backed off to get his shot. Bein climbed up a drainpipe on the side of the doorway and wedged the flag over the door while the cameraman braced himself characteristically and "shot" the action.

Bein jumped down self-consciously, as the photographer said to Johns, "Now—how about you saluting it?"

The Major stiffened to attention, threw a snappy salute to the flag, and faced about to return to the command post. There was no point in standing around in that murderous street any longer than necessary.

He went back to the antitank plan again. As he did so, Lieutenant Ellis came in to ask about an overlay for Regiment. The Major pushed the map away, saying, "The hell with it. Regiment will just have to take my word for it that we've done all we can to keep this place antiseptic. I don't see what I could do if I found something wrong anyway."

Ellis was looking puzzled and there was no one else in the room who could have any idea what the Major was talking about. Johns pushed the map still farther away and poked a finger into Ellis' chest. "You are now Red 2, 3, and 5. In case you don't know it, Weddle and Hoffman are both wounded, Grimsehl has a company, and Barnes is in command of our reserve. Your first job is to get that overlay fixed. You don't have an Operations Sergeant because Brooks folded up and I sent him back with Weddle. Now get going."

Ellis' eyes crinkled at the edges in a pleased grin. His heavy red-brown mustache bristled as he answered in his typical

Louisiana drawl, "Yes suh. Ah'll jus' do that right away."

The day was passing into history; but its passage was never quiet.

Barnes got into position with the 20-odd men he had somehow managed to scrape together. Mentzer was able to get him another radio so the commander of the reserve had direct communication with Battalion and with the two companies as well. The Major ordered Chadwick to move a few of his men as soon as he heard that 2d Battalion had finally got into the race track. Grimsehl felt better with Barnes near his rear. But they all knew that the town was held with the thinnest shell of a line along the outer edge, supported by a few tanks, tank destroyers, and part of the 29th Reconnaissance Troop. Most of the tanks and tank destroyers were placed to protect possible avenues of approach, hence could not fire at anything else although they would of course be invaluable in the event any sort of armored attack tried to come in over a road.

The town was being held by the artillery, really, as the infantrymen were little more than guards for the observation posts. Wire was laid repeatedly to the companies and to the rear, but it was seldom in for long, although the wiremen were out constantly, repairing breaks. The radios carried most of the communications load. Unfortunately there weren't enough of them to insure that each little strongpoint was a secure artillery and mortar observation post, at least not to the extent that they were after the wire was in.

The result was that the few officers and noncoms would call for artillery whenever they found a target and had communications. This occurred often, as the Germans tried to form up in the woods and ravines south and southwest of the town. If the wire was out and infantrymen had no other contact with the nearest forward observer they would send for him by runner and have him and his radio brought to their own observation post so that the forward observer could see and fire upon their targets. That kept the forward observers moving around but it got the job done.

The enemy fire did not slack off with the end of the day. It pounded the companies, moved in to its favorite spot around the command post, then ranged up and down the road to the rear before going back to work over the companies again. Mortar shells arrowed in silently to burst here and there throughout the town. No man could feel safe unless he was covered on all four sides and on top.

Mentzer moved the rear command post into town as soon as it was dark, but it was the next day before Major Johns knew where it had been placed.

The forward command post was in a chaotic state. Ellis was out at the companies, getting precise dope for the overlay, which left the Major to carry the entire load of all the thousand and one reports, orders, and requests that came in. In addition to the usual messages from the companies, he was now harassed by the tankers, the tank destroyers, and an occasional stray cavalryman from the recon outfit. They all wanted something— ammunition, gas, batteries for radios, litters, food, water—and Battalion was the nearest place to ask for it. They never got anything except a reference to Regiment. The Major was willing but unable to help. Besides, he was far too concerned with the problem of holding the town, from the standpoint of pure combat, to worry about supplies.

He didn't mind handling all these matters except for one thing. It kept him pinned tight in the command post. He started out the door a hundred times to visit the companies, but he never saw a single position. Each time he started to depart, a message would come over the radio, a runner would come in, or Regiment would call for some information. After St. Lo the Major always appreciated his staff much more than he ever had before.

During the night, infantry patrols probed the front, which they found well occupied by the enemy. Grimsehl tried to get across the river, but discovered that this was not feasible. Contact was maintained with the 2d Battalion in the race track, which was a bare 500 yards from the 1st Battalion command post. Also, something was said once about a unit of the 35th Division's being just outside the city on the north. But as far as the men of the 1st Battalion were concerned, those other units could as well have been on the moon. It was still a personal war between them and the Germans with no help except what they gave themselves and what they got, thank God, from the artillery. They were still clay pigeons.

The Major stayed awake to take reports as long as he could. It was around three in the morning before the nervous and physical strain of the last four days got the best of him. Things had slowed down a little—even the enemy wasn't throwing in quite so much as they had been. Finally he frankly gave up, to stretch out on the hard wood floor with a single blanket under him. In a moment he was sound asleep. The mortar round that fell on the roof of the building just behind the cafe failed to disturb him an iota although the concussion rained plaster all over him.

It was after dawn when he woke. The first person he saw was a strange major, sitting at the table. He blinked a few times, sat up and rubbed his eyes, then got to his feet, still looking at the stranger.

Getting to his feet the newcomer put out his hand. "I'm Major Weller, sir, Malcolm Weller."

Johns introduced himself, staring at the visitor inquiringly.

Weller explained, "I got in here late yesterday evening, trying to get through to the 175th Infantry. They're a couple of miles east of town. But I found out I couldn't get out that road so I stuck around. I ran into your companies, where I met both Chadwick and Grimsehl. Tried to give 'em a hand once or twice."

Major Johns peered at Weller more closely. He looked like a prizefighter or a wrestler. His nose was pushed in a bit, his face was square, and his jaw firm while giving a general impression of amiability. He had the broad but rounded shoulders of an athlete who looked as if he could be right tough if he wanted to be. Johns decided he liked the visitor.

"What were you going to do when you joined the 175th?" he asked.

"I was supposed to be the new Exec of the 2d Battalion. I used to be with the 116th, but they needed a new man over in the 175th, so they sent me."

"Hell, I need a new Exec as bad or worse than they do; why don't you stay here with us for a while?"

"Looks like I might have to. It suits me, anyway."

"Good. Consider yourself Lagoon Red 5 until somebody tells us different."

They shook hands again.

The commander checked, to find that nothing serious had happened while he slept. Having devoured a K-ration, he started out the door to visit the companies. The phone, in at the moment, rang. The operator called after him, "Major, Regiment wants to talk to you."

It was the Colonel. Johns was to come back and see him right away. Somebody reported that the Major's jeep was in town, so a runner went out to look for Pete, the driver.

The Major found the regimental commander in the depths of a huge old building, next to an enormous vat. The Regimental Commander didn't want anything in particular, just a resumè of the situation in general. Johns gave him the whole story, winding up with a request for a few men to hold in the rear as a reserve just in case something should push through the companies. The Colonel very cheerfully stated that there were no reserves. Hence the 1st Battalion would have to hang on with what it had. There was no change in orders—just hold what they had.

Major Johns felt it necessary to say, quite truthfully, "Okay, sir, but I'd be remiss in my duty if I didn't tell you that a determined, full-size platoon could come through us any time they wanted to badly enough, if we didn't find it with artillery first."

The Colonel replied that it would, therefore, be a good idea to fire on every possible attack with the artillery before it could get started. Johns promised that if it were humanly possible it would be done. He had already explained the artillery setup and asked for more radios.

That ended the interview. The Major started back for the town, still anxious to get out to see his men. At the entrance to the Regimental CP he ran squarely into an old friend from the American Intelligence Service, Lieutenant Colonel Tom Crystal, Corps Assistant G2.

Tom was his usual ebullient self, as full of ideas as ever. When the congratulations and backslapping were disposed of, the current idea was for Johns to make a recording for the British Broadcasting Company people,* who had an instrument truck outside at the moment. Would he mind cutting a record?

"No, I won't mind. There's nothing shy or bashful about me. What do you want me to say?"

"Just tell 'em what your outfit has been doing and how you got into St. Lo. But be careful not to say anything about your condition or strength because the record will go on the air in a couple of days and it might be of some use to the German intelligence people."

They went out to meet the BBC sound man. He was a pleasant, cheerful individual, who enthusiastically approved the Major's off-the-cuff dry run. The technicians set the machine to turning, whereupon the Major spoke his little piece into a hand microphone. He meant to say something funny about fire and maneuver, about how the Krauts were providing all the fire while his men were providing all the maneuver. But at the moment the punch line was supposed to come out the Germans threw a very high air burst over the command post, which caused Johns to look up just long enough to lose his train of thought.

When they played the record back he thought it sounded corny as hell. But as the air burst registered very clearly, he thought it would add a note of authority to the recording if they would explain, when they played it over the air, that the

---

* Allied units in Normandy received newscasts and entertainment from this source.

flat little explosion was not the sound man dropping a C-ration on an empty water can.

The BBC man promised to cable the Major's parents before the record was played over NBC. It seemed it was to go to the States as well as to Britain. Tom Crystal thought it was all just marvelous. He promised to come up and visit Johns just as soon as he could—he was too tied up at the moment to come along. Johns listened to the faraway crunch of three mortar rounds, decided they had hit not far from his command post, and grinned at Crystal. Then he mounted Pete's jeep and drove off back to St. Lo, leaving the staff officer to his urgent business at Regiment.

Shortly after Major Johns returned to his command post both A and P ammunition trucks were hit by artillery fire. They exploded, killing or wounding several Ammunition and Pioneer Platoon men. While the Major was out looking at the wreckage another man was killed and three more wounded outside the command post.

He decided that the command post had to move. That street was just too hot. He sent Mentzer word to find him another place. And to do it fast.

Half an hour later the S1 came up to lead him back to his new home in St. Lo, which turned out to be an imposing mausoleum in the cemetery! On the facade were two words Johns would always remember, "Famille Blanchet." He balked at the idea of moving in with the Blanchets; but when he looked inside he decided it was the best command post he would ever have.

The walls were of polished marble blocks 18 inches thick, with a heavy door set back under a small but equally solid portico. There were no windows to be blown in, so that only a direct hit on the front steps by something big would have any chance of hurting anyone inside. It would take a bomb to damage the building itself.

Inside, on the ground floor, was a small chapel. Though the room was only about 10 feet by 15 feet in size, it would hold everyone who had legitimate business there. Furthermore, there was plenty of room outside for the runners to dig foxholes so there would no longer be any excuse for bunching up. Under the chapel was a crypt, reached by a narrow flight of stairs leading down from one side.

This vault was largely occupied by an enormous stone sarcophagus. The thing sloped upward toward the entrance, the high end having a flat surface on top which was at an awkward height but would do better than nothing for maps. A small stone tablelike affair was set into the wall opposite that end, with barely room for one straight chair. The crypt was cramped, but it would do.

Space around the sarcophagus itself was limited. A man could walk by without touching, or lie down full length and be comfortable, but two men could never pass one another.

The Germans had used the vault, too. Empty wine bottles lay about, and a half loaf of hard, dry bread took up space on the little table. Johns ordered the place cleaned up, then went back upstairs to where Henderson and Bein had already set up shop. The former's switchboard frequently was idle, as the wires were out so much, but when one or two circuits were in they were in constant use.

As he reached the top of the steps an officer, whom he recognized as Captain Purnell of the 110th Field Artillery Battalion, came in the door. Purnell said that he had come down to take over as Liaison Officer until the St. Lo show was over.

"Say," he queried, "did you see the show up in the square by the cathedral this morning?"

"No. What show?"

"They put Howie's body there to lie in state."

"Howie? Who's he?"

"He was a major in command of a battalion up on the ridge somewhere to the west. Got killed yesterday during the fighting."

"Lots of good men have died here. What's special about Howie?"

"Well. He was a helluva nice guy, who had been with the division for a long time. Somebody says he said 'See you in

St. Lo, and walked out of his command post right into a mortar burst. When the General heard about it he ordered them to get a coffin and carry Howie into town after the task force so his word would be good, or something like that."

Purnell was quiet for a few moments. He had known and liked Howie for a long time.

The Major, out of respect for a fellow battalion commander whose luck had run out, was quiet too.

Guardian Angel / 18

THE GERMAN fire was picking up. It grew in volume until everyone in the command post was conscious of it. Every wire to Henderson's switchboard was knocked out and every wireman in the battalion was out in the artillery fire, trying to find and splice the breaks.

The Battalion radio to Regiment had not been able to make contact for some reason that was baffling Sergeant Wilson. Captain Purnell's radio was also out. That meant absolutely no communications from Battalion to the rear, either to Regiment or the artillery. Then the forward observers' radios began to go out, one by one. The one with Able Company got hit by shell fragments, another fell off a building. A third just quit.

This was disastrous. The clay pigeons were now completely isolated from their artillery, which at that time constituted their major source of defensive power.

The company 300's to Battalion and to the mortars were all working, but artillery support was absolutely essential. The reassuring sound of shells passing overhead on the way to the Germans slowed, then ceased except for big stuff going out to harass faraway road junctions.

Barnes had called in a few minutes before to report a counterattack forming up in the edge of the woods along the draws south of town. He could see that area better than either Chadwick or Grimsehl. Through his observations the artillery had broken up the attack in short order except for a few foolish fanatics who tried to keep coming. These diehards had fallen easy prey to the machine guns and mortars of Baker Company, as soon as they had come into the open.

Now Barnes called in again. This big, good-natured officer had far less knowledge of how to operate a radio and how to adjust artillery fire than the rawest recruit in the battalion. But he was intelligent, and he got the job done despite his ignorance of the Signal Corps' precious "radio procedure." His idea of using a radio was that it was a substitute for a telephone and should be used accordingly. The Major had finally got him to push down the butterfly switch long enough to let the tubes warm up, but nothing else seemed to impress him. He would just pick up the handset and start talking. He always talked directly to the Major, regardless of whether the Major happened to be talking back to him or not. Bein might tell him a dozen times that the Major was not there, but he would go blithely on just as if they had been standing face to face.

This time he said, "Hey, Major, there's Krauts up on the edge of that big draw down by the river again. Lots of 'em."

Johns answered, "Okay, boy, what are they doing?"

"Looks like they're getting ready for an attack. Gimme some artillery on 'em, quick."

"We are temporarily fresh out of hay in that department, old boy, but stick around until we send out the wagon and we'll get you a new deal."

The slang and double talk were intended to confuse the German monitors, if any. It got so bad sometimes that even the people doing the talking didn't understand one another. Johns blithely figured that the poor Germans didn't have a chance!

"Okay, boss, but I sure would like to bust that balloon down there."

They were silent for a few minutes while the wiremen worked frantically on the lines to the rear.

Then Barnes came back again. "Hey, Major, you better get that jalopy fixed but quick because those SOB's are swarming all over the place. They've got an 88 with 'em, a self-propelled job. It's shooting up here now."

The sound of explosions came over the air before Barnes released the switch.

"Okay, boy," said Johns. "I hear you talking but I can't scratch your back."

The urgency in Barnes' voice sent cold fingers into the Major's guts. He couldn't help thinking that it would be heartbreaking to lose the town now, in more ways than one. In the first place, he did not expect to give it up while a brave man remained alive, and in the second place it would cause someone else one hell of a lot of trouble to come and get it back again. He felt that his battalion had almost sneaked it away from the Germans as it was, or they wouldn't be trying so hard to get it back.

Chadwick and Grimsehl both checked in to say that they had heard Barnes' transmissions and were aware of the situation. Chadwick calmly informed the Major that the "Stove pipes* weren't burping any more, either," and nobody seemed to know why. The mortars, which had been shooting almost constantly ever since they had been in the town, stood to beat their own record of some 4,000 rounds fired the night of the Dufayel attack and during their own attack the next day. Now they had suddenly stopped.

The minutes dragged on. Each officer and man felt his nerves screw up a little tighter. Barnes called again to report that they were shooting everything they had—rifles, machine guns, and 60-mm mortars. But they weren't doing much good. The Krauts were too numerous and they had too much cover against flat-trajectory fire.

Major Johns sent a messenger to the mortars, a few hundred yards away, giving them a target area and telling them to fire for effect at once. As the messenger started out the door, a flap dropped on Henderson's switchboard. The operator snapped a plug into it and listened intently while every eye in the command post was on him. Breathing almost stopped.

Henderson turned to the Major. "Sir, it's the wire crew. They say they have found the break but it's a big one and all the

---

*Mortars.

wires are snarled up on both sides of the road. It'll take 'em half an hour to sort out the lines, so they're going to tie us in with the first one they find that goes clear through. Is that all right?"

"Tell 'em hell yes, anything is okay if it goes to the rear."

In a few seconds Henderson spun his crank again. His voice rose in excitement as he spoke into the transmitter. "This is Lagoon Red. Who've I got?"

Johns made no attempt to take over. Henderson knew as well as he what was wanted. The one-sided conversation went on.

"Angel? Who's Angel?"—pause—"Are you artillery?" Henderson's voice rose to a squeak on the last word. "What kind?" . . . "Damn it, man, this is Lagoon Red in St. Lo and we need artillery worse'n we ever needed anything in all our lives and we need it right now. All our lines to the rear are out and our wire people spliced one and got you. Now quit asking damnfool questions and tell me if you can shoot for us in St. Lo?"

Henderson was masterful. His small body was so tense he seemed to be radiating sparks. Then he screeched with excitement, "155's? Thank God! You CAN?" He turned to the Major. "Sir, I've got a battalion of 155's, who can shoot anywhere on our front. They have an observer up here but haven't heard from him for some time."

Johns nodded to Purnell, who was ready with the proper information. The captain took the phone. He was excited too. "Give me all you can at 48.8-62.7 and don't ask any questions. This is an emergency. We need fire at once to break up an enemy attack."

The Major called Barnes on the 300. "Hey, boy, here comes a whole load of hay for you! Big, tough hay."

"Judas, Major, it'd better hurry. They're getting in damn close now."

In a very short time the 96-pound 155-mm shells roared overhead with a sound like a freight train passing through a tunnel in the night. The sound of their bursts rolled back like thunder.

Barnes called in, excitement high. "That was wonderful—wonderful! Only it didn't hit any of 'em. Move it across the river to this side. Most of 'em are over here."

"How was the range? Was it too far or too short?"

"Okay—that part was good—just move it over the river."

Purnell heard and looked at the map. He gave the correction over the phone, "Right 300, repeat range."

It seemed forever before the freight train went overhead again. The infantrymen, accustomed to the rapid fire and adjustment of the smaller 105's, were jittery because the 155-mm howitzers took somewhat longer to load, lay, and fire.

The thunder rolled back. With it came Barnes' call. "That was right in there with 'em, Major! That rocked 'em! Give me some more a little closer in."

"How much is a little?"

"Make it 200 yards."

Purnell caught it, said "200 over," then listened. Angel Fire Direction Center was questioning the adjustment. The correction would bring the shells inside the No-Fire Line, maybe on friendly troops.

"Hell yes, we got doughs on the edge of town. Who do you think wants this stuff, anyway?" The artilleryman was frantic, afraid the safety rules for the big guns would make them stop just when they were needed most. "Please, sir," he pleaded, "just put it out there. The infantry battalion commander is standing right beside me, praying for more of it. That last volley was right in there but the Germans are still coming."

Although that seemed to satisfy the Fire Direction Center, the next wait was still longer than before. The roar, when it came, was comforting—it was such a BIG roar, even if it was late.

Barnes called again. "That was marvelous! Do it again some more."

Purnell said into the phone, "Repeat range. Fire for effect. Give us all you have and give it quick. You're breaking up the attack, and you are all we have."

Barnes was still talking. "That stopped 'em cold! We had

'em slowed down. The dumb jerks were all bunched up and that hit right in the middle of 'em. They flew every which way. Man, that big stuff is wonderful. Give me some more!"

He was still yammering, as excited as a kid with a new toy, when the next volley hit. The sound of the bursts came sharply over the radio and rumbled in the door a few seconds later.

"That fixed 'em permanent! Nope, wait—they're running into a woods on the left about 300 yards—some of 'em are going into a building in there—put some on the woods quick or they'll get away."

The fire was shifted, but not quite so quickly as Barnes would have liked. He kept begging for haste, "before they all get away." The next volley hit in the woods whereupon the lieutenant, perhaps a mite overenthusiastically, reported, "That got *all* of 'em. . . . NO . . . One of 'em is getting away. Damn it, I knew it. That big stuff is wonderful but it's slow. That Kraut is going to get clean away."

The tension in the command post vanished. The counterattack had been broken. They could afford to laugh—and did. The Major said that was SOME artillery fire that could knock off all but one of a hundred or more Germans. Purnell relayed the story to Angel and got a belly laugh from that end of the wire.

Barnes then switched his attention to the 88, which had been sitting behind a thin woods firing regularly into the Baker and Charlie Company positions along the high ground. Chadwick called in to cheer Barnes along when he started gunning for the 88 because, he said, the bastard had taken a whole wall off their command post a few minutes before, and it was getting drafty in there. Angel gave Barnes one howitzer to adjust on the 88. After a few rounds had been fired, Barnes was able to report that the self-propelled gun was headed for Berlin with smoke pouring out its back end.

Just about that time mortar fire blanketed the whole area where the Germans had been. Barnes said it was very pretty, but just a little late. However, it would stir up the pieces if Angel had left any.

When the little show was all over, the Major and Captain Purnell sat very quietly for a few minutes just looking at one another. Their luck was unbelievable, from finding the wire to the remarkably accurate and effective fire from the big, strange guns.

The Germans seemed to quit for awhile after that last try. Even their fire died away. The battalion's wire lines were repaired, one by one. Regiment called in about something trivial. Johns took the opportunity to tell the Colonel about what had just happened, by way of pointing up their need for some reserves. The regimental commander was impressed. He didn't want to lose the town either. He agreed to let them have a platoon from K Company.

That settled, the Major started for the companies. At the door he met Don Whitehead, a war correspondent he had known while back with Division, and Lou Azrael, of the *Baltimore News Post*. They wanted to know all about what had been happening to the battalion, so Johns gave them a brief resumè, adding, "They call us the Indestructible Clay Pigeons now— because we're always out front where everybody can shoot at us. I admit we're a little chipped around the edges, but we're still flying."

Don used the remark in his story. As a result when the clippings came over from the States the men began to call themselves "The Clay Pigeon Outfit—always out front!"

By the time this chat was over it was beginning to get dark. The Major talked with the companies by telephone instead of visiting them. They reported that all was well. Chadwick said he had a new and better command post but the German 120-mm mortars were bothering him there. Did the Major know of any Krautproof locations in his area? Johns replied that the mausoleum was as Krautproof a place as any he expected to find but it was much too good for a tough young second lieutenant who was supposed to eat Germans alive. Chadwick laughed and rang off.

Just after dark General Sands, the Division Artillery commander, came in. The Major had moved downstairs by then and was talking over the telephone with Grimsehl when the General walked into the room. Before Johns could get Weller to take over, the General said, "Hello, nice going, stay with 'em, I see you're busy," and sailed out again. Major Johns was sorry to see the General leave so quickly because he had a very high regard, considerable admiration, and a great deal of affection for him. General Sands was a big, robust man who had a reputation for being tough as a boot with his artillery people, but he had been damned nice to Johns. They had come across the Channel on the same landing craft, and the General had had a plentiful supply of cigars, with which he was not stingy. Johns had blessed the artillery commander many times for the pocketful he had given him just before they hit the beach.

Now the General was down on the front—and a very dangerous front it was—to see that his people were doing their jobs. The Major knew that General Sands had gone forward to see the observation posts, but wished he could have talked a few minutes with him to tell him just how well the artillery people had been doing—and maybe to ask for a few extra radios.

About an hour after the General left, a strange messenger came in looking for Major Johns. He gave him a brown paper sack which he said General Sands had sent. The Major thanked the man, set the sack on the base of the sarcophagus, and went on with the war. Hours later, having a breathing spell, he remembered the sack. He opened it curiously to discover a half dozen cigars. He got a lump in his throat as he looked at those cigars, evidence that the General was not too busy directing all the artillery of the division to remember that one tired battalion commander loved them and hadn't had any for weeks. He thanked God that there were a few men in the world as considerate and thoughtful as Bill Sands.

Some time after General Sands' visit, a lieutenant from K Company reported that he had a platoon of 23 men assigned as a reserve for the battalion. The Major told him to have his men dig in along the back wall around the cemetery and stay within call at all times.

Shortly after that the sound of small-arms fire came from the direction of A Company, but there was no answer to a query sent on radio and phone. The battalion commander dispatched a messenger to find out what the trouble was. Chadwick, having heard the radio call and the firing, reported that all was quiet on his front and that he would also send over to see what was going on in Grimsehl's area.

Before the messenger could return, Grimsehl phoned to report that he had been out to a listening post which had reported sounds that indicated the enemy were forming up in the same draw again. He thought the listening post was right and had asked for a TOT* on the ravine. Chadwick called in at the same time with the same information, so Purnell called back to the artillery, through newly laid wire lines, and gave the fire mission. In a few minutes shells coming overhead from several directions crashed into the draw.

Grimsehl and Chadwick called in to say the possible attack had apparently been cancelled for good and sufficient reasons. Once more the artillery had staved off an assault on the town.

After that there was nothing of importance for a long time. Then, very suddenly, a call came over the radio from Able Company. The wire was out again. The call came in the hoarse, panicky voice of a new Able operator who was spelling Higley: He screamed, "Counterattack! Counterattack! Send us reserves."

Major Johns was puzzled. He went to the door of the command post to listen. There was a little firing from the direction of Grimsehl's company, but not enough to account for the frantic message. He called back and asked for more information, refusing to send the reserves. The operator said he would call Able 6.

Chadwick, mildly disturbed by what he too had heard over the radio, reported that he was having a few "visitors" but there was nothing to get excited about.

The Able operator then repeated his yell, "Counterattack! Send us reserves," but without giving any more information. In

---

* An artillery concentration plopped down suddenly, all pieces firing so that their shells will arrive at the same "Time on Target."

the meanwhile the small-arms firing increased somewhat, though it still did not seem to be of dangerous proportions. The Major did not send the reserves.

The Able operator, now nearly hysterical, called a third time, pleading for help. This time the Major, who was now standing under the portico of the command post, from where he could hear the sound of firing, heard the clump of grenades. That was more serious. He called for the K Company lieutenant.

"Lieutenant," he said, "A Company is yelling for help. I can't tell what's going on but they seem to be having some trouble. Take your people and follow their runner down there. It isn't far. Do whatever you find necessary to straighten things out. As soon as you clean the trouble up, come back here. And don't let them talk you into leaving any of your men down there."

The lieutenant ran off into the darkness, followed by the A Company runner.

A few minutes later the Luftwaffe made an appearance. Usually one or two planes came over just after dusk, flying quite low over the lines. Very often they dropped no bombs, indicating that their mission was reconnaissance. The men called this plane Bedcheck Charlie. His path was always marked with the rising spray of tracers from .50-caliber machine guns and the fast-firing 37-mm and 40-mm automatic antiaircraft cannon. The 1st Battalion never suffered damage from this nocturnal visit, and the men usually watched the ack-ack display with awe and admiration, even though it rarely hit a target.

Tonight, however, there was a feeling that the enemy planes weren't up there for the ride. This feeling was quickly justified. Flares blossomed out from below the planes and swung in the sky over the town. The enemy turned and came back and the rustle of falling bombs filled the sky.

The Major was still standing outside when the bombs started whistling down. Bein was near him. A guard was supposed to keep out all persons except those who had specific business. Now this became impossible. Men from all over the cemetery made a wild dash for the inside of the solid marble walls.

Johns shouted, "Damn it, stay the hell out and down. Do you all want to get killed at once?" He shouted it again and again, but they paid no attention. Before the bombs hit he was forced back inside and found himself pinned against the altar, sputtering with rage.

The solid walls of the mausoleum shuddered under the concussion as a string of bombs hit 200 or 300 yards away, past the old command post on the way to A Company.

As soon as the flurry was over, the Major's first thought was for his precious communications. He called, "Bein?" The answer came quickly and cheerily, "Yes, sir." "Henderson?" "Yes, sir." The switchboard operator's tone matched Bein's.

Then he turned to the men who had run into the chapel. He threw them out, physically and verbally, collectively and individually. "Do you idiots want to wreck every wire in the battalion and my radio too? Do you want to cut the whole works off and let the riflemen fight this stinking war all by themselves? Do you want to get yourselves all killed at once? Damn it, I'll shoot the next man that runs into this CP."

The men slunk out into the darkness where most of them dug their foxholes a little deeper and kept their heads down. The Major wondered who they all were anyway. He never could understand where all the people came from who were around a battalion headquarters, but there were always a lot except when you needed them most. All command posts he had ever seen were alike in that respect but all men he had questioned, which were dozens, had always had a good reason for being around. Long ago he had given up trying to solve this mystery.

A messenger came panting into the chapel. He was from the K Company platoon. The bombs had hit right in the middle of their column. The lieutenant was dead and only eight men were left alive and unwounded.

There went his reserves—a lot of good men. Raging at this tragic fate, he called for all available litters and aid men and sent the runner to lead them to what was left of the reinforcements he had wanted so badly.

As he was doing this, he caught a glint of starlight on what looked like a major's leaf on the collar of a man standing out-side the command post. Grabbing the man by the arm he looked at him closely. "Who are you?"

The stranger gave his name and said he was from an engineer unit the CO had never heard of. 'Have you any men with you?"

"Yes, sir."

"Good. How many?"

"One hundred and forty."

"One hundred and ———. Great Caesar's ghost! Do you know that I am in command of this town and all the American forces in it?"

"Yes, sir."

"Well, you have just become my reserve. Put your men in the cemetery or near it. Don't you get more than 6 feet away from me from now on. You may not like it but you're dough-feet tonight!"

He did not even ask why the engineers were in the town. Here were 140 men, more than half as many men as he had on the line altogether! As far as the Major was concerned, St. Lo was safe. With 140 men, even engineers, they could hold it against anything the Germans could scrape together now. Praised be the artillery and the engineers—good old "supporting units" for the Queen of Battle!

The Major stomped into the command post to find out what had happened at A Company. Grimsehl was calling as he went in the door. The lieutenant casually reported that they had had an engagement with a strong enemy patrol that had gotten in fairly close and had refused to go away until they had been convinced, individually and personally, that they were unpopular with A Company, not to say downright disliked.

Johns listened in wonderment. "Didn't you ask for reinforce-ments a while ago?"

"No sir, not me. I knew I could handle it."

"Well, your radio operator sure did—three times, and with gestures."

"Wait a minute, sir, I'll check up on that and see what hap-pened."

His voice was apologetic when he came back on the line. "Sir, the radio operator is a new man, who did what he thought was right when he called you. Nobody told him to, but he heard all the shooting, and as I was away running the show, he thought we were about to get run over. So he called you on his own."

The Major felt an attack of apoplexy coming on. An officer and God knew how many men killed and wounded because one new radio operator had gotten his wind up. Then he subsided. There was no use telling Grimsehl about it now; it would just upset him, and the damage could not be undone.

All right, George, but you get rid of that man right now. Give him another job. He's too excitable to be in a position of responsibility like that. Don't you ever let an operator send such a message without orders from you."

Laying the handset down he buried his face in his hands as he sat down for the first time in hours. He couldn't help thinking of the death and agony to so many men, so needlessly. It hurt damnably, deep inside.

There had been rumors ever since early afternoon that the 35th Division was going to relieve them. Major Johns had put no stock in these whispers, but had ordered that they not be repeated as they could lead to a tremendous drop in morale if they proved to be unfounded. But now the rumors became fact. A liaison officer from Regiment came in with a lieutenant colonel, his staff, and all his company commanders. They were from the 134th Regiment of the 35th Division, which was to relieve the 1st Battalion at once. Johns could hardly believe it, even when he saw his replacements standing there looking fresh and confident. He was beginning to think the Clay Pigeons were supposed to go on forever, fighting all alone except for the artillery.

He sent the company officers of the 134th out with the runners to warn all the companies that they were having friendly visitors. Then he gave the new staff all the information he could, which wasn't a great deal, other than the location of the companies and the occurrences of the past 36 hours.

The new battalion commander wondered about Major Johns' staff, as both Mentzer and Weller were doing things in the rear and his S4, Lieutenant Bogle, was rarely at the front. Regiment had grabbed Ellis for something and never had let him go again. Johns explained, and as he did so he reviewed in his mind all that had happened in the short thirty days since that first attack in the Bois de Bretel.

His whole forward staff was gone. Newcomb, Sadler, Carter and McCarthy dead; Weddle and Hoffman wounded. Grimsehl out commanding a company. Nabb, Ryan, Todd, Stoen, Kordiyak, Kenney, and Dettman all wounded, besides God knew how many other officers he had never even known by name. The company commanders from four companies, killed or wounded, mostly in the space of seven short, action-packed days.

He stopped talking while he thought for a moment of all those fine people. When he glanced up, catching himself, he thought he was looking at a ghost. There stood Kenney, the shadows on his face wavering as the candle flickered in the faint breeze of his entry.

In an instant his troubles—his preoccupation with the relieving officers—were forgotten. "Kenney!" he cried, "What in God's name are you doing here?"

"Well, Major, I heard you got into town all right, but were sort of short of company commanders. I saw Todd, Dettman, and Kordiyak back there, so I thought I'd better get on up here and see if I could do anything. The docs will let you go these days if you can stand up straight for two minutes without falling down."

The Major saw that Kenney was exhausted in spite of his cheerful attitude. He found out later that he had walked alone in the dark all the way from the division clearing station, several miles to the rear, in order to get back to the battalion. His back and legs were covered with bandages under his new shirt and pants.

He said, "Well, old man, there isn't anything you can do right now. These nice people have just come in, so we're going to be out of this rat trap in a little while. You just go back behind Mrs. Blanchet, here, and lie down and get some rest. You need it."

Kenney did as he was told. The strain had begun to bend even his indomitable will.

Johns turned back to the lieutenant colonel from the 134th and went on with the exchange of information. When he was through, he looked around the command post. The dry bread, the old wine bottles, and the inevitable K-ration boxes were still there. Barbeaux had been kept busy with more important duties than acting as janitor, and he himself had never noticed the debris. After all, there *had* been a right smart little war going on.

He looked at the relieving commander and grinned weakly. "I don't ordinarily leave a CP like this. I hate to do it now, but we've been busy."

The new man nodded. He seemed to understand.

At 0440 the Major reported to Regiment that the 134th Infantry had taken over. The wiremen took out the phone, the Major shook hands and said goodbye and good luck to the new arrivals.

Then he and Kenney followed the companies down the hill. Just seven days ago they had numbered 800. Now there were only 450 proud, tired men—the Clay Pigeons who had taken the Corps objective.

Appendix

"For the benefit of those who came in late"

ORGANIZATION AND ARMAMENT OF A WORLD WAR II INFANTRY BATTALION

The Tables of Organization and Equipment for an infantry battalion in 1944 called for some 900 men and 28 officers. The battalion contained five companies: A headquarters company, a heavy weapons company and three rifle companies. Three such battalions made up a regiment. The rifle companies and weapons companies were lettered consecutively throughout the regiment. Thus A, B, and C Companies were the rifle companies of the 1st Battalion. The Weapons Company was D Company. E, F, and G were the rifle companies of the 2d Battalion, H being the Weapons Company. I, K, and L (there is never a J Company) were always in the 3d Battalion and M was its Weapons Company.

This organization was standard throughout the Army. The battalions were always known respectively as Red, White, and Blue for 1st, 2d, and 3d, respectively, and anyone familiar with the organization of course knew at once which battalion any given company would be in. One would say, "M Company of the 115th Infantry." It is not necessary to say, "A Company of the 1st Battalion of the 115th."

The headquarters companies were designated by battalions, as, "Headquarters Company, 1st Battalion, 115th Infantry, 29th Division."

Each rifle company was made up of 6 officers and 186 men —on the Tables of Organization and Equipment. Actually it is questionable that any company ever had exactly that number of officers and men in it; usually a unit was understrength, though on rare occasions it may have been overstrength. Certainly, no company in combat stayed at the same strength for very long. The official strength was merely a point of departure, a measuring stick to determine how many replacements were required. The "Clay Pigeons" of this story actually varied in strength from well over 1000, for a very short time, down to as low as 241 at one time during the eleven months of fighting in Europe.

Each rifle company was divided into three rifle platoons and one weapons platoon, each headed by a lieutenant. There was an executive officer and, of course, the company commander. The company commander was often a second lieutenant, though the position called for a captain.

Each rifle platoon comprised three squads. The weapons platoon contained two light machine gun squads and three 60 mm mortar squads.

The rifle squads, of 12 men each, contained one Browning Automatic Rifle, or BAR, in addition to the rifles carried by the rest of the men in the squad.

The weapons platoon of the rifle companies was equipped with two light machine guns and three 60 mm mortars.

The Heavy Weapons Company provided a total of eight heavy machine guns and six 81 mm mortars.

There were three .57 mm anti-tank guns in the Headquarters Company and a total of 24 rocket launchers, commonly called "bazookas," scattered throughout the battalion.

Officers were officially equipped with pistols as were machine gunners and a few other individuals. Many of the Headquarters and Weapons Company personnel were supposed to be armed with carbines but the majority acquired and used the heavier but more reliable and authoritative M1 rifle.

Medical aid men are not assigned as an integral part of the infantry battalion. They are attached in the form of a detachment from higher medical units. This battalion detachment included a surgeon, first aid equipment, company aid men, and a limited number of litter bearers.

Glossary

BRIEF EXPLANATION of some of the abbreviations and military expressions appearing in the narrative.

A and P—Not a grocery store. Refers to the Ammunition and Pioneer Platoon of Battalion Headquarters Company.

Ack-Ack—Antiaircraft guns, fire, shells, etc. Term adopted from the British; taken from their telephone code expression meaning AA (antiaircraft).

Ammo—Ammunition.

AP—Armor piercing.

AT—Antitank.

Ballistic crack—Sharp sound made by any object, such as a bullet or missile, traveling through the air faster than sound (1100 f/s).

BAR—Browning automatic rifle.

Bazooka—Slang term for a hand-carried rocket launcher used principally for AT fire.

Big picture—The general situation. Known only at higher echelons; sometimes used to cover ignorance of what was happening at the front.

Bird dog—A staff officer sent from higher unit to investigate and/or harass lower unit.

Burp gun—German machine pistol or submachine gun. So called because of the Brrrrp sound made by its high cyclic rate of fire.

BBC—British Broadcasting Company. An unusual outfit employing no commercials.

C & R car—Command reconnaissance vehicle—a cumbersome five-passenger touring car looking like some prehistoric monster. So difficult to turn around in narrow roads that it was largely supplanted by the ubiquitous jeep .

CE—Combat exhaustion. Very real, and not funny, but unfortunately it could be faked.

CG—Commanding General.

CO—Commanding Officer.

CP—Command Post.

C-ration—Accurately, a field ration consisting of sufficient food for 1 man for 1 day, but often used loosely to designate 1 meal. Came in cans.

D-bar—A delicious (?) chocolate bar issued as an emergency or "iron" ration. Not enjoyed, even in emergencies.

Exec—Executive officer; second in command. Also acted, in an infantry battalion, as administrative officer.

88—A German 88-mm cannon, high velocity. Was a dual-purpose gun for firing at aircraft or tanks. Also used in lieu of ordinary artillery.

FDC—Fire Direction Center.

FO—Forward Observer.

Foxhole—A rifle pit used by individuals or 2 men.

Goose eggs—Roughly circular or elliptical figures drawn on a map to designate targets, objectives, or position areas.

HE—High explosive, usually TNT.

High Port—Refers to a ready position of the rifle, held diagonally in front of the chest.

I Section—Intelligence Section.

Jerries (also Heinies, Krauts, bastards, SOB's)—Germans.

K-ration—A precooked emergency or field ration packed in waxed cardboard containers.

Lagoon Red 6—CO 1st Battalion 115th Infantry.

LD—Line of Departure. The jump-off for an attack.

LO—Liaison Officer.

Luftwaffy (Luftwaffe)—Correct pronunciation, Looftvaffah; literally "air weapon"—German Air Force.

M1—Semiautomatic, .30 caliber rifle carried by individual infantrymen.

NBC—National Broadcasting Company. Uses commercials.

NCO—Noncommissioned officer.

Nighthawk—110th Field Artillery Battalion.

OD—Olive drab—color of US uniform.

OP—Observation post.

Overlay—Sheet of tracing paper or other transparent material on which are plotted lines, positions, etc., transferred from map.

PX—Post exchange.

Queen of Battle—The Infantry.

Recon Troop—Division Reconnaissance Troop, an armored cavalry unit mounted on halftracks, armored cars, and other light vehicles.

RJ—Road junction.

Replacement—Man sent up from "repple depple" to fill vacancy in unit depleted by losses.

Roger—Communication code expression meaning literally "Message received," but popularly adopted to mean "Okay," "Understood."

SCR 300—Walkie-talkie radio used at company and battalion level.

SCR 536—Handy-talkie radio used at company and platoon level.

Shellrep—Shell report.

SP—Self-propelled vehicle.

Stovepipes—Mortars.

TD—Tank destroyer.

10-in-1 ration—Food for 10 men for 1 day. Contained large cans of some items, and was far more desirable than the C- or K-rations.

Zero-in—To adjust fire on.

The Stackpole Military History Series

THE AMERICAN CIVIL WAR
Cavalry Raids of the Civil War
In the Lion's Mouth
Witness to Gettysburg

WORLD WAR I
Doughboy War

WORLD WAR II
After D-Day
Airborne Combat
Armor Battles of the Waffen-SS, 1943–45
Armoured Guardsmen
Arnhem 1944
The B-24 in China
The Battalion
The Battle of France
The Battle of Sicily
Battle of the Bulge, Vol. 1
Battle of the Bulge, Vol. 2
Battle of the Bulge, Vol. 3
Beyond the Beachhead
Beyond Stalingrad
The Black Bull
Blitzkrieg Unleashed
Blossoming Silk Against the Rising Sun
Bodenplatte
The Breaking Point
The Brigade
The Canadian Army and the Normandy Campaign
Critical Convoy Battles of WWII
A Dangerous Assignment
D-Day Bombers
D-Day Deception
D-Day to Berlin
Decision in the Ukraine
The Defense of Moscow 1941
Destination Normandy
Dive Bomber!
Eager Eagles
Eagles of the Third Reich
The Early Battles of Eighth Army
Eastern Front Combat
Europe in Flames
Exit Rommel
The Face of Courage
Fatal Decisions
Fist from the Sky
Flying American Combat Aircraft of World War II, Vol. 1
For Europe
Forging the Thunderbolt
For the Homeland
Fortress France
The German Defeat in the East, 1944–45
German Order of Battle, Vol. 1
German Order of Battle, Vol. 2
German Order of Battle, Vol. 3

The Germans in Normandy
Germany's Panzer Arm in World War II
GI Ingenuity
Goodbye, Transylvania
The Great Ships
Grenadiers
Guns Against the Reich
Hitler's Final Fortress
Hitler's Nemesis
Hitler's Spanish Legion
Hold the Westwall
Infantry Aces
In the Fire of the Eastern Front
Iron Arm
Iron Knights
Japanese Army Fighter Aces
Japanese Naval Fighter Aces
JG 26 Luftwaffe Fighter Wing War Diary, Vol. 1
JG 26 Luftwaffe Fighter Wing War Diary, Vol. 2
Kampfgruppe Peiper at the Battle of the Bulge
The Key to the Bulge
Kursk
Luftwaffe Aces
Luftwaffe Fighter Ace
Luftwaffe Fighter-Bombers over Britain
Luftwaffe Fighters & Bombers
Luftwaffe KG 200
Marshal of Victory, Vol. 1
Marshal of Victory, Vol. 2
Massacre at Tobruk
Mechanized Juggernaut or Military Anachronism?
Messerschmitts over Sicily
Michael Wittmann, Vol. 1
Michael Wittmann, Vol. 2
Mission 85
Mission 376
The Nazi Rocketeers
Night Flyer / Mosquito Pathfinder
No Holding Back
Operation Mercury
Panzer Aces
Panzer Aces II
Panzer Commanders of the Western Front
Panzergrenadier Aces
Panzer Gunner
The Panzer Legions
Panzers in Normandy
Panzers in Winter
Panzer Wedge, Vol. 1
Panzer Wedge, Vol. 2
The Path to Blitzkrieg
Penalty Strike
Poland Betrayed
Red Road from Stalingrad
Red Star Under the Baltic
Retreat to the Reich

Rommel Reconsidered
Rommel's Desert Commanders
Rommel's Desert War
Rommel's Lieutenants
The Savage Sky
The Seeds of Disaster
Ship-Busters
The Siege of Brest 1941
The Siege of Küstrin
The Siegfried Line
A Soldier in the Cockpit
Soviet Blitzkrieg
Spitfires & Yellow Tail Mustangs
Stalin's Keys to Victory
Surviving Bataan and Beyond
T-34 in Action
Tank Tactics
Tigers in the Mud
Triumphant Fox
The 12th SS, Vol. 1
The 12th SS, Vol. 2
Twilight of the Gods
Typhoon Attack
The War Against Rommel's Supply Lines
War in the Aegean
War of the White Death
Warsaw 1944
Winter Storm
The Winter War
Wolfpack Warriors
Zhukov at the Oder

THE COLD WAR / VIETNAM
Cyclops in the Jungle
Expendable Warriors
Fighting in Vietnam
Flying American Combat Aircraft: The Cold War
Here There Are Tigers
Land with No Sun
Phantom Reflections
Street without Joy
Through the Valley
Tours of Duty
Two One Pony

WARS OF AFRICA AND THE MIDDLE EAST
The Rhodesian War

GENERAL MILITARY HISTORY
Battle of Paoli
Cavalry from Hoof to Track
Desert Battles
Guerrilla Warfare
The Philadelphia Campaign, Vol. 1
Ranger Dawn
Sieges
The Spartan Army